THINK WEALTHY

Master the Money Mindset That Creates Millionaires and Billionaires

By Todd Havens

Wealth is the ability to fully experience life.

- Henry David Thoreau

For Chris: There's no one I'd rather journey with more on the road to financial freedom.

For Sydney: I wrote this book so you never confuse your net worth with your self-worth – your true value is infinite.

Table of Contents

Preface

When I learned how to Think Wealthy, I saved my life.

That may sound dramatic, but when you get completely out of debt for the first time in your life, fully fund your retirement accounts, know you will never again have crushing financial stress and you become known as the "rich uncles" in your family as first-generation millionaires, you have achieved more money milestones than you ever dreamed were possible.

When I learned how to Think Wealthy, I saved my life because I was finally able to *breathe*, to pause and actually plan the life that I wanted to live – not the life that an employer or credit card or private student loan (shark) company wanted for me.

This is the book I wish someone had given to me in high school, in college and every five years after that so I could have been reminded throughout my adult life that financial freedom was always within reach, one step at a time. Had I known then what I know now, I would've been even MORE financially independent – just so much earlier.

I don't know about you, but growing up as I did in my close Midwestern family, rich and wealthy people were always put on a pedestal, admired like a rare gem on one hand and mildly resented and feared on the other. I had major work to do to retrain my brain to allow the money I made (or collected, as we'll see) to flow through me for a higher purpose of creating safety, security and, ultimately, financial freedom in my life.

When my mindset started to flip, I wanted to learn *everything* I could about money. I devoured all the personal finance classics, but quickly realized that many of them sounded like they were written in a different century – because they were! – my eyes still glosssssssssszzzzz over just thinking about that man in Mesopotamia or trying to Wattle my way through the science of wealth.

If those outdated classics work for you, great! I simply found many of them to be inaccessible snoozefests, considering the incredible rate of change in the late 20th and early 21st centuries.

Consider *Think Wealthy*, then, a modern retelling of timeless wealth creation wisdom. I even invented a new, *super* easy way to set achievable financial goals by using just one number, what you pay each month in rent or a mortgage.

My perspective is uniquely American. I lean heavily on the bootstraps narrative because it worked for me and forever changed the course of my life. The core concepts of saving and investing, however, are global, and the four pillars of well-rounded wealth apply to any human being walking the earth. (That should include you.) You can think wealthy and implement change wherever you are in the world – you'll figure it out!

Many thanks to my amazing friends and family who have supported and informed this labor of love.

I hope you enjoy this book as much as I enjoyed writing it – now stay awake! I promise never to use words like "sex transmutation" within these hallowed pages. (Napoleon Hill, what were you *thinking*?)

Our Only Financial Job in Life

Our only financial job in life is to pay our monthly bills until game over.

That's it.

Even billionaires have monthly bills – and *lots* of them.

How do we pay our monthly bills after schooling ends, on through our years in the workforce and all the way through what might be decades of retirement?

That's all anyone working in personal finance is helping you figure out at the end of the day.

Statistically-speaking, most of you were raised in families (as was I) that approached this financial job of ours by thinking about it one month at a time – you saw your families JUST clear the hurdle of affording one month before they started planning (and worrying) about the next month – which is a very middle-class approach – and which is fine if that's all you've ever known.

The KEY to successful personal finance, however, is to think and to plan year-to-year, to have a longer time horizon in mind and plan of action in play. To do that is to Think Wealthy, which is the sole purpose of all the words I'm stacking next to each other in this tome.

If just one of these chapters can actually *shift* your thinking from scrambling week-to-week or month-to-month to confidently flowing from YEAR-to-YEAR, then you're well on your way to creating wealth and financial independence for you and your family for generations to come.

No joke – for generations to come.

It'd be my honor to help you get there.

Even if you don't end up leaving a few million to your heirs, at minimum you won't be eating cat food in retirement.

Unless you want to. (It'll be our little secret.)

Introduction

You're awesome!

How's *that* for an introduction?

You are awesome because you already have everything you need inside to become a millionaire – maybe even a billionaire. The financial puzzle pieces are all there, you just need to rearrange them as you learn to Think Wealthy.

You can LEARN to be wealthy because the rules by which you make money and your MONEY makes money are simple and only need to be learned once.

I'm living proof of that.

I went from being the poorest guy in any room to a self-made first-generation millionaire and I'm going to show you how we did it.

There are plenty of great financial planners out there (and you should work with one at some point), but what has protected me and my family and what will protect you, too, in the long run is for you to "get it" – for you to "get" money. Because once you get it, you got it...and you'll never forget it.

Tell me if this sounds familiar...

No one ever shared with you everything they know about money – how money works in the world, what it's really for and, most importantly, how to make as much of it as you want in your lifetime – I never heard it from my parents, grandparents or teachers or my creepy uncle Ron who always hugged me a little too tight (I don't have an Uncle Ron) and I'm guessing you never heard it, either.

Sucks to be just the two of us, right?

Turns out it's more than just the two of us as nearly 80% of Americans (!) live paycheck-to-paycheck which means they don't "get" money yet, either.

80% of Americans – or over 100 million people – live paycheck to paycheck in the wealthiest country the world has ever known – SAY WHAT?

If financial misery loves company, then there's a big 'ol party going on in the U.S. of A.

Which is exactly why I wrote this book – so we can stop commiserating in our negative net worth and start celebrating our financial freedom TOGETHER.

My Goal of Zero Net Worth

For years my highest financial aspiration was to simply break even and have a net worth of zero.

I can't believe I'm sharing that. It's pretty bonkers.

In my 20s and 30s, I LITERALLY used to dream about having no debt *and* no assets to my name. "What a financial god I'll be when I am finally worth ZERO dollars…NOTHING! I'll be asked to lead parades around town as people dance behind me, I just know it!"

My life's highest financial goal for the longest time was to JUST BREAK EVEN in the financial game of life.

Silly, goofy, money-unsavvy Todd. Now that we have our retirement years accounted for, the memory stings a little bit less, but it's still embarrassing to admit.

But you know what? How many people reading this right now might have the exact same financial goal that I did? "Man, if I can just get to a ZERO net worth, I'll be better off than everyone I know!"

All I had heard from my parents and teachers was to get good grades and work hard and that the financial stuff would take of itself.

That was a lie.

The financial stuff does NOT just take care of itself...at least not without understanding how money works in the world and how you can make it work hard for you in your own life.

From Poorest Guy in Any Room to 1st Generation Millionaire

I'll keep the details of my life to a relative minimum as we're here to talk about (awesome) YOU, but suffice it to say that since college where I double-majored in Linguistics and French in undergrad (a real money-printing diploma) followed by grad work in film at the USC School of Cinema-Television, I have found relative success in many different areas of the fickle and über-competitive entertainment industry in Hollywood, sticking with a particular career only until it no longer paid emotional dividends.

I worked in commercial casting and was a successful commercial actor appearing in spots for Volkswagen, Subway, Sears, Westin Hotels and on and on. I also traveled the country casting reality TV shows for MTV before transitioning to a Director of Marketing and Account Director role for a digital creative agency that worked with all the major movie studios and premium cable channels to help them market their shows and movies online.

I was even a 35mm film projectionist for a work-study job in college (did you ever see *Cinema Paradiso*?) and then to some of the wealthiest and most famous of the Hollywood elite when I moved out to Los Angeles. I used to drive to people's homes in Beverly Hills, Bel Air, Pacific Palisades, Malibu…homes worth tens and even hundreds of millions of dollars to project the opening weekend films for them in their plush, private screening rooms. (Before the digital revolution hit its tipping point and everyone started just pushing buttons at home.)

What's a few hundred dollars they would pay me for an in-home film screening of the newest releases when you're not paying that crazy upcharge on popcorn and soda at the local cineplex, amirite?

I used to peek out from the port windows at the lavish screening rooms filled with popcorn machines and innumerable jars filled to the brim with candy and think, "What is so different between them and me? What do they know about money that I don't? And how do I get to THAT side of life?!?"

Financially-speaking, I've had windfalls of money roll in over the years from residual checks as a commercial actor, I've been unemployed and collecting funemployment for months at a time in-between reality casting gigs and I have humbly lived with a stable six-figure income, replete with 401k and quarterly sales bonuses.

Through all those careers and adventures, I have seen both sides of the coin, having nothing to my name for decades when I was easily the poorest guy in any room, to seeing how Hollywood celebrities and "the other half" lived in their amazing mansions and now to making a beeline straight for a wealthy, happy and healthy life for myself and my family.

My partner and I have gone from a *negative* net worth of over $50,000 when we met fifteen years ago to being squarely on track to become 1st-generation multimillionaires.

We have zero debt and our FICO scores are well into the 800s. Life ain't bad on the financial front…and it's only getting better.

And yet, none of this would have been possible if I didn't learn how to Think Wealthy. Swing a dead cat (as the saying goes) and you could easily hit another couple with all the same life circumstances but who are now even MORE in debt.

What's the difference between us and them?

Thinking Wealthy

I'm fascinated by what's called the psychology of wealth…the idea that simply how you THINK about money directly affects how much money you HAVE.

Yet, it's absolutely true.

Regardless of how much I struggled to be better with my money than my parents were, for years (and years and years) I just barely got by.

Just like them.

Saddled with consumer debt, I lived paycheck to paycheck – just like them – and the almost 80% of the rest of Americans.

But who could blame my parents? If they knew better, they would have shared their most relevant financial lessons with me and my sister, too – they only wanted the best for us!

The U.S. is always touted as the wealthiest nation ever to exist in the modern era – but if we can't create and pass down our collective financial wisdom to successive generations, we don't deserve to hang onto that title for much longer.

What we're talking about in this book is having it ALL – more financial means than you need in one lifetime, an inner confidence against whatever life tries to throw your way (did I mention yet that I was diagnosed with incurable blood cancer in March of 2021? #nowthatsacurveball), being surrounded by a supportive, loving family and a wealth of true friends who get you and who inspire you (and whom you inspire) to be ever better people in the world.

It's what I call Well-Rounded Wealth and it's our ultimate goal – we'll talk more in-depth about this in the final chapter.

I didn't realize it at the time, for those decades of early adulthood, but debt always made me feel LESS THAN in life. For years, I mistakenly confused my NET WORTH with my SELF WORTH and as a wide-eyed man-child buried under $60,000 of consumer debt who was entering the labor force, I made way too many mistakes that kept me from growing up financially (and emotionally) – I was wrapped up in a diaper of debt.

Are you, too, wearing a diaper of debt? (I may be the first Financial Poet Laureate!)

As you can imagine, now that I've figured it out for myself, I'm over-the-moon excited to talk about money with everyone else.

I love the peace of mind that having money in the bank has afforded us. Heck, it created the space for me to not just *talk* about this book (everyone has a book or ten in them), but to actually sit down and WRITE it.

I wish I had read this book in high school, college and then again as I headed out into the world as a young pup (with the saddest excuse for a moustache anyone has ever seen).

I also wish I had this book at my disposal when I needed to be reminded of how powerful I was in creating my OWN life and doing it with confidence and purpose.

The biggest gift you can give yourself is confidence with all your money moves because it will mean you are also confident with the decisions in most every other area of your life, as well.

Besides, I've done the bulk of the work in writing it down – all you have to do is READ the dern thing and think about yourself! ;-)

The Goal of This *Think Wealthy* Book

My singular goal in writing this book is to change your entire relationship with money.

For the better.

Forever.

(I like to aim low.)

And we're going to have fun along the way because life just isn't that serious.

By the end of *Think Wealthy*, if I've done my job right, you will be excited about money, creating more of it, investing it, donating it…letting it flow through you to do good and make even MORE MONEY in the world.

And you'll do it all in good conscience so you can sleep soundly at night.

I envision a country whose citizens aren't on the collective brink of collapse, where its people AND its government don't spend above their means.

It sickens me that the majority of Americans do not have a spare $1,000 in a bank account or understand WHY they should – it should scare the bejeezus out of all of us because it *affects* all of us one way or another.

Luckily for you and for anyone who dares to crack the pages of this book, there are only a few timeless facts about money and wealth you need to learn. If you don't have these basics at the very center of your financial worldview informing the money decisions you make day in and day out, you'll probably never make a lot of money…or at least you won't keep much of it.

If you are tired of throwing your monthly bills across the room to hit the snooze button on the life you've always wanted, then let's grab a cup of joe or an awesome craft beer (it must be 5pm *somewhere*) and let's figure this out together.

It's time to pull back the curtain on your money mindset so we are all working from the same financial foundation.

Everyone who wants to be wealthy, bounce your eyeballs to the next page…now!

Chapter 1: Money Mindset Basics

Money is a terrible master but an excellent servant.

- P.T. Barnum

I love it. I'm so excited to talk about M-O-N-E-Y!

My money. Your money. Money flying around all over the world today.

Before we dig into what we THINK we know about money and creating a life of wealth and happiness, first let's get on the same page with our money mindset basics.

We need to build a strong financial foundation together and that starts by learning what wealthy people already know about money…that we simply may not know…yet.

The real beaut (pronounced BYOOT) of all of the money basics is that YOU ONLY NEED TO LEARN THIS ONCE.

No joke.

Wealth is learnable.

I'm dead serious.

And now I'm resuscitated-and-breathing-again serious.

The money rules we'll be discussing never change.

Just ask the 80% of all millionaires that are self-made (whether through entrepreneurship or simple saving and investing like us) – THEY know that wealth can be learned because they did it THEMSELVES.

Once you grasp these core money concepts and flip the switch in your brain to Think Wealthy, you'll be set for life, my friend, because once you understand them, you can't unlearn them.

The financial concepts we'll be covering may feel like common sense, but if you're not already following them then there's an emotional disconnect between what you know and what you do that we need to work on.

But I progress (getting ahead of myself)…

Money, Money, Money!

What a beautiful word.

If money isn't connected to every aspect of our lives, it sure feels that way: from paying our bills each month, to being able to take that little hottie out to dinner and drinks one night (after the global pandemic ends) because there was a crazy flash of chemistry between you two, to saving and investing your dinero today for the promised financial windfall of retirement later in life…or even just stressing about everything money-related because you know you're SUPPOSED to be smarter with your money, but you have NO IDEA where to start or what to DO with it.

Money enters our minds, if not our conversations, endlessly, on a daily basis.

It's everywhere!

Money is as important to our lives as water is to our bodies, yet we know almost nothing about it.

You want proof that we don't know much about money? Most of us go through life with completely "dehydrated" bank accounts – there's not enough water, not enough money, in them to keep us clear-headed and feeling really alive.

"But, Todd…"

"But, Todd," you say, "if I HAD more money, then I'd actually be good with it!"

To which I say, "Horsecakes!"

If you can't handle what you have now, giving you MORE money will only make things worse.

The reason is simple: You either "get" money and GET and KEEP more of it, or you don't "get" money and you SPEND and LOSE it.

I'll tell you why you're kidding yourself by thinking you'd be set if you only had more money (which is what I did for years, too), but first let's jump right into the green end of the pool and check out the top 5 things that the wealthy already know about money.

Yuck…or yay!

The 5 Things Wealthy People Already Know about Money

I've studied millionaires and billionaires for decades and I firmly believe that to pull yourself into a different socio-economic class, you need to emulate the underlying psychology and common financial habits of those who have gone on before you.

In this hyper-connected age, we have all the data points we need to create financial wealth for ourselves. We know that simple S&P 500 index funds tend to beat actively-managed mutual funds and overpriced hedge funds in terms of returns. There is also no shortage of detailed articles on how the wealthy have created and maintained their sizeable net worth – heck, we even know how Peter Thiel amassed a whopping 5 billion (!) dollars in a Roth IRA.

What we need on this planet – as an ever-more-intertwined social, global population – is to connect the financial dots *individually* so that thinking wealthy (and, therefore, *doing* wealthy) becomes second nature to the routine of our daily lives.

First, we need to clear out the cobwebs of old ways, or misinformed ways, of thinking about money. To do that, let's take a look at the five things that wealthy people know about money.

Truth #1: Money is not cash

All cash is money, but all money is not cash.

This is either a no-brainer for you or the first time you've ever thought about it.

Let's break this down…

CASH

To most of us, cash is the currency of bills and coins we carry around in our pockets, wallets and purses. It's the change we leave in our car so we can plug parking meters (they're still out there, those coin-based bandits) and what we find hiding in couch cushions that brings tears of joy to our eyes with newfound fortune.

Cash is the physical, tangible assets we often use without thinking much about it. We literally hold cash in our hands.

And what we do with cash is SPEND it.

Yep, we primarily handle cash to BUY things. Linguistically-speaking, we even CASH checks to pay for our monthly lifestyle.

Of course, you can also DEPOSIT cash into your bank account if you run a lemonade stand in your front yard or have an odd habit of breaking into vending machines (why would you do that?), but it's much more likely that you take cash OUT of your bank via an ATM or debit card to SPEND it.

Actual cash in the form of bills and coins (and basically every digital cent sitting in your checking account) is meant to be SPENT.

The key to CASH (which, again, is definitely money) is that it exists to be SPENT.

$$$

"Cold Hard Cash" Isn't Cold, Hard…or Even Cash!

For most people, cold hard cash is only used for small business transactions like buying lunch or a latte or, of course, if Trinity, that lovely pole dancer at the local Nips & Navels, has proven herself worthy of those singles that were just burning a hole in your pocket (after the global pandemic ends). Or perhaps the dancer's name is Maximus, an equally talented male dancer at the local Sax & Crax – no judgment in this book.

We rarely handle cash for much more than basic, day-to-day necessities, if at all.

Large cash transactions are so rare, in fact, that the U.S. Department of the Treasury's Bureau of Engraving and Printing (perhaps the *only* governmental office with a sense of humor given its moneyfactory.gov web address) hasn't circulated bills larger than $100 since 1969.

1969!

And they discontinued bills larger than $100 back then, WAY before the internet made online banking a feat of super awesomeness, because the bills larger than $100 were being used primarily for illegal shenanigans and wire transfers were already sufficient for moving around large amounts of money.

Isn't that bizarre? You can't get anything larger than a $100 dollar bill from your local bank since 1969.

1969!

That fact alone makes robbing banks sound so NOT worth the time and energy it takes to really excel at that line of work. The highest denomination you'll get your hands on (before the dye pack explodes or a handful of other security measures take effect) is hundred-dollar bills?!? Puh-lease. What's your time worth, amigo?

In case you need any more discouragement, the average amount of money stolen in a bank robbery is $4,000. Chump change!

And then you'll BE somebody's chump all those years behind bars.

We may be limited to 100s as the top bill in circulation today, but we once did have U.S. currency in denominations of $500, $1,000, $5,000 and even $10,000.

It's fun to think of reaching into your wallet and seeing a bunch of $10,000 bills staring back at you.

Not practical, perhaps, but a man-boy can dream.

These larger-denominated bills ($500, $1,000, $5,000 and $10,000) that were once in circulation do still make an appearance from time to time, much like a reclusive movie star, and they are still legal tender, but if a bank gets ahold of one, they will turn it into a Federal Reserve bank to remove it from circulation.

Go ahead and guess in which year these larger bills ($500, $1,000, $5,000 and $10,000) were last printed.

Did you say 1969?

Wrong!

They were last printed the year World War II ended…1945.

1945!

If you ever find yourself face-to-face with Salmon P. Chase on a $10,000 bill and it is in great condition, snicker at his name if you must (except for you, Mackerel McGillicuddy), but do NOT deposit it at your local bank as that $10,000 bill might be worth over $140,000 to a collector!

Also, of note (Dad Humor), the highest official bill EVER produced in the U.S. was the Series 1934 $100,000 gold certificate bill – it was only produced for three weeks in 1934-35 for interchange between the Federal Reserve Banks when they had an equal amount of gold in the Treasury…but the $100,000 bill never made it into public circulation.

Call me crazy, but I honestly thought a MILLION-dollar bill had totally existed at one time – didn't you?

Nope. Our country's Who's Who of millionaires and billionaires, those who have proven the possibility of the American (financial) Dream, have never held a legal tender million-dollar bill in their hands.

[wipes away lone tear from eye]

$$$

We've established that all cash is money, but not all money is cash.

What gives, then? What exactly IS money?

MONEY

To the wealthy, money is a much larger CONCEPT while cash is just one of the FORMS it can take.

MONEY has a much broader, higher purpose in your life.

If you've only ever seen your parents and your friends' families live paycheck-to-paycheck (or worse) and if you've done the same (or worse), you have probably thought about cash and money as pretty much being one and the same...you have logically collapsed the two terms together, thereby making money and cash indistinguishable from one another.

To those who are wealthy, though, money is much bigger (and exciting!) than cash.

Technically, money is nothing more than an intangible string of numbers separated by punctuation marks of commas and periods in our bank accounts.

We all get the period in our bank accounts for free ($0.00), but those commas to the left (i.e., $1,000.00 or $1,000,000.00 or even $1,000,000,000.00) are what separate the wo/men with a rockin' net worth from everyone else just making ends meet.

As I noted earlier, most Americans don't even have ONE comma of savings (or $1,000.00) to their name.

While cash is usually physical, money of any significant quantity is not physical – we can hold and touch cash, but money is really just a number or a lot of different numbers on bank computer servers and balance sheets.

We know if we go to an ATM and withdraw $40 or $100, those 20-dollar bills the machine burps out give us the ILLUSION that we could walk into the bank, close out an account and leave with wads of physical cash in hand...as if our money is sitting behind the counter waiting for us to claim it like a homesick kid at summer camp.

(Your money is not actually sitting there in the bank, of course. The bank immediately used it to pay for their overhead and make loans to businesses and other people. It's been sent out to do all kinds of other tasks and make even MORE money while you tucked yourself into bed and fell fast asleep dreaming of how safe and sound your money is at your local branch.)

But that is the first mistake many of us make…thinking that our money is ultimately just cash.

You can't be blamed for collapsing the two terms as there are still plenty of misleading turns of phrase out in the world…

As the real estate market tanked in the Great Recession and investors swooped in to buy up properties (which they're still doing, P.S., and driving up housing markets across the U.S.), you'd hear talk of homes being "bought for cash." What being "bought for cash" really means is that there was no mortgage needed through a bank, no need for debt financing, the usual path to buying a home.

Trust me, U-Hauls were not backing up to people's homes so forklifts could unload pallets of cash in the form of 100-dollar bills and bags of wrapped coins for the lucky seller. It was all done through a wire transfer or check into an escrow account. No actual CASH was involved when it was "bought for cash"…but a whole lotta MONEY was!

As for the peacock fan of plastic debit and credit cards we carry with us and the paper checks we tear out of our checkbooks if we're rollin' it old school[1], those financial tools that FEEL like money, those are really

---

[1] Old school like that woman in line in front of you at the supermarket who pulls out her checkbook and you're all like, "Really, lady?!? I will give you the gosh-dern 12 dollars and 23 cents you've taken half an hour to write out.

just pointers to different bank accounts, ones that (hopefully) have the money in them you need in the case of a debit card or to a mini-loan with unconscionable interest rates in the case of a credit card.

As we become an ever more digital and cashless economy it may become harder for future generations to distinguish between money and cash, but it will ALWAYS be true that money is just a collection of numbers sitting on different bank servers and balance sheets.

$ $ $

The MONEY/CASH distinction is a FUNDAMENTAL difference in how wealthy people view money…

All cash is money, but not all money is cash.

It is a life-changing distinction to make if you've never thought about it…to separate and pull apart the two concepts, one from the other.

There is a world of difference between cash which is meant to be SPENT and money which has a higher and much more powerful purpose in your life.

Money is not just cash.

Do you see the distinction yet?

$ $ $

Consider it your personal invitation to the 21st century from me and everyone else in line behind you."

This is why I am so excited by MONEY, but not necessarily by cash. I mean, I LIKE cash…it's great at its job…but I LOVE money.

So, what is money's "higher purpose" (that I keep rambling on about)?

Truth #2: Money is freedom

We all want more money.

We share our dreams of being rich with friends and family and tell them what we would do with all the money we are going to have one day.

And by that, I mean we tell them everything we would BUY with our newfound loot. We tell them what we would SPEND it on as if it's a big pile of cash.

"I'll get a bigger house in a better part of town, get that llama farm in Texas I've always talked about, buy three gas-guzzling SUVs, season tickets to the local NFL team (when the global pandemic ends), travel the world (when the global pandemic ends) with my family and a bunch of cousins I never knew I had until they saw that I won the lottery…"

This is the stuff that financial daydreams are made of.

The reality, though, is:

Only people without money think money exists just to be spent.

After we jump onto a bed covered in 100-dollar bills (since that's the biggest bill a bank will give you since 1969…1969!), what do we DO with it next?

What is money FOR, really?

Does money just exist for us to spend on things, experiences and other people?

Of course, that is one SIGNIFICANT use for money…for spending. We do it as we create our standard of living each month when we say, "Yes, please. This will do just fine." Whether we can afford it or not.

The very strength of our US economy DEMANDS that we spend our money. With 70% of our economy dependent on consumption, on people buying things that they may or may not need, don't expect the federal government to spend many of your tax dollars convincing you to beef up your savings accounts.

To the truly wealthy, money is not just for spending – money serves a much higher purpose.

That higher purpose, and perhaps the biggest secret to money that the wealthy already know…and know in their bones…is that money is FREEDOM.

Money is personal freedom.

Money is freedom from living someone else's life.

The more money you have, the more free you are to live YOUR life on YOUR terms.

Think about that for a second. Doesn't that sound amazing? Isn't that what every Millennial and Gen Zer has set their sights on – their life on THEIR terms, sitting in the lotus position on top of a mountain of organic avocado toast?

To the wealthy, CASH is for spending just like everyone else, but Money with a capital 'M' is FREEDOM with a capital 'EFF-YEAH!'.

$$$

Wealth Warning: *Wealth does not equal materialism.*

There is a correlation many people mistakenly make that wealth equals materialism, that the more money you have, the more things you have to OWN.

You may hear non-wealthy people say (as they shiver through a harsh winter with their feet crammed into oven mittens to save on their gas bill), "What do I need more money for? I've already got everything I NEED!"

My mom used to say it all the time...minus the fashionable oven mittens.

"What do we need with more money?" she'd say to us, "We live a comfortable life – we don't NEED anything more."

The one thing she and my dad have never had, however, was any sense of financial security, let alone freedom.

There was just no wiggle room in their finances – they had the tangibles in place, a nice house in a good neighborhood and two working cars – but there were no intangibles accounted for (savings, retirement, long-term care insurance, etc.).

To my mom, extra money would have to be spent on *something*. To my dad, any extra money that did come in WAS spent on *something* – lots of model trains. (Don't ask.)

This erroneous idea that wealth must equal materialism results from the same origin of not growing up with any money – since every dollar earned was spent just to keep the lights on and the family bellies full, any MORE dollars earned than what the family needs must ALSO just be spent – after all, there's always something that could be repaired or replaced or upgraded.

When there is never enough money coming in, there is no value placed on a stash of cash simply sitting on the sidelines for the breathing room and stress relief it provides.

Do not equate having more money with spending that money on more and more things – you can be wealthy and not have anyone know it from the outside looking in. In fact, many mega-wealthy families are humble and very private about their financial affairs.

This is a MAJOR POINT to absorb:

If you want to be financially wealthy, you can be the same YOU you are now…just with a sky-high net worth. You don't need to buy things with big price tags to "be" wealthy. You don't need a Lambo in your driveway when you have the money to afford it – you're just showing off for someone else at that point.

To those who know how to make money and take good care of it, money simply makes them feel SAFE and SECURE and FREE.

It frees them from the addiction to a weekly or monthly paycheck, from living their boss's life instead of their own.

To have more money does NOT mean you have to spend it.

$$$

It's ironic that in the grand experiment that is America, the home of the free, that most Americans DON'T FEEL FREE at all…they feel insecure, indebted and powerless…feeling FREE is one of the last adjectives to make the list in the 21st century for most Americans.

They don't feel free because they don't have a stash of F-U money within reach to help them navigate out of a bad situation.

They feel as helpless as my then two-year old daughter when we put her in her car seat (that she'll be in until she graduates college based on manufacturer's recommendations): "STUCK!" she'd yell as she pushed against the restraints.

She didn't understand us much back then, but I'd always look at her lovingly, smile and say, "Of course you're stuck, Honey. My job is to keep you safe – does this car look like a freakin' bouncy house to you?"

The wealthy don't grow their net worth so they can buy more and more things – what the wealthy know that those in debt or living paycheck-to-paycheck have not yet learned is:

Money in the (bank's) safe is safety.

More money in the bank is security.

Even more money in the bank is freedom.

Money in the bank[2] gives you more choices and options on how you want to live your life.

Money in the bank puts a person in charge of their own destiny because they have the financial freedom to make their life a choose-your-own-adventure story.

---

[2] By money in the bank, I'm not just referring to checking and savings accounts, but having significant assets on your balance sheet (retirement accounts, stock holdings, real estate, etc.) that you can tap in an emergency or for the rest of your life.

If the wealthy do carry any DEBT (as you'll often hear), it is merely a tool that they use in their favor, it is not the indentured servitude it is for the majority who can't get out from under their payday loans, revolving credit card debt and, for so many now, student loan debt.

So, what is money ultimately FOR to the wealthy?

Money is for safety, security and freedom.

This is a key point I'll be repeating and expanding on throughout this book...that money is for short-term SAFETY, long-term SECURITY and ultimately financial FREEDOM.

When you grasp how powerful your money is to provide those three key things, you will start to look for every opportunity to not just make or earn or collect more money in your life, but also at how to KEEP more of it and to GROW the money you do have.

$ $ $

Have you ever thought about money just sitting in the bank as being freedom?

This is beyond saving UP for something. This is just money sitting in a bank to help you weather an unpredictable life. (And life is supposed to be unpredictable...otherwise what fun would it be if you knew exactly what would happen day after day?)

Whether it's one dollar ($1), a hundred dollars ($100) or ten thousand dollars ($10,000)...every dollar stored up in the bank behind what I call your Money Dam is a dollar of safety, security and freedom.

Money is not what you make in a month or in a year and money is not what you spend…MONEY is what you KEEP for yourself because it, in turn, KEEPS YOU SAFE.

And once you start to feel SAFE, you have the breathing room (and thinking room) to define the life you want for yourself and pursue it.

For people who LIVE this line of thinking, the first thing they do with each paycheck is pay THEMSELVES first by moving a chunk of dough into their savings account. They understand the underlying and lasting power of Money versus the transience of Cash.

They also understand that it is THEIR money first BEFORE they pay the landlord and the 72-month car loan (I'm kidding…a 72-month car loan, people?!?) and the insurance company, etc. – they pay themselves *first* because they are the top priority in their lives.

If you get this at its most fundamental level, your entire relationship with money will change right here.

$ $ $

The Money Dam

I find the idea of a money dam to be a very powerful metaphor for thinking about your own money, so powerful that I'm going to be referencing it throughout this book – it'll be our visual metaphor as we dive deeper (yuk-yuk) into our money mindset talk.

Much as the same water is always recirculating throughout the world and you statistically drink some of the very water molecules that made their way through Julius Caesar ("Et tu, reader?")…or through a dinosaur (RAWR!)…money is always in a similar flow around the globe.

The Money Dam™: This is a simplified version of The Money Dam that we'll be expanding on later in the book. For more information, check out Appendix A.

Think of the accumulation of your money as water being saved up behind a dam, thus creating a lake. Just like water in a real reservoir, any money you have in the bank is in reserve.

Much as dams let water through to generate electricity or to fulfill contracts to provide water downstream, you do this, too, when you pay for…well, anything! The biggest dams don't completely block the flow of water, after all, but they do limit its flow downstream from what they receive upstream.

Water behind a dam is stored up as potential energy.

Likewise with money, before you steer your car through a McDonald's drive-thru, for example, and rejoice in the industrialization of the common meal, your money was just potential energy twiddling its thumbs and waiting for you to tell it what to do, just chillin' like water behind the dam.

Now, a few people have a Hoover Dam/Lake Mead of resources at their disposal (Elon Musk, Bill Gates, The Zuck, Warren Buffett, Martha Stewart…any billionaire, for sure) and many people have a reservoir that could last perhaps a decade of income drought of retirement, but most Americans and many people around the world have at best a few twigs of good intentions bunched together that don't stop any of the water from flowing right past them downstream.

People with a NEGATIVE net worth and little to no income, which was my situation for years when I was saddled with student loan debt, feel like there's only desert as far as the eye can see. For this latter group, there is no dam to build because there has never been any water to hold back!

Yet.

What we'll soon see is that we need to build our dam as high as we can first and for that we need nothing more than our own minds.

As I like to say, "If you don't give a dam about your money, no one else will!"

If you don't put in the work and learn to Think Wealthy…to build the mental dam in the first place…you will never be in control of your own life.

Money is Energy

Money is just a tool because money is energy. That's all.

If you think about it, you pay your bills by shifting numbers from one bank server to another.

"Yo, electric company, grab those numbers from Bank of America and leave me alone for another month or two, ya' dig?"

That's all you're doing at the end of the day.

Even if you write a check, it's just a note of instruction for a bank: "Take that number in the box over there and move it from the account and routing number in the funky-looking font[3] at the bottom of the check to this OTHER account…(yawn, checks are SOOOO last millennium)."

Money is ultimately just a tool – nothing but a catalyst for making people exchange objects (goods) or take actions (services) for one another.

---

[3] That funky-looking font is the MICR font, or Magnetic Ink Character Recognition font, created so that both machines and humans alike could read it for ease of processing. It's like a legible bar code system for banks.

There's no reason to get too woogy-woogy about this – money is not that unique a form of energy in the world:

We only see the wind in the objects that it affects.

We only see electricity via the heated filaments or agitated gas molecules of light bulbs, the spinning of a motor or whichever of the million amazing things it does when it flows through a wire or a circuit board.

We only see magnetic fields on a compass yet the Earth, our home, is just one huge magnet that (thankfully) deflects most of the sun's life-zapping solar wind.

So why should the force of money be any different?

Money makes the world go 'round and is everywhere in our lives, but before this moment, very few of us have thought of it as being a form of energy.

Yet it is.

Money is energy flowing in every direction at once. It is in a constant state of flow in a mind-boggling and never-ending cycle.

$$$

The Super-Sized Power of Your Money

Let's say you go through that McDonald's drive-thru I was just talking about because you're hungry, want something fast and dependable(ish) and don't feel any guilt about it because you don't live in Los Angeles, like I do, where eating fast food is a sin you must confess to your yoga/Pilates/spin/Zumba/clean colon-obsessed/Keto instructor.

For the sake of simplicity, you hand over $10 after super-sizing your Extra Value meal. Your $10 transfers to the restaurant where it shatters into a multitude of uses: it goes to pay for the employees working there, their health insurance plan, the workers' compensation insurance, the employer's contributions to Social Security and Medicare via payroll taxes, the plethora of income taxes levied on the employees themselves as W-2 wage earners, the raw (frozen) food materials used to create your Extra Value meal, the utilities of that particular building to heat up the deep fryers that make the world's most amazing French fries, franchise fees for the 80% of McDonald's restaurants that are franchised, for state and local sales taxes and on and on and on…

And on.

And still buried deep down in there is enough profit from your $10 that the franchisee and the national corporation all smile a little on the inside. Which, in turn, makes all the shareholders who own shares of McDonald's stock (NYSE: MCD) smile.

Your simple $10 bill or swipe of your card did ALL that!

Did you have any idea?

It exploded out of your account like a shotgun blast to fulfill so many different needs at once.

And every time you spend money it does just that.

Money is always in motion.

You thought you were just dropping by for a quick meal after a long day of work at the office (when the global pandemic ends) and here you actually funded your state's bullet train initiative via state sales tax that you voted against but that passed anyway and your local government's electric bill next holiday season to keep the nativity scene, Christmas tree, menorah and Kwanzaa candles all burning equally bright and the U.S. government's military efforts in the war on…whatever war they're fighting this year.

That $10, and ALL of your money, works hard!

$$$

Your money is potential energy

Before we Super-Sized our triglycerides at McDonald's, our money was just POTENTIAL energy until we reached the drive-thru window and we agreed that what we ordered was worth $10 from our wallet or bank account.

Money is potential energy because its value is stored up like water behind a dam. The more money we have saved and invested…which is the bigger goal…the bigger the reservoir behind that dam is all.

This is why I say money is so dam sexy. (Sorry, you're stuck with me now.)

Our money is "digital" because we so rarely touch tangible, physical money in the form of cash these days, "potential" because it doesn't DO anything until we tell it to and "energy" because it causes a good to be delivered or service to be performed for us while remaining emotionless and aloof, like a rising teen actor.

It's a little odd, but after the U.S. untethered its currency from the gold standard in 1933 to help pull itself out of the Great Depression and then fully abandoned the gold standard in 1971, there is absolutely nothing backing the money that we spend day in and day out except our mutual trust that the very next person you give your money to will honor it at the same value.

In theory, you could take a roll of toilet paper, mark "$100" on each sheet and use that to pay for goods and services in your community. The only thing needed is a shared communal agreement, trust in its most basic form, that a sheet of your toilet paper is worth $100 of goods or services.

Of course, if you grew up in Hawaii like my father-in-law did, and lived through hurricanes that made landfall, you knew to stock up on toilet paper before the hurricane hit as it might be weeks before the cargo ships could deliver any more. Hawaii doesn't have the resources to make (much of anything, really) on its own – so a sheet of your toilet paper being worth $100 isn't so far-fetched, after all!

[A stockpile of toilet paper in Hawaii definitely comes in handy in a pinch.]

[And as we saw at the beginning of the coronavirus pandemic, many Americans viewed toilet paper as if it WERE rolls of hundred-dollar bills! We had 60 rolls stockpiled in our garage for months on end – turns out you don't use as much as you think you do.]

Once you see that money is not cash, that it is neutral and a tool that is waiting for YOU to tell it what to do, you start to take responsibility for where you are in your life...all the good and all the bad...and you realize:

Money does not, and cannot, control you – YOU control IT.

It's YOUR money.

(You can't see me right now but I'm pounding on my desk because that's how much I want you to get this.)

The money you earn is YOUR money.

[Pound, pound.]

You better believe that wealthy people all understand this very clearly: YOU control your money – it does not control you.

Of course, you have financial priorities to pay the bills each month, but your money is YOURS to do with as you see fit and if you start CHOOSING to pay your bills (as opposed to HAVING to), you will forever change your relationship with money in an instant.

For years, every check I received had a big job to do: there were student loans to pay down, credit card debt to make a dent in…I'd open every envelope, look at the check and immediately feel my soul deflate because the money had already "been spent."

There was no joy in the receiving of money for a job well done, there was only resignation and defeat that it was spent before the check even cleared.

My debt and my lifestyle were in charge of my life and I was just a casual, handsome observer to it all.

To turn my financial life around I had to literally reset my money mindset. When I would get a check, I would hold it in my hands, force a big smile on my face and act giddy that I now had that amount of money (no matter how small) in front of me.

It didn't matter that the money had plenty of places to go – in the moment I was thrilled to receive it – I was unclogging the pipes of money circulation in my own mind.

For one of the first times in my adult life, I was grateful for all the money heading my way.

I was grateful that flipping a switch in my apartment always turned on a light, that the toilet always flushed, that I was making a living in a city on the other side of the country from where I grew up and I had made great friends and was able to afford amazing adventures.

I had gratitude – I was grateful for my life exactly as it was.

That's when my life started to turn around financially.

I started CHOOSING every bill that came my way, after learning to ACCEPT and APPRECIATE the money flowing to me, and suddenly I felt like I was in the driver's seat of my financial life. For the first time ever.

The more grateful I was for my INCOME and the more I chose the OUTCOME (or outflow of my money), the more expansive my mind became about the role that money played in my life.

$ $ $

Do you ever consciously CHOOSE to pay your bills?

Or do you feel, like most people, the burden that you HAVE TO pay your bills?

Does your financial life consist of one OBLIGATION after another, or do you pause with each bill to think about what you're paying for and how you benefited from the product or service?

Flip that switch in your brain to CHOOSING to spend your money the way you do, to being GRATEFUL for all that you do have and see how that feels.

As a wise person recently said, where most of us are right now in our lives was little more than a dream even a few years ago.

The world will only reward you for pausing to be grateful for where you are in your life.

It's empowering. And it's a crucial first step to taking control of your (financial) life.

$ $ $

This is true for everyone. When you are grateful for and love the flow of money in your life, and really respect it, what you're actually doing is loving and respecting YOURSELF.

Truth #3: Money is a magnet to value

This is the foundation for understanding how to create, earn and collect as much money as your heart desires.

Money is a magnet to one thing and one thing only, and that is to VALUE.

We tend to think that money rewards the smartest of us or the greediest of us or the luckiest of us, but money is only attracted to one thing: value.

Rather than putting anyone who is wealthy up on a pedestal, think of them, instead, of simply having created enough value in the world to collect a big sum of money for it.

Money flows toward value. [4]

The fact that money flows TO value may seem quite commonsense, but it revolutionized the way I think about it.

A light bulb lit up in my noodle and I smelled ramen. (That or I had just had a stroke.)

Once I understood that money flowed to value, I could trace its path anywhere and everywhere and follow it back to the source: the repair work on my car, the electricity and water I used from local utilities, the craftsmanship in the $10,000 engagement ring for my sig other (As if! we got our rings on Amazon for $20 each and everyone compliments us on them…now there's some value for you!).

Wherever I looked and whenever I pulled out my wallet or signed into online banking, I saw value being exchanged for my money.

AND by watching where my money flowed, I saw what I VALUED in my own life based on how I was spending my money. In many cases, I didn't actually *value* the things or experiences that I was spending money on. So, I stopped. Bam!

That $20 monthly subscription to Publishers Marketplace that I held onto because I felt it kept me connected to the publishing industry even

---

[4] There's a fair argument to be made that certain products or services don't really produce any value, yet still attract vaultfuls of money. Bernie Madoff, the psychopathic and remorseless Ponzi schemer who was discovered in the crash of the Great Recession, only created "perceived value." Legions of people sent Bernie their life's savings and thought they were earning a 12% return – but it wasn't real value, only perceived value. This is an extreme case, but it's a fair point that billions of dollars flow to areas of perceived value every day, both good and bad.

though I had long moved on from the idea of publishing an earlier book? Canceled.

A big and expensive birthday dinner for a friend of a friend when I had no money to my name? Maybe next year.

Gifting any family members with money at the holidays that I couldn't afford because I felt guilty I didn't travel back to see them more often? Now, no one exchanges gifts so problem solved!

The concept of value...and what we each find value in...is the ever-shifting variable here, but that's what makes us all unique.

Of course, this is also the exact reason that money causes so much friction between couples and is the **number one** predictor of divorce, greater than any other subject – you both need to be on the same page when it comes to what you VALUE in your life and where you are headed TOGETHER....what your SHARED VALUES are...and, therefore, where and how you should spend your money.

I spent so much of my life imbuing money with mystery and intrigue...into how money was "made" and how the rich and wealthy became that way as if they were from another planet...and here was the culprit all along – VALUE!

It also provides a couple of formulas for entrepreneurs and business owners for creating wealth:

Provide value to millions and you will make millions. *

Provide value to billions and you will become a billionaire. *

* If you know your own worth.

The more people you provide value to, the more money you will earn...or collect.

It's why the sharks on ABC's Shark Tank are always looking for businesses that can scale (up) easily. From their point of view, the more quickly you provide value to ever increasing numbers of new and happy customers, the more of a return your investment will make.

If money is attracted to value, then you are paid at your job commensurate with the level of value that you bring to the company you work for, based on current market rates. You are being paid what the market and your company thinks your job is worth at this time. [5]

You can also see that by providing MORE value at work or by creating a side business that creates value for others, the sky's the limit to what you can earn.

$ $ $

Money flows to value in your own life.

View a recent bank or credit card statement of yours and scan down the list of transactions. Do you really VALUE everything that you spent your money on? Can you cut out anything next week or next month of LOW value and instead put that money behind your Money Dam because you value feeling safe and free MORE?

What about your job or career? Do you bring as much VALUE to the position as you think you do...would you hire YOU if you were asked

---

[5] Being born and presenting female or a POC (person of color) or one of any other type of employment discrimination, notwithstanding. C'mon, people, it's 2022 – let's work in earnest to spot and resolve this dinosaur thinking.

to interview candidates to fill your current job?

$ $ $

Looking at money as an exchange of value helps to take the emotion out of a lot of financial decisions, too. When deciding whether a product or service holds any value for you, if you remove the emotion, it often becomes a very easy and binary (yes/no) decision to make. No guilt, no shoulda/coulda/woulda…just a yes or no answer to the question of value.

Money has no emotion, but YOU do!

We all have a very complex and intimate relationship with money. After all, we've used it our whole lives to express who we are to the outside world by how we dress, the cars we drive, etc.

Yet if I asked ten different people to talk about money, I would get ten different (emotional) responses, most if not all of them about how they struggle to make more of it, to keep what they do make, wishing they knew how to manage it, hoping that one day their lottery ticket is going to hit and on and on and on.

You'd be hard-pressed to find someone who *doesn't* have a negative, emotional relationship with money and who thinks that every problem of theirs would be solved if they only had more of it.

Poor, poor money.

It's not easy being green.

But that is OUR mistake…adding emotion to money.

We think money is finicky, temperamental, cryptic, even mean-spirited! But money doesn't CARE about anything, of course.

Including you!

You can love it or hate it but realize that is your choice to make in the matter because:

- Money is 100% neutral.
- Money has no emotion.
- Money is not bad.
- Money is not good.
- Money is just money.

We, on the other hand, have been in a psychotic love affair with money our entire lives.

It logically follows that if money is completely neutral and is neither good nor bad then:

Money doesn't have morals.

That doesn't mean that money is amoral in the "money is evil" chorus so many of us have been led to believe.

Of course, money doesn't have morals. It's neutral, emotionless.

The real question here is: Do YOU have morals?

It's up to YOU and the people you do business with to have integrity and stay on a moral track.

Money doesn't have morals, PEOPLE do.

And some people don't.

But should.

And that's just life.

"But, Todd…"

I know. I know. The idea that money doesn't single-handedly "turn" people to the dark side is a real doozy for most people.

Be careful not to BLAME money itself and think it is inherently immoral (fraud, embezzlement, political corruption, etc.) any more than that money creates philanthropy and all the good that it can do in the world, too.

MONEY is not moral or amoral…PEOPLE are moral or amoral.

If a real saint of a person you know comes into a lot of money and they suddenly become the spawn of Satan, don't blame the money. Your friend was never much of a true-hearted saint to begin with.

I've always been fascinated with first-generation millionaires and billionaires and have listened closely to Oprah Winfrey and other ultra-high-net-worth individuals when they talk about their relationship to money and the one thing in common they all say is:

Money just makes you more of who you already are.

Bam. Mucho money in the bank just turns up the volume on your personality.

So, if you're kind and generous with a little money, you'll be even more kind and generous when you're wealthy. And what a great contribution to the world and the human condition you will be! (There are plenty of news stories of wealthy people doing good in the world if you keep your eyes and ears open for them.)

And if you're a raging d-bag with a little bit of money who's about to sell his or her company for a major profit, look out, World!

But money doesn't TURN you into a kind-hearted philanthropist or a mean sonofagun. Those seeds were always there in a person's character, and money merely watered them.

I say life is too short and no one gets to the top of the money pile without the help of many, many other people so let's get over ourselves and just treat people the way we want to be treated, agreed?

(Instant better world! That was easy.)

$ $ $

Clear your mind and think about the word "money."

What is the first sensation you feel?

Does your chest tighten or do you feel a knot in the pit of your stomach because you really NEED or want more of it? Or because you've witnessed its power to break up couples and destroy families? (Again, arguments about money are the leading predictor of divorce.)

Or does the thought of money excite you because of all the new opportunities it represents? Money may equal travel and meeting new people (after the global pandemic ends), moving into a different socio-economic class than you were raised, etc.

This early in the game (and in this book), you are most likely to have an unconscious, underlying negative relationship with money. Which is PERFECT for now – if the thought of money gives you the heebie-jeebies or completely confuses you or if it just feels utterly mysterious and confounding, accept it all, laugh about it, and keep reading because you're RIGHT where you're supposed to be.

Since money itself is completely neutral, it's important for you to see at this point what YOU are bringing to the table in our discussion of money, one way or the other.

$ $ $

What I hope you learn as we poke around under the hood of your money mindset together is that whether you give money positive or negative connotations will directly determine not only your net worth, but even more importantly, your very own happiness in life.

Truth #4: Money is abundant

This is one of the most difficult truths about money to accept if you've been told all your life that "money doesn't grow on trees" or you were eternally, rhetorically asked by a parent, "What – do you think I'm made of money?!?"

When all you've seen and heard is lack and scarcity surrounding money, the idea that money is actually abundant in the world sounds like wishful thinking or that a genie has just granted you an unbelievable wish.

But it's true. Money is abundant in the world because people will always be in search of the value that either solves a problem that they have or that makes their life easier in some way.

Money is never locked away like water in an iceberg (except in retirement accounts as I'll later explain) – money is always in flow around the globe in search of value…and it always will be.

Money is abundant in the world.

This was one of the most difficult beliefs for me to absorb because I was raised to believe that if you earned $200 then someone else didn't earn $200 – the money scales always had to balance out which meant that your gain was always someone else's loss and, well, how could you knowingly take money from someone who needed it MORE than you? How selfish of you, Todd!

The belief I grew up with was a relativistic one – there were money winners and money losers because there was limited supply and the only humane thing to do is to not ask for too much and take too big a share of the pie.

What is becoming clear is that only people without much money in the bank say, "Well, so-and-so needs it more than I do" – even as they dance on the razor's edge of financial ruin.

A wealthy-minded person may take the money they have earned and endeavor to turn it into even MORE money, creating new businesses and jobs for others, all the while donating to the causes and charities that are dear to them – they're helping themselves while also helping others.

Even if you were to believe that the money scales must always be in balance, think of an Elon Musk or Jeff Bezos or Warren Buffett, some of the world's wealthiest people, and realize that regardless of their astronomical personal net worth, their combined wealth is not even a drop in the bucket of money flowing throughout our global system at any given moment.

The wealthiest people alive on our planet believe that money is abundant...so much so that when they occasionally lose it all on a risky bet that goes south, they simply go back to the drawing board and make even more the next time around because they understand how to provide massive value to get it back again.

This is not a support for or indictment of the tremendous wealth inequality that exists in the United States and in other parts of the world. For the first time ever, in 2019 the 400 richest Americans paid a lower total tax rate than any other income group. Which is absurd but not surprising when politicians continually pass tax legislation that benefits the 1% and above.

It's apparent that the tax code is out of whack and needs to be addressed. In fact, many of our country's wealthiest people whose names I've mentioned in these pages repeatedly call for tax reform for the ultra-wealthy. There are volumes of books dedicated to issue of wealth inequality so I don't intend to address it within these pages except to say that the distribution of wealth on a macro-economic scale is unsustainable in the long-term.

As I write that, I'm staring at a book next to me titled *Ten Thousand Years of Inequality: The Archaeology of Wealth Differences*, edited by Timothy A. Kohler and Michael E. Smith. Maybe wealth inequality IS sustainable in the long-term, it just demolishes empires is all. I'll read it and let you know what I find out later...if the United States is still standing by then...

All this being said, it remains true that there is an infinite supply of money in the world, ever more accessible to individuals and companies based on globalization and the interconnectedness of the world's financial markets – that should only be more apparent now than it has ever been.

If you still don't believe that money is abundant and infinite, just ask the Fed (the Federal Reserve) and the United States Treasury whenever the country leans toward recession:

> *Sorry, I can barely hear you over the printing presses in the next room creating trillions of dollars out of thin air, but yeah, we'd agree that money is pretty abundant. We should know – the buck doesn't stop here, it actually starts here!*
>
> *- Teddy the Treasury Worker*

Of course, it's not *really* noisy where Teddy works – any talk of the government printing money out of thin air only happens on a balance sheet as it adds credit to its member banks deposits to create more liquidity in the markets.

All modern money "printing" is digital.

But you knew that already, you genius, you.

$$\$ \ \$ \ \$$$

Money is abundant, but you don't really believe that, do you?

You can be honest with me…I'm your money buddy…you don't REALLY think money is in complete abundance in the world.

I know. I feel your pain.

Imagine if that were actually true, though. Imagine that there is as MUCH money out there waiting for you as you can lay claim to. And all you need to do is HELP enough people, provide enough VALUE, to rake it in.

With such a positive and optimistic outlook, perhaps a creative part of your brain is already racing to figure out how you can get there?

What if, right?

$ $ $

If money is flipping around all over the globe, why is it in abundance everywhere but in our own pockets and bank accounts?

Because we don't know how to effectively COLLECT it yet is all.

And unless we understand and change any of our negative views and opinions of money and wealth, we'll never keep any of the money we DO collect.

So, let's help you capture more of it so you, too, can feel the safety and security of a blossoming bank account and net worth as water rises up behind your financial dam.

Because...let's say it all together now...if you don't give a dam about your money, no one else will!

Truth #5: Money makes money

Money makes more money.

And your money NEEDS to make more money.

The wealthy look to every opportunity to foster and capitalize on the fact that money makes more money.

Money makes money for the simple fact that money COSTS money as it zips around the globe.

You might best know this as the interest you get charged by a bank for using your credit cards or for a car loan or a mortgage if you buy a house.

This is a tale as old as time…like the one where Beast loans Belle money to get a nose job so Disney will cast her in the live-action movie version and he charges her a nominal interest rate until she pays him back.

Since money costs money via interest to borrow, the wealthy, in effect, are acting as a bank when they INVEST their money.

Money multiplies when it is invested correctly.

Like anything that replicates itself when you turn away from it for even a moment…zombies or Mogwai…money makes more money.

And more money makes even more money.

And the mostest money makes the mostiest money.

This is what banks do – they lend money out and charge interest. You can do the same with your money when it's invested – let's ALL be the bank!

$$$

Wealth Tip: *Think of "Saving" as Investing in Yourself*

I was always told to SAVE my money for a rainy day, or if I wanted something to SAVE UP for it, the implication of which, and the one that I followed for most of my life, was that you were just setting extra money aside until you BOUGHT something with it in the FUTURE.

Just "saving" money kept it in a spending purgatory waiting for the Judgment Day of shopping.

Saving money for a rainy day made money only a temporary friend in my mind as opposed to a long-term member of the family.

Don't think just of SAVING or SAVING UP your money, think of it, instead, as you INVESTING in yourself. There's action and growth toward financial freedom in thinking of it that way.

Saving is passive. Investing in yourself is active.

$$\$\$\$$$

You want your money to make more money at every chance, even while you're sleeping (like the wealthy do). Saving your money won't really do that…only investing it will.

Of course, you don't need to earn a seat on ABC's *Shark Tank* to invest your excess dollars, you start by "investing" them in a simple savings account so that your money is making some money (albeit a small amount of interest as we recover from low interest rates from the Great Recession and now the economic tailspin of the coronavirus pandemic), but at least it's DOING something and WORKING for you.

In our family, we have a chunk of change in an online money market account because we may need it for a down payment for a house in the next couple of years and that's the most secure place for it. It's returning under 1% at the moment, which may not feel like much, but it has returned $1,000 or more various years by just sitting in that account.

Does a $1,000 seem like not much money to you? Considering that you expended no energy to earn it and it was 100% safe and insured by the federal government? Would you say no to it?

We will pay ordinary income tax on the "interest income" but it was still free. Free!

Our money sat in a bank and free money was made while we slept peacefully through the night (depending on whether our daughter was sick that week or not).

You always want your money to make more money because your only financial job is to pay your monthly bills until you die. But you don't know when that will be.

Investing your money is the only way to hedge for the long term.

Of course, our money makes the most money with the help of the two most beautiful words in any wealthy person's vocabulary:

Compound Interest

If they're not your favorite words yet, they better be by the end of this book!

Compound interest is quite simply the interest your money makes sitting in an account, compounded (you making interest off the interest!) and growing exponentially year after year, over whatever time horizon you have.

Compound interest is why a 25-year-old can drop $50,000 into a tax-advantaged retirement account and never add in another cent yet wake up a millionaire just in time for retirement at the age of 65 (assuming an 8% average annual return on those investments).

$50,000 turns into $1,000,000 with an 8% annual return over 40 years. That's $950,000 of free money! (Tax free if it's in a Roth IRA.)

Are "compound interest" your favorite words yet?

You should love them so much you're going to lobby your congresspeeps for legislation to let you MARRY compound interest.

"You may now kiss your double-digit returns." [cue Mendelssohn's Wedding March]

$$$

Wealth Warning: *Compound Interest in Reverse*

Millions of people feel the effects of compound interest on the FLIP side of the equation – it not only works on the positive side like we've just seen, it works in reverse, too.

If you have $5,000 of credit card debt (which is about average as of 2020), you probably have a minimum payment of $200 a month.

If you had no interest accruing on that debt each month, you would pay off that $5,000 in 25 months (or 2 years and 1 month). ($200 per month x 25 months = $5,000)

BUT, because you have a 17% interest rate on your credit card, it will actually take you 10 years and 10 months to pay off the same $5,000.

Compound interest in reverse tacked on an additional 9 YEARS of minimum $200 payments!!!

Not only that, but by the time you pay off the original $5,000, you will have paid an additional $2,627 in interest. So, if you thought you were buying the latest and greatest TV for $5,000, it really cost you $7,627 and it kept you in debt for over 10 years!

All because of compound interest in REVERSE.

That better be God's gift to televisions for all those hours you spent at the office (before the global pandemic started) to afford it. Oof.

Compounding interest in reverse is the WORST.

This is why debt can be so difficult to climb out of. It's all compound interest, either you're paying it to a credit card company and the bank is earning it or someone is paying it out to you in an investment and you're earning it. I know which side of that equation I want to be on.

Compound interest is very, very powerful. You just want to make sure you're on the right side of it…that you're EARNING it and not PAYING it.

You see why compound interest has been called the eighth wonder of the world. It's highly dubitable that Einstein ever said this, but the sentiment is spot-on so forget about the saying's attribution and let's just live by it:

Compound interest is the eighth wonder of the world. He who understands it, earns it … he who doesn't … pays it.

- (Not) Albert Einstein

The wealthy rely on their own money to make more (free) money for them at every opportunity – the money they worked hard for, in return, works hard for them – that's where they see free money, in investing their money.

And nope, don't even try it with me…lottery tickets are not investments. End of story.

So that is the glorious revelation of compound interest, to introduce it to you for the first time or to remind you to look for it at every opportunity so your money can grow and grow and GROW.

Two Money Enemies

Why all this talk about INVESTING our money, anyway?

Since many people are distrustful of banks and the global financial engine after the Great Recession, why not just stuff our money under our mattresses at home where at least we know it's safe and we can keep an eye on it?

The reason we always…ALWAYS…want our money to make MORE MONEY has to do with that seducer of our dollars and cents, that lothario known as inflation.

Money Enemy #1: Inflation

If you keep your money in cash at home stuffed under the mattress, inflation is going to walk into your bedroom and seduce the hell out of your cash stash, leaving it feeling used and exhausted, unable to provide the same purchasing power it once had…and leaving you the poorer for it before you know it.

Inflation, quite simply, is the upward creep of the price of goods and services over time.

(Your eyes may have glossed over at the boringness of this section title…of talking about inflation…but when I tell you you're always LOSING MONEY because of inflation, that should wake you up!)

That loaf of bread that Grandma yammers on about paying only 5-cents for that is now $3.99? Inflation!

A gallon of gasoline for the lawnmower that Uncle Clyde paid $0.75 for that warm summer day when it accidentally whacked off his right thumb (true story), that gallon of gas that now costs $3.25 a gallon? Inflation!

That happy ending your great-grandfather shelled out $5 for in that Paris red-light district after storming the beaches of Normandy in WWII that today costs $50 (after the global pandemic ends)? Inflation!

There are two primary types of inflation, price inflation and monetary inflation, but only one is relevant for us here:

Technically-speaking, we're talking about **Price Inflation** which is nothing more than the month-to-month difference in the Consumer Price Index. This data is published every month by the Bureau of Labor Statistics, but price inflation is almost always discussed in terms of a yearly or annual percentage.

Monetary Inflation, on the other hand, is when a government floods the markets by consistently "printing" more money and thereby devaluing whatever money is currently in the system through simple supply and demand economics.

The takeaway here is that your money starts to LOSE its purchasing power as soon as you get it because of INFLATION.

And stashing it under the mattress won't solve the problem.

Phrased another way, price inflation means your money will always be worth LESS tomorrow than it's worth today unless you invest and

GROW it because it starts losing value as soon as you receive it.

Think of inflation to your money as evaporation is to water sitting behind a dam. Evaporation causes water to "disappear" as water vapor into the air just as inflation causes your money's purchasing power to "disappear" into the air.

Evaporation and inflation are both just facts of life and...

There's nothing you can do about inflation.

Nothing.

The wealthy understand that their money is always LOSING MONEY (or losing value) if it's not invested because of INFLATION.

It doesn't mean they're obsessing about what inflation is clocking in at each year (2-3% is the goal in a healthy economy), but they do understand its long-term effects on their money.

There is a great debate among economists and their brethren and sistren (that's Middle English fer ya, look it up!) about whether inflation is a good or a bad thing. So often the knee-jerk response it to decry that inflation is bad, but if your salary at your job rises at the same level as inflation (that 3% cost of living raise you should be getting each year), then no one's losing anything...it's all in lockstep and everyone is happy.

If you're starting to see why the people who understand and are "good" with money are always on the lookout for ways to keep their money growing to at least match inflation, then you're already clicking into the right money mindset.

Woohoo – we're not even through the first chapter and I smell the smoke of progress wafting out of your ears!

In truth, inflation is more of a back-burner concept. It's messy trying to peg the inflation rate each year and just because some goods and services inflate in price doesn't mean they ALL do so this isn't one to get your pantaloons in much of a bunch over – it's a fact of life and is more of a motivator for always making sure your money makes MORE money year after year.

$ $ $

As I write this, the rate of inflation for the 12-month period ending December 2021 is 7%. (Ouch.) That's the highest rate in 39 years!

Did any money you have sitting in a savings or retirement account grow by at LEAST 7% last year? Your answer is most likely NO to the former (savings) and YES to the latter (retirement).

Have you ever even thought about it that way before?

I want you to get into the habit (and mindset) of knowing where your money is and what return, if any, it's making. If you've never thought of it that way before, welcome to the WEALTHIER YOU.

As I already wrote, our family has some change sitting in an online money market account returning under 1% a year. (It was returning 2.2% annually until the pandemic spooked the markets and the Fed rolled the fed funds rate down to almost zero.) But that is all we "need" to do with that particular savings account as it's for short-term safety, so a guaranteed return that was beating inflation (until very recently) with NO RISK is actually pretty solid. Smiles all around.

$ $ $

Again, inflation is generally expected to clock in at about 2-3% a year.

I would try not to lose any sleep over inflation, but just know that it's there chipping away at your purchasing power like a total financial d-bag.

Money Enemy #2: Taxes

The other enemy to your hard-earned money is taxes.

The two inevitables of life, as the saying goes, are death and taxes.

Now we all know that we need to pay taxes. We WANT to pay our taxes because we want the firemen to show up when our house is on fire, we want safe bridges and roads to travel on and we all want our retired parents to get their Social Security checks on time…and on and on and on.

In essence, we all need to pay taxes to keep this amazing experiment of a country moving forward.

Every country (I'm talking to you, select European Union nations in a Mediterranean climate) needs to pay enough into their government to keep it running as smoothly as it can from a purely financial perspective.

That's a given.

Of course, no one LOVES paying taxes. But we do NEED to pay them.

The upside to this money enemy, which stands in opposition to the enemy of inflation…which you have no control over…is:

There is a lot you CAN do about taxes.

The wealthy know this better than anyone.

While inflation is totally out of your control, the taxes you pay IN to all levels of the government (local, state and federal) are much more malleable and somewhat under your control. The more money you make and the higher your net worth, the more reliant you will be on various tax specialists to help you strategize throughout the year to minimize your tax liability.

Let me say that again – the more money you have to your name, the more you'll be thinking about taxes THROUGHOUT the year and not just on April 15 in the mad dash to file on time. Or July 15 as it happened in 2020 because of the pandemimania.

Regardless of whether you have read that there are 74,000 pages or 2,600 pages to the US Tax Code, either way it proves that the Internal Revenue Service (IRS) understands that there are many, many, (too) MANY shades of grey in the computation and collection of federal income tax.

Between taking full advantage of those shades of grey and paying the least amount you owe – or TAX AVOIDANCE, which is legal - and finding ways to not pay your fair share – or TAX EVASION, which is illegal – is why many people describe accounting and tax preparation as more art than science.

And here you thought accountants and CPAs weren't creative! Their knowledge of the tax code and their ability to save you from paying MORE tax than you need to is why a good tax accountant and CPA are worth their weight in crypto – I mean, gold.

What the majority of wealthy Americans pursue is TAX AVOIDANCE – they take this deduction here and that one there, run expenses through their companies, all to keep their tax bill on the lower end so they can use the rest of it for living life…and for spending and investing to keep driving a strong American economy, the world's largest.

It Costs a Lot to Make a Lot

The crazy thing about paying taxes is that you never stop doing it! Your money is taxed to infinity and beyond.

When I earned exactly six figures (or $100,000 a year), I saw only about 60% of that in my monthly checks. It's one thing to say you make $8,333 a month (or $100,000 a year) and another to see the resulting $5,200 deposited into your account each month. What happened to the missing $3,133 every month? Or $37,600 each year? Federal and state taxes happened...among others!

After maxing out my 401(k) and a Roth IRA, I was left with $37,000 in actual take-home pay each year for rent, insurance(s), food, etc. Still more than many people make, but not exactly the gold mine that $100,000 sounds like, is it?

This gets at the very heart of a core mistake many people make when they talk about their finances. They know they make $100,000 a year on paper, but they don't distinguish that they only take home around $60,000.

That means that if their actual lifestyle costs $80,000 but they're only taking home $60,000...they're short each year by $20,000. And that has to come from...*somewhere.*

You'll hear on financial shows that they always clarify gross income (the $100,000) versus net income after taxes ($60,000), or "take home."

If you're not already thinking in terms of net income...of what is really going into your pocket each month or each year...you need to get on that train because it's already left the station.

Reserve the GROSS INCOME conversations for salary negotiations and the income fields on applications that make you look and feel wealthier than you are – but always think in terms of NET INCOME when calculating what you have to work with month in and month out.

If you want to annoy your friends by talking taxes (like I do – naturally), whenever someone mentions how much the lottery is worth or how much someone won, always be there to say, "Yeah, but after taxes, that 150 million dollars is only about 75 million."

I get yelled at for being a party pooper (and I love it because there's no sugarcoating that the tax man wins the lottery with you!), but it's important to always be thinking of NET, NET, NET income.

The difference between gross and net is why starting your own business and running applicable expenses through it is often very financially-savvy because those expenses are being paid with pre-tax dollars instead of post-tax (or net) which is NIIIICE for your bank account.

Taxes, Taxes Everywhere!

Taxes lurk around every corner and if you're not aware of them throughout the year, you might be letting thousands of dollars slip through your financial fingers.

Let's say you live in Los Angeles (like I do) and you spend $20,000 a year buying the things you need to keep your lifestyle afloat – how often do you also think to include the sales tax of almost 10% that will zap an additional $2,000 from your wallet?

And that's just in sales tax which is obvious because we see it printed out on receipts.

There is a whole list of products and services that have the taxes already baked into the prices:

- Flip on a light switch or turn on the TV (which you paid sales tax on when you bought it): electricity tax!

- Watch a show on cable ("On what?!?" I know): cable tax!

- The cable goes out and you pick up the house phone ("A what?!?" I know) to call the cable company to complain: federal and state landline phone taxes!

- Use your cellphone, instead (because who has landlines nowadays besides that lady who paid for her groceries with a check – ugh!), to complain about the cable being out: federal and state cellphone taxes!

Argh! You need to relax – try taking a shower:

- Turn on the hot water: natural gas tax!

Ugh! Get out of your over-taxed home already!

- Fill up the tank of your economically-minded Honda Civic: federal and state gasoline taxes!

- Thank God you don't drive an SUV: gas guzzler tax!

- Sounds like you could really use a cigarette right about now (even though you don't smoke): cigarette tax!

- Screw it, where's a glass of Arrogant Bastard, your favorite craft beer: alcohol tax!

You can't even travel to get away from the tax insanity because…you guessed it… more taxes! As in, taxes on the entire trip (after the global pandemic ends):

- Flight airfare

- Rental car

- Hotel room

- Gambling

Is it starting to sink in yet?

I hope so, because that sink was taxed, too!

It costs a lot to keep the wealthiest nation the world has ever known running, doesn't it? (And every other nation, for that matter.)

This is just the "basic living" part of life. Most of these are taxes we don't even think or know about...but they're everywhere.

But we're not done!

In terms of INVESTING, any money made in the stock market or most any other investment scenario is taxable, too, when it is not within a tax-advantaged retirement account![6]

I'm not here to make a case that any of these taxes are un-American or anti-American or that the federal government is doing anything sneaky or blatantly wasteful (resist...another footnote...you...can...do...it) or

---

[6] Good luck getting through any discussion on taxes without knee-jerking to the use of a few dozen footnotes. In this case, it is a sweepingly broad statement to say that any money made in the stock market is taxable as there are many fun and zany rules that dictate the who, what, where, when and why of taxation there, but this statement is true, in general.

that we should all grab our old-timey farm pitchforks and rise up together to JUST. SAY. NO.

I just want to point out the reality of taxation on your dollars in modern life.

Taxes in various forms have been around for at least 5,000 years – one of the earliest written records of taxation occurred in Ancient Egypt so it would be pointless for us to rail against taxes themselves. They appear to be a necessary component to living in a civilized society.

What the wealthy already know and understand about taxes, however, is that our tax code is infinitely complex and there are many ways to MAXIMIZE income and earnings and MINIMIZE tax liability LEGALLY.

Why would anyone pay MORE in taxes than they need to?

This is one reason why financial planners and your Uncle Larry are always trying to convince you to put as much money into a tax-advantaged retirement account (IRA, 401(k), etc.) as possible so that your money can grow tax-free or tax-deferred.

IT. IS. THAT. IMPORTANT.

It's a jungle of taxes out there and anything you can do to keep the tax man at bay will only benefit you financially down the line.

Summary

We made it through the money mindset basics! That wasn't so painful, now, was it?

Here's a quick recap of everything we talked about and that you only ever need to learn ONCE:

- Money is as important to your life as water is to your body. No modern, large-scale economy with a highly specialized division of labor like ours has ever existed without some form of monetary system in place.

- If you're not "good" with money now, just giving you more of it won't solve the problem.

- Money Truth #1: All cash is money, but Money is much bigger than cash.

- Money is no thing. It's nothing but numbers on different bank servers. Ultimately, money is just energy waiting to be told where to go and what to do.

- Only people without money think money is primarily for spending.

- Money Truth #2: Money matters because it can provide you with a feeling of short-term safety, long-term security and eventually total financial freedom. With anything less than freedom, you're living a form of financial servitude to someone else.

- Think of your money as a reservoir of water sitting behind a dam and just how dam sexy that is. The question is how high will you build your dam? It happens in your MIND first.

- Money is completely neutral. Money is only a mirror for any positive or negative feelings you have about yourSELF or your lot in life.

- Money just makes you more of who you already are.

- Money Truth #3: Money is a magnet to value – it always has and will flow to value created, mostly in the form of goods sold or services provided. The more value created, the more money you receive – provide value to millions and you will make millions.

- Money Truth #4: Money is as abundant in the world as there is air to breathe.

- Money Truth #5: The beautiful secret about money that every wealthy person understands is that money makes more money.

- Once you understand the power of compounding interest (in both directions), you are now as smart as (not) Albert Einstein who claimed (no, he didn't) that it was the eighth wonder of the world.

- We always want our money to be making more money so we can protect it from inflation (which is out of our control) and so we pay the least amount of taxes possible (which is often WITHIN our control).

The One Financial Takeaway to Know in Your Bones

We've covered quite a bit of ground in this first chapter, but I want to make sure that there is ONE financial concept that you know in your BONES.

If you get this and truly understand it, it makes the price of this book the smallest of investments that will pay compounding dividends for the rest of your life.

What you need to know in your bones is that:

Money exists for safety, security and freedom.

What that means is every single dollar you earn gives you the CHOICE of the future you want to make for yourself – will it go toward making you feel SAFE in the short-term, SECURE in the long-term or financially FREE to create any life you want?

Most people don't understand this on its most powerful and fundamental level or they wouldn't be living paycheck-to-paycheck – they would fight like mad for financial safety, security and freedom as if their LIVES depended on it.

Do you get that yet? Ya' kinda gotta get it before we move on. In fact, I genuinely ask that you not move onto the next chapter until this has really sunk in - it's <u>that</u> important.

But if you do got it, then let's go!!

$$\$\$\$$$

But FIRST, go play "THE MILLION DOLLARS GAME"

in Appendix B at the end of the book.

$$\$\$\$$$

Chapter 2: Understand Wealth

"I can understand wanting to have millions of dollars, there's a certain freedom, meaningful freedom, that comes with that. But once you get much beyond that, I have to tell you, it's the same hamburger."

- Bill Gates

As excited as I was to talk about money in the last chapter, you can imagine that my eyes are teetering on the edge of their sockets now that we're talking about WEALTH.

That one word inspires me into action day after day after day, but maybe not for the reasons you'd think.

Wealth of anything is just an abundance of that thing - it is a great quantity, a plentiful amount - and while this book is called *Think Wealthy* because we are focusing on financial enrichment with money as the fuel for feeling safe, secure and free in our lives, it's important to remember the importance of wealth in ALL areas of a well-rounded life.

What good is a mountain of growing financial assets if you don't have the loving support of family and friends, children who enjoy spending time with you, peer relationships with people you respect and admire and strong mental and physical health so you can actually savor your financial surplus?

Of course, "wealth" is back to being a dirty word. (Truth is it's probably always been a dirty word to the financially-disadvantaged.) People may cheer the success of a newfound millionaire or billionaire for proving the American Dream we all hope to achieve, but the daggers come out soon after.

When many wealthy people have significantly *increased* their net worth in the global COVID-19 pandemic, while millions have lost their jobs (their careers, their loved ones, even) and many are months behind on rent or mortgage payments, the system does seem as if it's rigged.

As I stated in the first chapter, we won't be looking at money and wealth at a macro level in this book as my focus is on you, the reader, the person responsible for navigating your own financial waters. I'm not denying the very real inequalities that exist in the United States of America and the disparity that has continued to grow unchecked for decades now throughout the world, I'm merely concentrating on you and your family on a personal, micro level to help you create lives in which you feel safe, secure and free.

Back on topic, we're going to spend this entire book unpacking what it means to be wealthy.

Be careful, though, not to confuse wealth with EXCESS.

Excess is TOO MUCH of something…kind of like when Kanye (now officially Ye) speaks at an awards show...whereas wealth is limitless abundance.

Wealth is limitless abundance. Excess, on the other hand, is too much of something.

This is the difference between a family who has rather quietly kept financial wealth flowing throughout the generations by learning how to diversify their investments and grow their pool of wealth versus a family that is suddenly blessed (or cursed) by winning the lottery and they make every wrong decision with the excess of money they've been handed.

Also, let's not confuse financial wealth with materialism (as we saw in the first chapter) because HAVING money and SPENDING money are two totally different animals, really a MEOW and a MOO comparison. Still, many people conflate those two ideas and pay dearly for it.

This is a BIG ONE to grasp if you grew up with nothing...wealth does not (necessarily) equal the buying of things or the buying of more stuff than you need.

Wealth and materialism are NOT the same thing.

You can live exactly as you do right now with either $10 or $10,000,000 dollars to your name – the choice of HOW YOU LIVE is always yours to make.

My mom would often respond to the idea of financial fortune with her customary gasp and, "My word! What would I DO with a million dollars? I HAVE more than I need as it is." But there would still be a smile on her face that some deep-rooted fantasy had finally come true.

Not that a million dollars signifies real wealth any longer, but the larger mental mistake that she would make is that having more money meant that she would have to purchase more things. She was an educator, a savvy accountant and an incredible mother who always craved financial security, yet she never understood the value, the power, even, of money just sitting in a bank for safety's sake and invested in a diverse portfolio for a feeling of long-term security.

I've a suspicion that she did understand it, but that she and my dad were just never on the same page with their financial goals.

As my parents have aged up, I have taken over the responsibility of handling their finances and although they may have a house full of things (not TOO many things, thank God – they never became hoarders), they have always skated on the razor's edge of financial insolvency.

In theory (and in practice), most millionaires look like your neighbors. In fact, they very possibly ARE your neighbors. I don't mean mega-millionaires, but people living what appears to be an average lifestyle without the need for the glitz and glamor that we so often associate with celebrities and wealthy people who live their lives in the public eye.

In terms of the *personal wealth* that any of us can achieve, we can have a wealth of friends, a wealth of love and support from our family, wealth of happiness and excitement when we're in love, spiritual wealth when we tithe at church to guarantee our spot in heaven – kidding! – I know Martin Luther already cleared this one up with the Reformation, but talk about VALUE for your money, you could literally BUY your way into heaven!

And, of course, a person can be wealthy without having any dough in the bank, too.

Let's say someone who donates all their time and energy to a non-profit that benefits the homeless and is only paid minimum wage, but who impacts hundreds or thousands of lives – they can certainly be considered wealthier on one level than the man or woman who amasses millions of dollars in the bank but is never emotionally available to their family or who never gives a dime to charity from their heart.

Remember, there will always be financially wealthy people who are unfulfilled, miserable SOBs since money just makes you more of who you already are.

It should be a great relief to learn that money only AMPLIFIES your core values (or lack thereof) as that supports our upcoming conversation that wealth of MONEY and wealth of HAPPINESS are not one and the same.

My personal goal and our collective goal together during our Tilt-A-Whirls around the sun, then, is to have wealth in ALL areas of our lives.

That's what I call well-rounded wealth (oh, what the heck, I might as well annoy one more Amazon reviewer with my all caps love affair)…ahem, that's what I call WELL-ROUNDED WEALTH, which is not restricted to just monetary wealth, though they are definitely inter-connected.

You may not yet think it's possible because of your past conditioning, but you CAN have a bursting bank account, a loving family that you spend a lot of time with (if you want to), great friends and a life lived at the stress level of your choosing.

Your life truly is an à la carte menu and the meal's on the house!

(I really don't know what that means, but it sounds profound.)

Does Money Equal Happiness?

This is a perfect time to bring up the perennial debate that very few people are actually able to weigh in on from experience.

The answer to the question "Does money equal happiness?" is not as cut and dried as you'd like to hear. Besides you're still going to think that more money WILL make you happier, but here goes:

Money does not equal happiness.

This is a real doozy for most people until they make their first ten million dollars, pinch themselves and then say:

"Huh, nothing feels different. I'm still pissed my dad abandoned us at an early age, I have no sense of who I am now that I sold the company I built investing 80 hours a week of my time in for the past ten years and I still resent my bratty kids because we gave them everything they wanted…and more…and they STILL bark at us like we're servants."

Money does not equal happiness for the simple reason that happiness comes from within and when we peg our own happiness against external benchmarks (like how many dollars we have in the bank or whether our boss pats us on the head and tosses us a treat for a job well done), it is only an illusion of happiness because external benchmarks are moving targets beyond our control.

Happiness, rather, is feeling pride in our work, learning and gaining confidence in our skills and abilities, seeing how we are actually helping others while expecting nothing in return, being lost in the flow of a creative project or making incremental progress toward the goals we care about most.

Happiness has nothing to do with the number of commas in your net worth, but everything to do with whether you see the abundance in your own life WHEREVER you are, WHEREVER you look and feel genuine gratitude for it.

Right now.

And now.

And now.

What IS true is that money can equal less UNHAPPINESS if by unhappiness you mean stress about how and when the bills are going to be paid and a family's basic needs met month after month and year after year.

But money equaling less UNHAPPINESS is not the same as money equaling HAPPINESS.

I didn't want to believe that money doesn't equal happiness, either, my friend. I STILL occasionally think that I'll be happier when every future financial concern is pulverized by a net worth that I could never spend in this lifetime...forgetting that with financial wealth comes a greater responsibility and a whole new set of concerns.

Think about it for a second. With true financial wealth, suddenly your alma mater is hounding you to fund a building in your name where they can research retinal cancer in frogs, everyone in your family expects you to pay for every dinner out and every vacation together (after the pandemic ends) and ALL your neighbors expect you to donate handsomely to their pet causes...which are often LITERAL pet causes like ending discrimination against purse dogs at the opera.

But the evidence is overwhelming that money does NOT equal happiness from those who have blazed the trail before us.

I can personally attest to a great sense of RELIEF and euphoria when that final student loan payment cleared, but that was an endorphin-fueled rush of a long-term goal being accomplished, not happiness, per se.

Even now when I look at my family's net worth, I feel safety and security, but happiness is not part of the equation – just no stress at the thought of having to cover a financial emergency.

$$$

Stop and think, "I have a million dollars in the bank."

Or if you want to over-achieve, you little teacher's pet, think "I have TEN million dollars in the bank."

Imagine yourself opening a banking app on your phone right now and seeing $1,078,552 just sitting in there. (I gave you a little extra because it's not realistic to see an even $1,000,000. You're welcome.)

How do you feel in this exact moment thinking about that money sitting in there? Do you feel happy…or do you feel relief?

Maybe you would feel happy SPENDING money on yourself or buying gifts for friends and family, but the money itself really just provides a sense of relief, doesn't it? Relief and that feeling of safety and security I keep rambling on about.

When I do this exercise myself, I stop and wait to see what feeling rises within.

For sure there is an adrenaline rush of excitement of "I did it! I knew I could!"

And then, "Suck it, high school bullies!"

(Wow. This just got uncomfortable. Maybe I have a few things from my past to reckon with.)

But then I wait a few seconds and think, "Okay, but our car still needs to be filled with electricity (c'mon, we live in Los Angeles) and my daughter still needs new clothes because she's growing like a weed and needs to be picked up from school just like every other day. I'm still me, I just now have more breathing room to pursue my dreams which are still just as much of a work in progress as I am."

Take as long as you want to daydream about what it would feel like to have a million or ten million buckaroonies to your name. Is it genuine happiness or something else you feel?

$$$

When you have more money in the bank than you "need," you have to know who you are and what you ultimately want out of life so you can pursue it…or you're going to be just as miserable and unhappy as you were the day before your account ballooned with all that fake money I gave you.

You'd be surprised at how many multimillionaires have found themselves in this same situation – they have more money in the bank than they know what to do with, their lives haven't changed much from before when they DIDN'T have money and they're shocked that they're the same person as the day before. The question that hits them next is, "So NOW what?!?"

In fact, if you talk to millionaires who had always dreamed of hitting the million-dollar benchmark, as soon as they reached it, they often felt emotionally let down – many even experienced depression – as the big ticker tape parade welcoming them to the club never happens - they're the same person, just with a fatter net worth.

Todd Tresidder, the man with a helluva first name and the founder of Financial Mentor, often blogs about this very topic. After selling his hedge fund and making enough money to never have to work again, some very interesting things started percolating to the surface for him.

Sure, he took a year off and traveled the world once he became a multi-millionaire, but he soon realized that he no longer had any EXCUSES as to why he was not happy with his life, in whatever area he felt the lack.

He woke up FEELING like the same person he was before the financial windfall, but from that moment forward he didn't have anything or anyone to blame for any unhappiness he felt; as he says, his life had now become *self-determined* (he could do anything he wanted and create his days however he chose), it was no longer *pre-determined* (working five or more days of a classic workweek, answering to others, that most everyone can relate to).

With nothing to HAVE to do, he was surprised to find himself 100% responsible for how he felt about his life. And THAT was a major wake-up call for him that we can all learn from...now...before hitting it big.

Of course, once you have more money in the bank than all your closest friends, good luck getting any sympathy regarding any of life's hardships. We've witnessed this many times behind the backs of people we know who have a net worth in the tens of millions...there is no sympathy from the outside looking in...because people without much money mistakenly assume that MORE money will solve all their problems.

With a worldview based on that common assumption, they don't want to hear people WITH money bitch about…anything, really.

But you and I know better now, right?

RIGHT?

Remember that what you may create for yourself in financial wealth one day, you will equally lose in sympathy from anyone who has less than you. And them's the breaks.

It's an interesting problem to have and one that is echoed throughout the books and blogs of the newly wealthy.

When we can no longer blame lack of money for our unhappiness, we realize WE must have been at the source of the unhappiness all along!

But you won't believe me that money doesn't equal happiness until you get there so GO FOR IT - chase money and keep telling yourself that once you have x million dollars in the bank, then you'll be happy. And when you're still not happy, buy me beers (that plural is not a typo) and we'll chat and figure out where to go from there.

Looking back on my own life, I never felt that my partner and I were going to have any significant money to our names since I carried consumer debt for so long, but as we become first-generation millionaires, we can definitely say that we are not any HAPPIER, but we are certainly LESS UNCOMFORTABLE and less stressed in the money department.

Speaking of financial stress, for the calendar year ending 2021, I received over $2.2 million in health care services for the diagnosis and treatment of a relatively rare cancer called multiple myeloma, an incurable blood cancer that lives in the bone marrow – because the global pandemic wasn't disorienting enough, I guess?

Besides making it a real whirlwind of a year, physically and emotionally, one thing that has NOT stressed us out is the financial aspect of it all – we had health insurance in place and have been able to weather the medical bills that continue to roll in with our monthly cash flow.

And the bills keep rolling in – case in point, in mid-December we received a bill from the physician's assistant who delivered the awesome news to me that my MRI turned up "more tumors than the radiologist could count." How much might one pay to hear the worst news of their life? A cool $500 is how much. And due to the incredible (sarcasm) American health care system, that bill showed up exactly 9 months after the date of service – just as we thought we were done with surprises from the Postal Service. Merry Christmas, Todd!

(This story does have a happy-ish ending as that bill had not yet been billed through insurance and it should be covered by the emergency room copay, but HOW MANY PEOPLE wouldn't think to check on it and would just start paying that $500?!?)

The truth is that we were incredibly happy when we had nothing...we learned very early in our relationship that we didn't need to spend money to have fun – just spending time together was what mattered most. Even home-coooked meals were often better than what we'd get at a pricey restaurant.

What money in the bank DOES do is help you sleep at night knowing that the money dam has been tested and that it'll be quite a while before you would ever go thirsty again.

Would You Rather Be Rich or Wealthy?

The two words *rich* and *wealthy* are often used somewhat interchangeably, but I want to distinguish one from the other before we move on.

I get it. When others can describe you and your family using either term, you're not going to care one way or the other, right?

Or as my grandfather would bark out in a loopy diabetic rage, "I don't care what you call me…just don't call me late for dinner!"

Although both rich and wealthy indicate an abundance of money, there are important distinctions we should make between the two.

Rich is visible. Wealth is discreet.

Someone who is rich may very well show off their riches via the clothes they wear, the cars they drive and the home(s) in which they live…whereas the wealthy, who may certainly enjoy all these things, don't derive their sense of self or a sense of satisfaction from the exhibition of these things - they are more modest in outward display.

You can SEE rich people whereas the wealthy aren't big on show.

Wealth does not carry with it the novelty of newfound riches.

If being rich is a statement to some people, being wealthy is an adjective like any other that someone may use to describe a person or family.

Rich is an event. Wealth is a habit.

A rich family is the couple down the street who win the lottery or sell the family business and take home a cool 5 million smackeroos. They won't be wealthy, however, until they turn that 5 million into 10 million because they understand and respect money and make it grow through smart investments to create generational wealth.

It is said that rich people make the news when they get money – wealthy people only make the news when they lose it.

Rich is a number. Wealth is a range.

The rich can more accurately count their money whereas the wealthy have so many assets of ever-changing value that they don't know what their exact net worth is.

I learned this while reading *How To Get Rich* by the late Felix Dennis, a thought-provoking and hilarious tale by one of the world's self-made multimillionaires. He remarked that the truly wealthy cannot determine their own net worth because of the ever-shifting value of the assets they've parked their money in, not including all the various tax scenarios of cashing out those assets, so they find it quite amusing when the editors of magazines and papers [cough...forbesbloombergwallstreet-journal...cough] peg their net worth with such confidence.

A rich person may be worth 12M, but a wealthy person may be worth anywhere from 200M to 300M on any given day. Heck, Mark Zuckerberg's wealth fluctuated by 3.1B (that's billions) in a single week because so much of his net worth is parked within the somewhat illiquid asset of Facebook company stock. Three billion dollars that was here one day, gone the next!

And then back again. And then gone. And then back again...

That's the reality of so-called paper wealth, when an outsized portion of your portfolio is based in paper assets such as company stock and other market-indexed assets.

Rich is transient, wealth is enduring.

All the nouveau millionaire coders and techies in Silicon Valley are rich, but not yet wealthy.

A person or a family who is wealthy implies a sophistication and history with money. The Du Pont family and its heirs are wealthy as is any family that uses their money to set up foundations, erect new buildings on college campuses and fund PBS shows that use the word "verdant" in the intro that sends us all scrambling to our dictionaries.

The wealthy have found the causes they believe in, and they are known as major philanthropists within their communities.

The wealthy understand the responsibility to help others that comes with their fortunes whereas the rich may be sitting on a pile of millions like deer in the headlights thinking, "Uhh...I made an app where you flick Cheetos into the bras of sorority girls...I guess I'll take the $10M I made in in-app purchases today to Vegas and...bet it all on red?"

It's a good idea to distinguish the differences between being rich and being wealthy to provide the right context for our conversations together.

Rich and riches denote a certain youth of financial wisdom whereas wealth connotes a longevity or generational quality to it, and an acknowledgment of the responsibility that comes with amassing a sizeable fortune.

The expression of someone being "filthy rich" even highlights the nuances we're exploring as it makes money feel dirty, greedy and crass, whereas wealth feels refined, calm and serene...you almost hear classical music playing behind the word "wealth."

In the end, a lot of *cash* makes you rich, but a lot of *money* makes you wealthy.

Are You Waiting for $uperman?

"C'mon, Todd, why are we even talking about monetary riches or wealth at all? This is the era of social good, being green, leaving the planet a better place for the families we're not creating until our late 30s, if at all – 'money' is a dirty word...like 'carbon footprint' or 'vaccination.' And don't even get me started on the global pandemic that has devastated millions of households around the globe!"

Yes! But money is important, and always has been, and always will be, because it is as life-sustaining as water is for your body. But I hear you. I feel you. (Heck, I'm the one who just wrote that!)

If we never take charge and manage our money so that it provides a level of safety and security for us and for our family, we will always be dependent on handouts from others (bosses, our credit cards/banks, friends, the government) to get by.

There was an eye-opening documentary about the American educational system in 2010 called *Waiting for "Superman"* that followed several children as they attempted to make it into their local charter school, their best chance at pulling themselves and their families out of poverty through a good education. It is a very compelling film.

It was titled *Waiting for "Superman"* based on one of the educators in the film recounting how frightened he was to learn as a kid that Superman was a fictional character (spoiler alert) who was NOT coming to save him and his family, after all. The realization that it was up to him to be the change he wanted to see in the world was a sobering and defining moment in his life.

With Social Security now acting as the major source of income for most of the elderly in this country, we ALL need to wake up to the fact that there is no financial Superman (or $uperman) coming to save US, either.

$uperman does not exist. He is not going to fly in to fully fund your Roth IRA for the next five years nor will he pop out of a local phone booth (a what?) to rescue you from any reverse compounding interest you're paying to a credit card company.

The sooner we get this into our heads and understand what that means, the sooner we can take action to make sure we, too, are not dependent on the federal government or anyone else to cover our basic needs in our latter years.

Re-TIRED-ment

What went "wrong?" Why are so many people dependent on Social Security well into their golden years?

Two answers:

1) We're living longer than we ever have.

If you retire at 65, there's a good chance you'll live for another 30 years. 30 years!

Yet you were only in the workforce for 45 years (if you work from ages 20 to 65) so in those 45 years of generating an income you needed to be saving and investing enough to live during the final 30 years when you're not producing an income – basically every year and a half of employment needs to fund an entire year of life post-retirement!

2) The traditional financial blueprint for a happy retirement has changed.

A successful retirement used to consist of a three-pronged financial approach: a company pension, personal savings and Social Security. With pensions having mainly gone the way of the dodo bird, that three-legged stool is now a two-legged stool: savings and Social Security, yet 62% of us don't even have $1,000 in savings so most people are sitting on a one-legged stool.

Have you ever sat on a one-legged stool? It's called a pole and it hurts when shoved up your caboose.

In essence, the first leg, pensions, became too expensive for corporations to maintain while continuing to show ever-increasing profits for their shareholders so Congress came up with the company 401(k) "defined-contribution plan" in 1978 – that pushed the responsibility of the primary leg of retirement income onto the shoulders of the employee – YOU!

Thanks (again), Congress!

That 401(k) your company offers is your pension – but now you're in charge of funding it and nurturing it up through retirement.

Even the "safe" pensions that still exist today are routinely gutted and raided when the corporations, cities and institutions that fund them realize they have big bills due today and so they grab from tomorrow's dollars which were already promised to someone else.

For the second leg of retirement planning, personal savings, wages have not increased over the past few decades beyond keeping pace with inflation or the general rise in the cost of living. With no real gain in middle-class wages for 30 years (which is a crime in itself) there is no extra income to set aside for a healthy savings account.

What about the third leg of the stool – Social Security?

Not surprisingly, nowadays Social Security is the major source of income for most of the elderly in this country, a burden for which it was never intended.

We hear all the time about the impending demise of Social Security and that it may not make it to the day when our children are retiring, but it seems unrealistic that it will simply run out of money one day. Steps will probably be taken to keep it solvent for the long haul once it becomes a crisis that can no longer be ignored by our elected officials – but, for the sake of this discussion, let's assume that Social Security WILL be there as a sturdy-ish stool leg.

Any way you slice it, the onus of retirement has been transferred from the corporation into the money-uneducated hands of the employee/consumer…YOU. And ME.

The bold truth everyone is now facing is that we are completely in charge of our own financial future. And…

No one is going to fly in and save you financially.

There is no $uperman.

And there never will be. Even if you inherited a majestic sum of money or came into a sizeable windfall, it's still up to you to manage it and make it last through your remaining trips around the sun.

This is not meant to scare you – you make all the choices in your life the same as everyone else.

It's just a reality check so you understand that you have plenty of options beyond the shaky Social Security check from the U.S. government. Which isn't a very sizeable monthly check, anyway.

Revisiting the fact that the United States is the wealthiest nation in the history of the world, doesn't it sound totally ridonks that the majority of the elderly depend on THEIR GOVERNMENT to keep them financially afloat (and even then, just barely!) through the last years of their lives?

I'm not okay with that for me and my family. I will not be an elderly child waiting for my allowance each month from my overly-bureaucratic, bipolar (Democrat/Republican) and…let's call a fig a fig and a trough a trough…total creeper of a dude Uncle Sam.

Regardless of what the future of Social Security looks like, in my own family we are fully planning to save and invest enough to create strong cash flow from our assets to keep us spending and enjoying our lives all the way to our dirt naps.

What surprised us…and may surprise you, too…is that it only took us about 2 years of aggressive funding to build up our retirement reserves due to the power of compounding interest and the time we have left until we need to tap those funds. That is true for everyone – the sooner you start investing, the less you need to set aside.

Since there is no one coming to save us with a big bucket of money, that gives us a few options:

a) We can learn to like the taste of cat food for our stay at the state-run Crusty Roach Convalescent Home.

b) We can marry someone super-rich in a community property state and kick and scream against signing a gnarly pre-nup.

c) We can dive head-first into the super simple Wealth Equation that every wealthy person knows by heart to create the financial safety and security we crave.

I hope you'll agree that C is the obvious solution here.

The great news it that it doesn't matter how old you are as it's NEVER too late to turn things around.

N.E.V.E.R.

The Wealth Equation doesn't require a long time horizon or a lot of money, it only requires a strong desire to turn things around.

The ONLY Wealth Equation You Ever Need to Learn

Hear ye. Hear ye.

There will only ever be ONE AND ONLY ONE financial formula you need to know to become as wealthy as your heart desires. And it is so fundamental that even our distant cavemen forefathers figured it out.

Heck, even other species understand this universal law – it's why squirrels store nuts for the winter, dogs bury bones and on and on and on.

The next time you look at your credit card statement and shake your head because you can barely make the minimum payment, call Mister Paw-Paws over for some solid financial advice.

No wealthy person in the world has EVER become wealthy without this magical formula:

EARN > SPEND

Earn more than you spend. That's all you need. I even made the SPEND side a little smaller to drive it home graphically.

There it is, folks!

You may know this more commonly as SPEND < EARN (spend less than you earn). It's the same equation, but we're talking about the creation of wealth and you can always EARN more because money is abundant, but there does come a point where you can't spend any less, so I flip-flopped the equation for emphasis on the EARNING side.

Notice the wealth equation is not EARN = SPEND which is living paycheck to paycheck or EARN < SPEND which is why many people are up to their eyeballs in debt.

No, my friend, there are only two sides to the equation to work with.

Integrate this into your daily DNA and money will start rising up in your bank accounts like water behind your own Money Dam. You will never go broke if you follow this equation.

Which is why I say:

Earn more than you spend – dam it!

Dam it up!

It's the most powerful equation that exists for creating the safety, security and freedom that a rising net worth can provide to you and your family.

Even in retirement you need to earn more than you spend because you don't know how long you'll live and this wealth-building equation will help keep you feeling safe and secure even as you transition back into diapers. (Ever the financial poet laureate – I promise to humbly accept any and all awards.)

Our Only Financial Job in Life

A reminder to us all that we only have one financial job in our lifetime and that is to pay our bills every MONTH until game over.

I don't care how many millions of dollars you may have in the bank one day, you will always have MONTHLY bills to pay and if you always have MORE coming in (INCOME) than is GOING OUT (OUTFLOW) each month, you will always feel safe.

We have the Ancient Egyptians to thank for this monthly bill-paying cycle because they decided to measure time by tracking the sun across the sky instead of the moon. Which is win-win for you and me because on a moon-based lunar calendar, we'd have an EXTRA month of bills every 2 to 3 years – nooooooo, thank you!

But that's it. Our only real financial job is to ensure our monthly cash flow for life – if we want to feel wealthy, all we have to do is bring in more than we spend each month and invest the rest.

See how easy life is?!?

The How of Modern Wealth

Now that we know the only wealth equation you ever need to learn (which is no big surprise to anyone who's managed their money on their own, but still it had to be said in a simplified form), how do we achieve wealth in our own lives? That's what we're REALLY talking about, isn't it?

Let's first take a look at how the accumulation of wealth has changed over the years.

In the great American heyday, with the arrival of the Industrial Age and the westward expansion across North America, there was endless opportunity to provide products and services that a growing superpower needed. Many of the men (you guessed it, across the board they were all straight, white men...to the best of our knowledge) who made fortunes for themselves and their families still sound familiar to modern ears in the institutions and buildings that their wealth has left behind.

Ever been to New York City and taken in a concert at Carnegie Hall? Or toured the campus of Carnegie Mellon University in Pittsburgh? Did you know that J. D. Rockefeller helped to found (and fund) the University of Chicago along with The Rockefeller University, also in NYC? Of course, Vanderbilt University should ring a bell, too.

All the captains of industry from America's Gilded Age like DuPont (gunpowder, textiles), Rockefeller (oil), Vanderbilt (steamships, railroads), Ford (automobiles), Carnegie (steel) and Mellon (coal, aluminum) sat at the top of the industrial and manufacturing food chain

– they owned the businesses that the growing American empire (and rest of the world) relied upon.

There were also incredibly wealthy financiers and investors like J. P. Morgan whose legacy remains with us today in the form of JPMorgan Chase & Co. (a.k.a. Chase bank).

Of course, this is the cream of the crop whose fortunes rivaled today's billionaires when you account for inflation. But back in the day they were just millionaires. (Just.)

Fun fact: The world's first billionaire was actually John D. Rockefeller who earned the "big B" title in 1916 primarily through his ownership stake in Standard Oil. Since then, there has been no turning back the financial pissing contest and the public's fascination with the ever-lengthening list of billionaires.

Another fun fact: America's first self-made female millionaire was Madam C.J. Walker (born Sarah Breedlove), a Black woman and entrepreneur who revolutionized the black hair-care industry – her assets were valued at over one million dollars at the time of her death in 1919. Her products are still available today at Sephora!

Third fun fact (and then I'll leave you alone): The first self-made female billionaire was Martha Stewart who achieved that title in 2000 after taking her company, Martha Stewart Living Omnimedia, public a year earlier in 1999.

A Million vs. a Billion

It's so easy to mistake the proximity of a million dollars to a billion dollars. They even sound like close cousins! But someone who has a net worth of one MILLION dollars is leagues apart from someone who has a net worth of one BILLION dollars in terms of underlying financial assets.

We know this conceptually – a billion is a thousand millions – but the numbers are so large and foreign to most people when they look at their Mint or Personal Capital account...or ATM balance if that's where they keep the majority of their net worth...the numbers are so alien to us that "million" and "billion" start to sound the same.

A post went viral on Twitter a few years back when @Paul_Franz tweeted that "people don't have a strong intuitive sense of how much bigger 1 billion is than 1 million. 1 million seconds is about 11 days. 1 billion seconds is about 31.5 years."

Whoa. That's a big difference!

Stated another way, if you spend $1 every second as a millionaire, you will run out of money in about 11 days, but if you spend $1 every second as a billionaire, you will run out of money in about 31.5 years.

There is a WHOPPING difference between 11 days and 31 years!

A billion dollars feels almost obscene in this context.

Let the record show that a net worth of a billion dollars is wildly more abundant (and some might say excessive) than a net worth of a million dollars.

Millionaires vs. Billionaires in the US

For the sake of simplicity, I'm going to keep the stats to the US population because it's the country with the most of each.

Although these numbers are always shifting:

Millionaires: There are over 20 million millionaires in the US.

Billionaires: There are about 614 billionaires in the US.

Those numbers alone show us how much "easier" it is to achieve a net worth of over one million dollars in assets in a person or family's lifetime than it is to join the billionaire's club.

The fact of the matter is that you can SAVE your way to a million dollars of net worth within one lifetime. Yes, it would take a high-paying job and a frugal lifestyle once you factor in the cost of being taxed on earned income, but it's possible.

What's easier, and how most Americans achieve millionaire status, is through a combination of saving (the lowest tier of The Money Dam which keeps us feeling Safe) and investing (the middle tier of The Money Dam which makes us feel Secure).

Most Americans sock away money into tax-advantaged retirement accounts so their money can grow at an average (and I do mean average given the wild fluctuations in the financial markets over the years) annual rate of return of 8%. They also own real estate: a home and possibly a secondary investment property, both of which should appreciate over time. This track to a net worth of more than a million dollars is pretty pedestrian and typically low-risk.

Most of those twenty million millionaires look like you and me because they ARE you and me.

Anyone who has reached a net worth of a billion dollars, however, has done so almost exclusively through owning so-called paper assets in the form of securities. Elon Musk, Jeff Bezos, Mark Zuckerberg and Bill Gates are synonymous with the companies they created. Their wealth and net worth are intimately tied to the stock they own in the corporations they currently run or once ran.

Billionaire investors also create their wealth through holding securities: Warren Buffett, Carl Icahn, Ray Dalio, George Soros, John Paulson. Mark Cuban first became a billionaire with the sale of Broadcast.com but has since multiplied his net worth via his investments in other businesses.

You *can* become a billionaire through owning real estate, but there are far fewer real estate investors in the B Club and they did it primarily by developing commercial, as opposed to residential, real estate. Their names don't show up in the media as often, but perhaps you've heard of Sam Zell, Stephen Ross or Donald Bren. Los Angelenos have all pretty much heard of billionaire Rick Caruso since many of us have shopped or dined at one of his outdoor shopping centers: The Grove or The Americana.

I'm stating the obvious, but there is simply no way to save your way into the billionaire's club – you must own assets that have no ceiling, or cap, on their potential growth.

Unless you have the luxury of time ahead of you and an unstoppable work ethic (or an already-wealthy parent in your family tree who you BETTER be nice to), there are probably few future billionaires reading this book – they're already out there experimenting and testing their ideas in the marketplace.

The rest of you will just have to be happy living as multi-millionaires.

But prove me wrong – go make a billion dollars and then give back to the world to leave it a better place than you found it. We dare you!

What equals Wealth these days?

Financial services company Charles Schwab released their 2021 Modern Wealth Survey after polling 1,000 people to see what they "think about saving, spending, investing and wealth" and their results are quite interesting.

That is, I was surprised at how ACHIEVABLE many of these numbers are with even a low-risk investment strategy. Here's what they found…

In terms of Average Net Worth:

- **To be considered wealthy, respondents felt $1.9M was sufficient** (DOWN from $2.6M in 2020).
- **For financial happiness, respondents felt $1.1M was enough** (DOWN from $1.75M in 2020).
- **To be financially comfortable, respondents felt $624K filled the bill** (DOWN from $934K in 2020).

Differentiating between financial happiness and financial comfortability feels a bit nebulous, but what surprised me, overall, is how LOW these numbers are. Maybe my living in Los Angeles for several decades has skewed my perception of what it means to "have money," but most people I know wouldn't consider themselves wealthy with a net worth of two million dollars.

What do YOU think? Are these numbers in line with your thinking or do you have higher financial aspirations?

The One Thing You Have in Common with All Wealthy People

Buckle up…here's the one thing that YOU have in common with all rich and wealthy people.

Are you ready for this amazing nugget of truthosity? I've studied this for decades – invested a lot of my time into this!

What the wealthy all have in common is…

Nothing.

Oh wait, let me double-check my facts.

I see, I was wrong, yes, what the wealthy *actually* all have in common is…

Absolutely nothing.

(Pregnant pause to let that sink in…and then the baby is born.)

How liberating to learn that the wealthy don't have anything in common, right?

Personally, I thought I had to have a brilliant mind to be wealthy.

You don't need to be a genius to be wealthy.

I thought wealthy people gathered together at their secret hideaway mountain lairs and pulled up a picture of me on some high-tech, spendy hologram device, studied my profile and then all shook their heads in unison while mumbling to one another, "That poor soul. If only he were a little bit smarter…if he just read one more book…if he'd just finished all the articles on the internet…then he could play in all of our amazing reindeer games. But alas, the Fates have cursed him with too few noggin neurons."

Then they would all break into laughter.

I got great grades in school and generally feel smarter than the average bear (don't we all…thereby leaving no average bear left…just all of us thinking we're smarter than everyone else?), but I have never considered myself to be too much of a brainiac.

Which is good news for me – and us!

The rich and wealthy are not any smarter than you.

In fact, in the Forbes 400 of the richest Americans, only 21 out of 400 completed an academic Ph.D. That is, just 5.25%, of the richest Americans have a Ph.D.

Those are terrible odds if you're hoping those three letters and two periods at the end of your name will make you wealthy.

There are other reasons why higher academic degrees are not prevalent among the financially prosperous, one of them being that masters and doctorate degrees have only risen to higher prominence in the past couple of decades, long after many of the billionaires on the list had already begun their financial journeys.

This was always my biggest mistake, though - I assumed everyone who is super-rich is brilliant beyond compare and that if I just had more formal education or read more books and magazines, I could get my brain ready for the day when it would crank out amazing money-making ideas.

What IS true is that the wealthy are often experts within their niches of specialization. It doesn't mean that they are generally brilliant *Jeopardy!*-winning individuals, but that they probably know their field of business forward and backward. And forward again.

I had always been told to go to school, get good grades and then get a good job. Obviously, the more education I crammed into my cranium, the higher my net worth, right?

You don't even need a formal education to be wealthy.

Out of those same top 400 wealthiest Americans, 63 of them, or 16%, have no college degree. 9% of them dropped out of college and the other 7% finished high school but never attended college.

So, you don't technically need a formal education to be wealthy, although you certainly seem to increase your odds if you do have one as 40% of the richest Americans did finish college and another 40% finished grad school, some of them earning multiple degrees.

Don't let this fact dissuade you from getting a degree as higher education has played a role in the vast majority of the country's wealthiest families, but also don't let it discourage you if college doesn't appeal to you and your parents are on board with you rolling the secondary education dice.

Speaking of rolling the dice…

You don't need to be lucky to be wealthy.

We'll take all the luck we can get our hands on, but most of the wealthy agree that people create their own luck by always being on the lookout for opportunities, taking calculated risks and trusting that they can always deliver value for others.

It's true that some wealthy individuals consider themselves positively drenched in the saliva of Lady Luck (poetry award, please!), but let's not use feeling like a lucky or unlucky person as an excuse for not even trying.

Go MAKE your luck, my friend.

You don't need to be a greedy, Type A personality to be wealthy.

This is an idea that has been created and supported by so many representations in pop culture and in the media – the mega corporation headed by the evil Mr. Burns, Gordon Gekko in *Wall Street*, the greedy old Mr. Scrooge of Christmas lore, Logan Roy of *Succession* fame – the concept that only greedy, bossy people who will step on whomever they can to get ahead is ubiquitous.

Every good story is rooted in conflict and to create conflict you must have both a clear protagonist and antagonist. In this paradigm, you can see how easy it is to take potshots at those in power, at those with more wealth than the protagonist. The wealthy and powerful seem untouchable because they've achieved what so many others have only dreamed of.

Don't believe it for a second.

Of course, some of the richest and wealthiest people in the world are greedy and some of them are larger-than-life…egomaniacs….because why? What have we learned?

Money just makes you more of who you already are.

Because money is 100% neutral.

There are just as many generous, introverted wealthy individuals and families out there so don't let this one hold you back - it's an excuse like any other.

Confession

I have a confession.

I lied earlier when I said the wealthy don't have anything in common. (And here you were just beginning to trust me – suckas!)

The wealthy do have one thing in common.

It's just not the traditional things that we think about.

The wealthy all believe that they are WORTHY of wealth.

The wealthy all believe they deserve to be wealthy.

I don't mean they feel they deserve it without working for it, but the wealthy all know they are worthy and capable of the responsibility of handling whatever amount of money they collect behind their Money Dams. In that sense, they know they deserve to be wealthy.

The truly wealthy are good stewards of money. They accept the responsibility and don't take it lightly.

This is the single greatest differentiator between the haves and the have-nots. Most people would say, just like my mom, "What would I even DO with a million dollars? I don't NEED that much."

They're confusing wealth with materialism and think they are being asked to SPEND the million dollars.

They don't yet understand that:

Money is just a tool that provides safety, security and freedom for yourself and others.

For the wealthy, when an opportunity comes along and says, "Hi Mr. and Mrs. Wealthy Persons, for x amount of time and/or $ of investment, I may have millions to give away down the line, now who would like to hear more about it?"

The rich and the wealthy all raise their hands.

These are the same opportunities not even seen by others, not necessarily because they didn't have the same access to them, but because of how they think – opportunities are routinely missed by people who are stuck in their heads, subconsciously, about how much they are or are not worth.

The wealthy say, "Yes, please! And if there's any overflow of opportunity (and money) that needs a safe and respectable home, I'll take that, too – dam it!"

So how did the rich and wealthy get to the point that they feel they deserve to be there?

Fundamentally, they all THINK similarly about money, perhaps differently from the way you do now. But that's all – they THINK differently and then act on it!

And when you learn to think the same way, you will be on the road to your own definition of wealth.

It all starts with your mindset which is zipping around up in that beautiful melon attic called your brain.

The one thing YOU have in common with all wealthy people (or will by the end of this book) is that you know you DESERVE to be financially wealthy. [mic drop]

We'll delve into some iron-clad steps to Thinking Wealthy in the fourth chapter, aptly called Think Wealthy, but first we need to put you back in touch with your inner billionaire!

Summary

Part of helping you to choose the way you view the world is understanding these key concepts covered in Chapter 2:

- Wealth is abundance in whatever form it takes – financially-speaking, there is no shortage of money in the world or value being provided to earn that money.

- Wealth and materialism are two completely, separate things. Having more money and spending more money do not go hand-in-hand.

- Money does not equal happiness, but it can equal less stress…or less *unhappiness*.

- Being rich and being wealthy are two different animals. Riches imply new money while wealth implies sound money habits and sincere philanthropy across the generations.

- There is no financial $uperman who is going to figure out your finances for you until game over. We are all responsible for building our money dams as high as we can, and it is never too late to get started.

- There is, and only ever will be, one Wealth Equation which is Earn > spend. If you simply earn more than you spend every month for the rest of your life, you will always be wealthy because you will never run out of financial resources.

- You build your mental money dam as high as you can by always Earning more than you Spend and understanding that money flows to value. Money doesn't discriminate on who has it or who gets it. Earn more than you spend, dam it!

- The only thing all wealthy people have in common is that they know they are worthy of, or deserve, financial wealth and that they will take good care of it. They are not smarter, more educated, luckier or greedier than anyone else – they simply view money as an asset, not as income, that can grow into more money over time.

The One Financial Takeaway to Know in Your Bones

I hope all this talk of wealth is getting your serotonin flowing, but there is one financial concept that I want you to know in your BONES.

Truly wealthy people all know they DESERVE the money they have because they will take great care of it.

And you need to know this, too, at whatever step of the journey you're currently on.

If people don't believe that they deserve the money they do have, they will soon enough lose it all. This loss or squandering of large amounts of money is all too common and most visible in pop culture with pro athletes and lottery winners.

If you truly know that you DESERVE to have as much money as you can legally earn or create via opportunity and providing value to others in your lifetime, then you're going to do everything you can to maintain a certain level of wealth, all the while keeping in balance any major purchases, gifts to others and philanthropy.

I need you to know that you deserve to feel safe, secure and FREE because of the money you are shoring and storing up behind your money dam.

It is your birthright to feel safe in this world and that includes knowing at your core that you are WORTHY of any financial wealth that you can collect on your revolutions through the Milky Way.

If you're not there just yet emotionally, we're going to address that in the next chapter on meeting your inner billionaire – it should remove any doubts from your mind and any past negative conditioning surrounding money and wealth that may be blocking you.

See you there!

Chapter 3: Meet Your Inner Billionaire

The reason I've been able to be so financially successful is my focus has never, ever for one minute been money.

- Oprah Winfrey

You read that right.

You have an inner billionaire.

We all do.

Now that we are starting to UNDERSTAND money and wealth out in the real world, it's time we BELIEVE in ourselves at our core, and for that we'll need to get acquainted (or perhaps reacquainted) with our inner billionaire.

Your inner billionaire is unique to you, but is fundamentally equal parts curious, modest, earnest, generous, goal-oriented, a good sport, a respected leader, fun to be around, adored by his or her peers and the very picture of **well-rounded wealth**.

Here's the thing, though: everyone's inner billionaire is a bit introverted.

As kids, our inner billionaires were on full display as we talked about how we were going to take over the world or be the best at x, y and z.

But then we were told not to dream so big or were shown many of the obstacles in our way to living a big life – and our inner billionaire shrunk back from the world.

They're still in there, but they need some coaxing and some encouragement to come forward again.

In this chapter, we'll make sure we're on the best of terms with our inner billionaire before tackling the key concepts of how to Think Wealthy in Chapter 4.

Like the most successful marriages, you two need to be aligned with the same long-term goals and desired outcomes in your lives so you can work toward it together, day after day, month after month, year after year.

Finding Your Inner Billionaire

Permit me to wax philosophical as I twist the ends of my non-existent handlebar mustache…

Everything comes from within.

Every feeling you have of love or happiness, every opinion, every judgment. It all comes from within.

Of course, it must – you're the only one thinking, feeling and experiencing YOUR life.

Problems can arise, however, when we lose sight of that fact and we start thinking that others CAUSE things to happen to us.

This is often called a victim mindset or mentality and most of us fall into the trap from time to time, if only temporarily.

Others often aren't doing anything TO us with their words (and actions), what we're doing is feeling a feeling within and attributing it to that person's words or actions. People may be TRYING to elicit a particular reaction out of us, but it's still up to us to create, feel and deliver that reaction back.

It's all we ever do, in fact, as we hand over so much of our pleasure and pain to be defined by other people in our lives: family, friends, significant others, bosses and on and on.

And whenever we feel things are happening TO us, we start to close down and stop sharing our beautiful and unique perspective with the world. Our "can-do" inner billionaire has no room to cheerlead us to our next victory. We feel that we must draw in to "protect" ourselves.

But what are we protecting ourselves FROM exactly?

We think we're protecting ourselves from other people's opinions of us, but those will be out there from the day we're born until we're pushing up a beautiful bed of daisies – what we're really protecting ourselves from…is the terrifying idea that our own worst thoughts about ourselves may be true!

The majority of us go through life like a pinball in a pinball machine bouncing off other people's opinions of us (based on what we're wearing, whether people laugh at our jokes, how smart we hope they think we are)…bouncing from one electrified bumper to the next waiting to see what the next person thinks of what we say or how they judge us for doing this, that or the other thing.

It's so much fun, riiiiiight? We spend our LIVES bouncing around and around and around from one person's opinion to the next.

As if high school, where everyone else's opinion was SO much more important than our own, never ended.

But it did!

Unless you work in Hollywood in which case you often STILL feel like you're in high school and seeking the cool crowd's collective approval.

If you don't work in Hollywood, however, this is your golden opportunity to finally forget all the bad parts of high school – talk about the gift that keeps on giving!

If you're an adult of relative sanity, it shouldn't be much of a leap to realize that NO ONE can make you feel happy, sad, worthless, excited, embarrassed, humiliated…anything, really…unless you LET them.

No one makes you FEEL anything unless you LET them.

Again, people may TRY to make you feel something, but whether you do or do not is totally up to you.

This is the classic sticks and stones childhood retort of yore – sticks and stones may break my bones, but words will never hurt me.

But words often do hurt us because we let them.

With that single realization...that YOU are in control...the world becomes a much less scary place because you TRUST that you can respond to any situation without your world come-a-tumblin' down.

YOU get to choose how you think, feel and respond throughout each day and throughout your life.

You have CHOICE now...and forever...as crazy as that may sound.

And when you realize you have choice, your inner billionaire comes out of hiding to help you dream and achieve again and you get your life back.

It's so interesting to think that if you're happy around your significant other, that happiness comes from within. They have only fostered or provided the context for its appearance from within you.

In theory, we should be able to be just as happy around our significant other as we are around our worst enemy. Of course, that person (our beloved and our enemy) is one and the same to WAY TOO MANY people, but that is a choice people make, too.

How you feel is always YOUR CHOICE.

Who You Really Are

It's easy to forget, or perhaps you have never been told, that the SUM of you is vastly bigger than any one emotion, mood, feeling, experience or event.

Vastly bigger.

We ALL forget this.

But, in fact, you are bigger than all your emotions, moods, feelings, experiences and events combined because you are a new person in each and every moment of your life.

And you are definitely bigger than all the opinions and beliefs you hold and all the commas that do or do not exist in your bank account. That may be hard to digest in a culture that idealizes the wealthy just for their net worth, regardless of whether they're decent people.

It may even be hard to digest in a book that promotes and seems to idolize financial wealth, but keep in mind that our goal is **Well-Rounded Wealth** which is much grander than just a net worth that would make your oldest friends blush.

You are always a brand new you…living and breathing right in this moment…with a world of CHOICE and OPPORTUNITY ahead of you.

Who you REALLY are is the pure potential in each new moment that arises.

This pure potential is your birthright. You needn't do anything to qualify for it other than to be alive.

Do you believe that?

It doesn't matter if you believe it or not – it's a universal truth and it's the reset button on a new life for many people once they truly get this.

If money is nothing (no thing) more than energy expended in an exchange of value and wealth is just abundance, then you are always ever your POTENTIAL to provide value and collect abundance of most any thing in your life, including financial gain, if you wish.

Be – Do – Have

If you haven't seen or heard this Yoda-sounding wisdom yet, it may just spark a new way of thinking for you.

I know I'm throwing a lot at you, but this is exactly how we start fist-bumping our inner billionaire.

By the way, the vast majority of our culture gets this Be-Do-Have backward so let's break it down together.

The reality of our lives…

When you grow to BE the person on the inside that you want to become, you will DO the things you need to do to create the life you want and you will HAVE (externally…it will manifest "out there") the wealth in all areas of your life as a result of what you're DO-ing.

So many of us think it's just the opposite, that it's Have – Do – Be.

We think that if we could just HAVE what we want first (money, fame, fall in love/find our soul mate, flashy bling-bling), we'll be able to DO the things we think we really want to do and we'll finally BE happy, healthy, loved, etc.

But we never get to HAVING it because we have the order reversed – HAVING is the effect or result of our thoughts and actions, not the beginning of the cycle itself.

I'll say it now to clear the air – money, wealth or even extreme wealth is only the RESULT or EFFECT of who you show up as in the world and what you're doing, it's not the origin or source.

If you get that, then you understand that:

Wealth is an inside job.

Wealth is an inside job. First, you must BE wealthy on the inside before you can HAVE (or allow into your life) material and other types of wealth on the outside.

To be wealthy or to live in abundance is to have a bigger life, and for that you must become a bigger you first.

And you become a bigger you by remembering who you are at your core (pure potential) which includes listening to your inner billionaire.

It's fascinating that where you are in your life right now has everything to do with how you think and feel about the world around you.

We each create our own set of rules about the world "out there" and then spend our precious time looking for and surrounding ourselves with others who basically agree with our worldview.

Motivational speaker Jim Rohn has famously said that we are the average of the five people we spend the most time with (beyond our immediate family).

For better or for worse.

And our net worth is going to generally be on par with that of the five people we spend the most time with, too.

Think of the five people you spend the most time with socially – is there a great disparity between everyone's net worth?

Probably not.

Our Invisible Rulebook

In terms of getting set in our worldviews, let's take the classic example of a person who has an alcoholic father and whose mother has enabled the addictive behavior – what is the likelihood that the child is going to find themselves in some sort of similar addiction/enabling pattern later in life?

We've watched Oprah and Dr. Phil and spent enough evenings listening to Adam Carolla and Dr. Drew on Loveline (back in the day) to know that the odds of that person repeating the addiction cycle are worth betting your entire 401(k) on.

(But don't! Crikey, that was close.)

The person from that family dynamic escapes the "craziness" of their home life and races out into the world, excited by all the freedom and opportunity they've been dreaming of, only to repeat the pattern over and over and over again. Because it's all they know on a subconscious level. It's as if it's hard-wired into our psyche.

This is true for all of us…we live our lives acting off of unconscious beliefs we picked up early in life.

In the process of growing up, life handed you an invisible rulebook which you read and said, "Why, yes, this is EXACTLY how I see the world, too! Such wisdom – sure to be a bestseller!"

We all live by our own unique, subconscious rulebook we received simply by growing up as we did, where we did, surrounded by our family and friends.

This rulebook gives us the beliefs that form the foundation of our lives.

As you can imagine, and as I already mentioned, these invisible rulebooks of ours often stop us from our true potential – they prevent us from feeling happy at our core, they prevent us from believing in our dreams and in creating the life we think we want for ourselves.

We think the rulebook is there to protect us, but it's also there INHIBITING us.

How My Rulebook Inhibited My Own Life

I grew up in Dayton, Ohio in the 70s and 80s. I knew I was different from a very early age, from about 4 or 5.

Turns out I was a gay kid in a time when no one talked about it except when referring to pedophiles (enter the Catholic Church priest crisis stage left to prejudice the public into thinking that anyone who is gay is sexually attracted to children) or when gay men portrayed in the media all had limp wrists and lisped with every sentence they spoke. This was before AIDS hit the scene and brought conservatives out in full force for their fight against "moral and sexual perversion."

So, there I was, a little pup, who knew he was different, but didn't know what it meant, or how to express it and who didn't see ANYONE like himself out in the world.

I grew up thinking that this part of me, that piece of my identity was wrong, that it was unacceptable.

I started to believe that not only was that part of me unacceptable, but that ALL parts of me were unacceptable because I saw no one like me except for the debilitating caricatures on TV and the occasional movie where the gay person was there for broad comedic effect, or even worse, playing the role of the killer because of their deep psychological instability - ha.

And I took that view that I was unacceptable with me out into the world, everywhere I went and with every person I met. Every situation I was placed in, the assumption I made from the get-go was that I was unacceptable and less-than everyone else around me.

Does that sound crazy? It IS, but it's what we all do on some level based on the invisible rulebook we get and the voice in our heads that gleefully reads it over and over again.

The moment I realized as an adult that it was ultimately ME who was bringing the feelings of unacceptance to every situation and wearing that as some sort of badge of shame, it gave me the power to be who I am today and the confidence to become whoever I *want* to be.

For the first time in my life, it didn't matter what other people thought because I was happy and confident and creating the life I wanted and DESERVED one day at a time. I finally understood that in each moment I was creating my own life exactly as I chose.

It is my birthright just as it's YOUR birthright to create each day anew exactly as you wish.

The Never-Ending Cycle

Kids think the darnedest things, don't they? And then they turn into adults who approach the world following that hidden rulebook that no one else can see.

We don't choose the rules when we're growing up – we're just observing and reacting to the world around us. And we certainly don't choose to suffer.

As adults, however, we CAN choose a new rulebook and choose not to suffer once and for all.

Everyone sees the world differently based on how and where they were raised, how many times they were picked first or last for teams in gym class, at what age their parents divorced or whether they stayed together when they should've divorced...and on and on and on with innumerable variables.

And that's life as it is. It's neither good nor bad – it is just our individual experiences OF life.

So, if the OUTSIDE of your life is not going the way you want it to, the only real place to effect change is from the INSIDE, with how you view the world around you and what you choose to do about it.

If you wake up each day hoping life will be different, it's not going to be...because what needs to change isn't "out there."

That, and hope isn't actionable. I know that 'hope' is a verb, but it's inert – it's all wishful thinking and ZERO action.

Much like Suze Orman always says that "hope isn't a financial plan."

Amen to that.

How Your Life Works

Here now is the generally-accepted flow of how you live your life. This is why we behave the way we do in the world.

And yes, this totally affects whether you will ever be financially healthy and financially wealthy...

Thoughts → Beliefs → Feelings → Actions → Habits

Imagine you don't think you're smart enough to ever become wealthy, like I did. Books start piling up in your home.

"Just. One. More. Book. To Read. Then I'll have all the answers."

The secret to wealth was out there somewhere, printed in a book – I thought I was surely getting close!

In the meantime, the repetition of the THOUGHT that I wasn't smart enough to become wealthy turned into a full-blown BELIEF which made me FEEL perpetually unprepared which meant I couldn't yet ACT or DO anything to bring wealth into my life because I wasn't yet ready.

What I didn't see is that that cycle set me up to NEVER be ready.

Playing off my rulebook from childhood where I thought I had no value to bring to others because I was unacceptable at my core as a human being, how could I possibly believe that I could provide the necessary VALUE to cause money and wealth to flow my way? A person who feels of no value has no way to create value.

Funny, no? (No, not so funny.)

You can't believe that you're too poor, dumb, gullible, unlucky – whatever – to become wealthy and ever hope that will lead to the actions and habits that will result in your finally becoming wealthy one day. And if you do happen into a stash of cash, you'll certainly never be able to hang onto any of it for long.

That's why we need to start at the very foundation with our thoughts – we need to meet, hug and empower our inner billionaire if we ever expect to create a life of well-rounded wealth.

Let's define each element on the list just to clarify the process:

THOUGHTS – At the level of thought is where it all begins. Unfortunately, most of our thoughts rise up unconsciously – we don't hear or see them – they're on autopilot unless we speak them out loud in an honest conversation with a friend or write them down for review.

For example, if you think that life is nothing but an uphill grind, then you will likely hear these types of thoughts echoing in your greyspace:

"Of course, that [bad thing] happened to me."

"Ugh, what's next?"

"Just my luck."

"Easy come, easy go."

You've surely heard people speak these out loud – be it you or someone else.

BELIEFS – A belief at its core is a repetition of the same thought. Beliefs form the foundation of how you see the world around you.

If you believe in leprechauns and that they guard pots of gold at the end of rainbows, then a big rainbow right outside your door is going to really make your day and drive you to feelings and actions that someone who doesn't hold that belief won't have.

You may also be bat-sh*t crazy, but you and I know the truth about our little, green-vested friends, now, don't we?

Thoughts that get a lot of airtime upstairs form the beliefs that ultimately drive us into action day after day.

Unless you're doing the "Lord's work" proselytizing and pounding on doors or handing out flyers that delineate your beliefs in glossy print, our beliefs tend to lie just under the surface – they remain subconscious most of the time which is why we so often sabotage ourselves in the money department – we have powerful NEGATIVE beliefs about money that we learned long ago – they just never reach the light of consciousness.

As it so happens, our underlying beliefs provide the springboard for our feelings.

FEELINGS – Negative beliefs make you feel defeated. Hopeless. They make you feel like grabbing a pint of ice cream and binge-watching The Housewives of Saskatchewan. ("It's really cold oot there, eh?")

Conversely, positive beliefs can be a major boon to any projects you're working on, to uplifting your family members, friends and coworkers and making you an all-around helluva person to be around. But for the sake of this example, let's get back to what negative beliefs can do...

How do the following beliefs make you feel?

"Life's not fair!"

"I can't trust anyone."

"I'm not smart enough to figure that out."

"I'm in danger - this alley is super dark and there's a killer on the loose!"

These beliefs stir up emotion, don't they? If you're a carbon-based life form with a heartbeat, they should.

Your repeated thoughts turn into beliefs which lead to feelings – emotions, stress, bursts of adrenaline or dopamine, etc. – which lead to actions.

ACTIONS – If you really believe you're in danger because there is a killer on the loose in your neighborhood and you happen to be walking down a super dark alley, you will take an action based on those beliefs and put an extra pep in your step while being hyper-aware of your surroundings. You'll probably also take the first chance you can to get to a place of safety.

Unless YOU'RE the killer! (Whoa! I didn't see that one coming.)

Your thoughts, beliefs and feelings lead you to take ACTION.

HABITS – The actions you take over and over again become habits.

Many of our habits become so deeply ingrained that they, too, become unconscious – this is especially true for money habits which are often seeded in childhood.

We are creatures of habit which is of necessity to maintain some semblance of order against the perceived chaos of life – some habits are just weaker or stronger than others.

Getting up at 6am every morning for a year to take a brisk jog around the block is a strong, healthy habit. (Unless you're the killer. Stop killing already!)

Getting to the end of each month with no money in your bank account is a weaker, unhealthy habit. (If the goal for you is to feel safe and secure in life, that is.)

What we're looking for within this personal finance book, however, is the gold standard where you start with the most powerful thoughts which become foundational, uplifting beliefs and create positive feelings which, in turn, create the strongest money habits for you which will run on autopilot because of your healthy relationship with money. And your healthy relationship with yourself!

Your thoughts and beliefs, the building blocks of how you see your life, need to be big, strong and powerful enough for you to build your biggest life on top of.

Remember that wealth is abundance and your life of well-rounded wealth requires a big foundation of the strongest thoughts and beliefs to hold it up and keep it steady through the good times and the bad.

Three Core Beliefs of Your Inner Billionaire

As our beliefs (or repeated thoughts) sit at the core of our subconscious worldview and extend out through every thought, feeling, action, reaction and habit in our lives, it's time we take a look at our beliefs surrounding money.

Let's go finally MEET your Inner Billionaire.

This is so awesome. It'll rock your world.

Is there anyone MORE important to meet than your inner billionaire? I'm drawing a blank.

A quick note that many of our core beliefs are based not on what our parents told us to BELIEVE, but what we actually saw them DO out in the world and in our world.

Same with our teachers, mentors, media portrayals, etc. Actions speak louder than words in terms of ingrained beliefs and learned behavior.

Regardless of which money beliefs we inherited, we need to replace them with the beliefs of those who are already wealthy, with those who are financially successful – we need to replace them with those of your all-knowing Inner Billionaire.

The naked (eek - close the door!) truth is that you may accumulate wealth with a weaker set of beliefs, but it will be extremely difficult to MAINTAIN financial wealth unless you have these beliefs in place to support it.

This is why an estimated 70% of lottery winners (and those who come into sudden financial windfalls) will end up broke within a few years. It's also why 78% of former NFL players and 60% of former NBA players teeter on the edge of bankruptcy in the years following retirement.

As we run through each of these core beliefs, check in with yourself on if you really believe them on a deeper soul level…as opposed to agreeing that they sound like good advice that you will just file away as wishful thinking.

Inner Billionaire Core Belief #1: I create my life.

I challenge you to find me a multimillionaire or billionaire who doesn't take responsibility for the successes and failures of his, her or their own life.

They know that they wake up each day with a choice of whether to respond and merely REACT to what they are given or to ACT in the world in pursuit of the larger mission and vision they wish to create.

As the saying goes, "There are no victims, only volunteers, in the Billionaire's Club."

Yet victimhood is the common currency for hundreds of millions of Americans day in and day out who feel helpless to the whims of the world around them.

Most people feel trapped and helpless while living their day-to-day lives.

Don't you feel that way, too, from time to time?

It's important to note that life is not just handed to us, of course. We are not entitled to anything we want WHEN we want it – we are only entitled to the life we CREATE for ourselves.

Which. Is. Awesome.

If someone handed you everything you asked for, you wouldn't respect them at the end of the day. And you wouldn't respect yourself for never having had to work for and achieve anything. Fact.

Getting something for nothing is hollow in the end. When you put in the time and energy – creating, problem-solving, learning and growing along the way – now that's rewarding!

That's also when you realize that the journey itself is the gift, not the effect, or prize.

It's the same reason that wealth, while nice to have, is really just the result of the right execution of great ideas, be they business ventures or investments.

You have a *greatness of purpose* within you. You were born with infinite gifts to share back with the world. And you have an amazing canvas – your life – upon which to do that.

You create your own life and I create mine.

If I create my own life, I also create my own luck.

Whether someone is lucky or not is often used as a catch-all excuse to explain away a wealthy person's long, intense journey toward reaching their goals.

To say that Mark Zuckerberg lucked out is to deny the years of intense thought, planning and good old-fashioned elbow-grease that he and thousands and thousands of people that have built Facebook into what it is today have put into it.

(As of November of 2021, Facebook is going through a bit of a PR and moral crisis [now hiding behind Meta?] for apparently choosing revenue over what some may call their obligation to do good/better in the world and Zuck is not doing himself or his company any favors in interviews – perhaps he has lost connection to his inner billionaire. Note to self: send him a copy of this book. And an invoice.)

To classify someone as lucky when it's meant dismissively denies them the recognition of the commitment and drive it took them to get there.

Luck is simply where opportunity meets preparation. And the more prepared you are, the more opportunities you are going to "see" spring up around you.

It's true that many wealthy people consider themselves just plain lucky or luckier than others, but I would guess we'd see a lot of preparation and seizing of opportunity if we peeked behind the curtains of their most successful investments, primarily of which is their investment in THEMSELVES.

If you really believe you create your own life, then you also know…

If I can dream it, I can achieve it.

Think about it – every consumer product and every service you use – everything in your house or apartment, every toy you loved as a kid, every book you've read that has affected you both positively and negatively – everything in our world first existed in someone's imagination.

First, someone envisioned it and then they created it. Or it was then created by someone else, at least.

Not only on the invention and design level, but *anything* that anyone has ever accomplished that you admire – whether you're a big NFL or NBA fan or a die-hard synchronized swimming aficionado – every physical feat by an athlete that you admire started as an idea and goal in someone's mind, too.

And if every product or service that makes our lives easier first started as a thought in someone's head, what great things do YOU have bouncing around in your noodle, too?

We so often devalue our own worth or our potential contributions to society because we feel small and insignificant within our ever expanding and inter-connected global culture of almost eight billion people.

But that's simply not true.

The next big thing, the next breakthrough in education or water treatment or solar cell technology or squirrel repellent could just as easily come from you.

If you can dream it, you can achieve it.

What most people overlook is that their biggest wealth-building tool is actually found between their waxy ear canals – their imagination. You create your life because you first imagine what it will be.

Bonus: Your imagination is totally free!

Inner Billionaire Core Belief #2: I am worthy of wealth.

We covered this comprehensively in the last chapter, but you are worthy of whatever abundance you create and acquire in all areas of your life.

The one thing all wealthy people have in common is that they believe they deserve to be wealthy because they know they can handle the responsibility that comes with acquiring ever larger amounts of money.

If financial wealth is just a byproduct, a barometer, of the value you have provided to the markets, to the world, AND you know that much of it will be earmarked for charities and causes close to your heart, why would you not feel worthy of it?

At the base of this and many of these beliefs is a self-confidence, a knowing from within that we can handle whatever heads our way.

In lockstep with this is the belief that…

Money is abundant.

Money is never locked away like water in an iceberg (except when I use that as a metaphor for retirement accounts later) – money is always flowing somewhat freely around the globe in search of value.

This was one of the most difficult beliefs for me to absorb because I was raised to believe that if you earned $1,000 then someone else didn't earn $1,000 – the money scales always had to balance out.

As we've seen, however, whatever money you have isn't sitting quietly in a bank vault twiddling its lil' green thumbs, the bank has already turned it into loans for others.

What's more, anyone of sufficient financial means is always investing in new companies, in startups they believe in, in art, other assets…their money is always back in circulation.

Money is abundant because there is, and always will be, a tremendous amount of value being created in the world – value that attracts dollars like a magnet.

The wealthiest people alive on our planet believe that money is abundant, so much so that when they occasionally lose it all on too risky of a bet (which is more likely to happen to fledgling millionaires who aren't diversified enough in their holdings as opposed to billionaires) they simply go back to the drawing board and make even more money the next time around because they understand how to provide the massive value needed to gain it back again.

The fact that money is abundant is perhaps the hardest basic money truth for people to grasp because they've lived so many years of their lives lacking money, wanting more and not seeing it, needing more and feeling passed over.

The idea that there is an infinite supply of money in the world, ever more accessible based on globalization and the interconnectedness of our world financial markets should only be more apparent now than it has ever been.

And the final piece to feeling worthy of any wealth you create, you need to be clear that…

Money is not evil or wrong.

We've also covered this briefly, but this is a doozy for many people. You simply must move past this one or you will always be trying to rid yourself of any money you DO accumulate because the more you have, the more evil and wrong a person you will BELIEVE yourself to be.

Yet we know by now that money is 100% neutral.

Money is nothing but a mirror.

Whether a person has two bucks or twenty million bucks to their name, it's always their choice to be a saint…or a d-bag.

One of the Biblical go-tos that everyone has on the tip of their tongue is that money is the root of all evil. Anyone who uses that line is validating their own low net worth and trying to justify some sense of moral victory over all the "evil people" who have more money than them.

The real Biblical passage is:

> *For the love of money is a root of all kinds of evil…* (1 Timothy 6:10)

The LOVE of money is A root of all kinds of evil.

Which is true! If someone loves money for its own sake, they're off track because money is only the effect or byproduct of a good or service that people need or want in the marketplace. Money is a tool of life is all – it's potential energy.

It also says that the love of money is A root of all kinds of evil…not THE singular root of evil. Big difference.

This is a Biblical passage that can easily be taken out of context to justify whatever end a person or institution seeks, even as there are a multitude of examples of rich, righteous kings and other players in the Bible who are blessed by God with financial wealth.

This saying irks me to no end. Not because of its religious origin, but because it's a catch-all saying to dispassionately justify the average American's financial life of debt and living paycheck-to-paycheck.

"Look how holy we are buried up to our eyeballs in a mortgage and consumer debt with no savings to fall back on. God must REALLY love us!"

This particular interpretation, that money is dirty or wrong, is perhaps the most buried of them all – it often only shows up with people feeling guilty after receiving an unexpected windfall.

Grrr…this belief drives me BONKERS. Can you tell?

If anything here resonates with you, take note of it as a key belief you need to be aware of – it'll sneak up on you just as you're negotiating an employment contract at a new job or wherever you have the ability to mediate your value in a particular marketplace.

Inner Billionaire Core Belief #3: I can handle any situation.

What we know by watching prominent and respected leaders and observing the wealthy is that they have an underlying belief that they can handle any situation – they will not break.

And you will not break if everything bad that you imagine happening actually came to pass – you would find the strength inside, surprise yourself and keep plugging right along.

Unless you're talking about zombie attacks – then you just have to RUN FOR YOUR LIFE.

So often we think we are on the brink of an emotional collapse, or our imaginations run wild and we envision all the traumas and crises that could happen in our lives.

Some mildly (or wildly) superstitious people (like my partner) say they think of all the potential pitfalls and outcomes so that they WON'T happen. To which I say to him, "Of course you do. And we thank you for that. You are so powerful, yes, you are! Who's single-handedly saving humanity day after day? You are!"

(Truth be told he's a producer and a damn good one BECAUSE he is always thinking about what can go wrong on a production and putting measures in place to prevent them from happening – it's actually a very valuable skillset for him!)

Many people seem to enjoy teetering just on the edge of losing it all emotionally, of not being able to handle…life. Their cup is always about to run over.

This third inner billionaire belief of being able to handle any situation and of not being about to break was a new one for me, one that I came to realize in the process of adopting our daughter. I never thought I would be a parent, but now that I am, and as soon as she was born and I cut the cord, in fact, I had an unshakeable core of parenting confidence, whereas beforehand I had always responded to the idea of parenthood with fear of the unknown.

What this belief that you can handle any situation does is it opens you up to life again. It opens you up to taking chances.

Now you know that if something goes wrong, a solution can be found – perhaps it can be found together with the help of others. An apology can be uttered, if needed. There is no situation that can't be resolved when you've acted with integrity and compassion toward your fellow man and woman and everyone else.

This doesn't mean that you won't run into conflict – sometimes your beliefs in the proper direction to take a company or a personal family decision will be met with resistance – but at least you can sleep at nights knowing that you stand behind your decisions and actions *because* you are a person of principle and integrity.

Trusting that you can handle any situation that might arise emboldens you to greet each day as the adventure and gift that it is. Yeah, that's right, you are mothertruckin' Indiana Jones deep within.

Yes, you are. And you will not shatter.

Because you got this.

You got this because…

What I don't know or understand, others do.

We live in an increasingly specialized world – which, interestingly enough, is how most wealthy people make their first million – they often become experts in one area, and they create their initial wealth based on that expertise within a particular market.

You can't know everything because no one does. And no one expects you to know everything. No one.

In fact, the less you realize that you know, the smarter you are to other smart people.

The REALLY dangerous people are the ones who think they know everything already.

This is why you'll often read and see that the wealthy are infinitely curious people – they know that their knowledge is limited and so they ask questions of other experts in their fields.

I can't tell you how refreshing it is to meet truly wealthy people in a social context and feel the genuine sincerity behind their questions of what I do and what I think about things. It feels like a peer relationship.

Many times, we think we have to know everything – about everything – before we start on the path to our dreams. But that is just fear, an excuse for why we haven't actually taken action yet.

Or even worse, we think we DO know everything, thereby allowing no room for anyone else's input, regardless of how necessary and helpful it may be.

Know what you know, surround yourself with people who know what you don't, stay curious, ask a lot of questions and you're well on your way to a constructive, creative and fulfilling life!

You also got this because…

My today and tomorrow are not determined by my past.

Your emotional past is not your present and it is certainly not your future.

What I mean by that is that you are not at the mercy of anything that happened in your past.

Friends of mine who are in their 40s still secretly hope that their divorced parents might get back together. Others are just aching to hear from one of their parents that they're proud of them, though the parent may be incapable of ever saying that – due to their OWN emotional past.

There's a saying that always stuck with me that goes…

The wake doesn't drive the boat.

The wake is the result of the boat's forward motion, but the wake is not pushing the boat forward. Similarly, your past doesn't push you into your future – you taking ACTION does.

Heck, you merely EXISTING, your birthright that we talked about earlier, pulls you into each future, beautiful moment.

The problem is that many of us spend so much of our time looking at the wake trailing behind the boat, talking about it, sharing it with others and analyzing it ad nauseum, that we seldom look ahead to actually STEER the boat to an awesome destination.

It's pretty easy, and quite comical, to envision an entire lake full of boats drifting endlessly back and forth all over the water, their drivers so focused looking back on what the wake means and how it makes them feel and on and on and on that they never plot an actual destination!

Instead of hanging off the back of the boat, be the bow. (That's the very front of the ship for all you landlubbers like me out there.) Be the bow and steer your boat exactly where you want it to go.

We covered this next one already, but it always bears repeating until it's drilled mega-deep into our grey jello molds:

No one can make me feel anything I choose not to feel.

Believing and knowing that you can handle any situation also rests on knowing that no one can make you FEEL anything.

Most commonly this means that no one can make you feel stupid or embarrassed or anything negative – and if they try to, it says everything about THEM and nothing about you.

That equally applies to praise. When you're in the zone, neither praise nor criticism will derail you from a laser-like focus toward your goals.

Of course, people can physically hurt you, but emotional scars are ours to process alone. This follows Buddhist teachings that pain in life is inevitable, given that we are sentient beings in physical bodies, but suffering, the ongoing mental reflection on the pain, comes down to a choice we make.

You can tell me I'm dumb or smart or an idiot or gifted – whatever – I will process your opinion, but I will run it past my own feelings of self-worth and if it doesn't resonate, I'll discard it.

There is SO MUCH chatter in the world right now through the glory of social media, a lot of insignificant and irrelevant talk for the sake of sharing opinions, gaining agreement, defining who this week's enemy is, etc. – but unless it serves to improve someone's situation or better the world at large, it's just chatter.

With the proliferation of celebrities on social media, I'm surprised at how often they get pulled into the echo chamber of other people's thoughts and opinions of them.

You, and they, always have the choice to listen to the negative yakking. Or not.

The choice – about everything – is always yours.

Your Inner Billionaire's Thoughts

We've been a bit abstract in this chapter so I figured it might be a good idea to list out some thoughts to help you recognize your own inner billionaire.

Now, give them some time to come out of their shell – it may have been a while since you two have connected. Ask them how the kids are doing before you jump into the deeper stuff.

Remember that your inner billionaire is pure potential – a problem-solver and team player with a giant heart who understands the value of themselves and, therefore, the value of others, too.

In no particular order, here are some of their thoughts:

- I deserve supportive friends who are my biggest fans (and I theirs) and who are the biggest supporters of my dreams and plans.

- I deserve a loving partner who shares in my enthusiasm for the journey we're on together.

- I deserve any life I can create for myself.

- I deserve the best.

- I forgive myself for mistakes I have made in the past and those I will make in the future.

- I trust myself to make the best decision I can in the moment.

- I can afford anything – if I truly want something, I will find a way and implement a plan to afford it.

- I am unique in all the world and my unique perspective can benefit others.

- I am an endless source of creative ideas and solutions.

- I am capable of limitless wealth because I am an endless source of creative ideas and solutions.

- I graciously share financial wealth back to the causes and communities that are close to my heart.

- I accept my physical body exactly as it is in this moment.

- I accept that my net worth is never a reflection of my self-worth.

- I see infinite opportunities looking out into the world.

- I love money because it makes me feel safe, secure and free.

- I like big butts and I cannot lie. You other brothas can't deny. (A test to see if you're paying attention!)

- I am a great manager of money and always take great of it.

- I am ecstatic just because I am alive.

- I love creating.

- My ideas and my passion easily attract financial wealth into my life.

- I know we are all in this together – no one is an island.

- I am grateful in every moment for what I do have, including what health, wealth and love currently exists in my life.

- I am exactly where I should be in this moment. I fully create my future moments.

- If I am pure potential – which I am – so is everyone else, though they may not know it yet.

I'll stop here, but that's only because I can see your eyes glossing over. I could go on introducing you to your inner billionaire, but that should get you off to the right start.

EXTRA CREDIT: If you really want to change your life, financial or otherwise, read your Inner Billionaire's thoughts out loud once or twice a day. And add in some of your own!

If you don't mind me saying, you have one cool-a$$ inner billionaire. Who WOULDN'T want to hang out with them? Such a positive vibe and glow coming off of them – wow.

I have a smile on my face from meeting them – I hope you do, too!

Summary

We veered off the straight money and wealth talk a bit from the first two chapters, but we need a strong foundation of beliefs to hold up the next chapter in our financial lives, so this is a necessary part of the journey together.

Lest we not forget what we just covered, here's a quick review:

- You have an inner billionaire, as does everyone else, that you have probably lost contact with over the course of your life.

- At your core you are pure potential in each new moment.

- How you view your life and the world around you and the people IN your life is only ever a choice that you make, day in and day out.

- You decide which way the world is, which way YOUR world is. You are that powerful.

- Most people get this backward, but to attain wealth, you must Be – Do – Have: first BE wealthy on the inside in order to DO the things you need to do so that you will HAVE financial wealth in your bank account(s).

- The road to riches, the way to wealth, is all about who you BECOME in the process.

- Financial wealth is an EFFECT of your thoughts $\rightarrow$ beliefs $\rightarrow$ feelings $\rightarrow$ actions $\rightarrow$ and habits in that order.

- We become wealthy on the inside by living the three core beliefs that all wealthy people already hold:

  ✓ I create my own life.

  ✓ I am worthy of wealth.

  ✓ I can handle any situation.

- Be the bow. Stand on the bow of the boat of your life and steer it in the direction you desire because it – your life – is always moving forward regardless of what has happened in the past. Most people spend their time looking off the back of the boat thinking that the wake (their past) is driving their boats forward.

- Your inner billionaire is a dreamer and a team player who only sees opportunity to make the world a better place and who expects to collect and protect the financial riches due in exchange for all the value they can create.

- The single greatest thing you can do to create wealth in your life after meeting your inner billionaire is to learn to Think Wealthy.

Of course, you can certainly become wealthy without thinking too much about it, but you'd be the exception, my friend, not the rule.

Now that you know that you create your own life day by day, know you deserve to be wealthy and that you can handle anything that comes your way, let's get our wealthy thinking caps together in the next chapter and throw the switch.

ZAP!

The One Financial Takeaway to Know in Your Bones

If there is one key concept, one mega-important takeaway, that I hope you can integrate into your own life, if you haven't already, it's this:

In each new moment of my life, I am the potential to be anything I want and to create the financial wealth I deserve.

In other words, the sky's the limit for your future REGARDLESS of your past.

This is not spiritual mumbo-jumbo or wishful thinking. This is one of the few facts of your life and everyone else's.

The only thing that keeps you from really believing in your dreams, financial and otherwise, is the concept of yourself that you have built over the years and that you take out into the world day after day.

I'm not saying that you can immediately be an expert in a particular field or industry that you have never worked in or studied, but that you can BECOME an expert if you so desire.

If you are five feet tall, your dreams of playing on an NBA team are probably pretty slim, yet you're close in height to the shortest NBA player of all time, Muggsy Bogues (1987-2001), who was 5-foot-3, so what do I know? Prove us all wrong, you anti-gravity slam-dunker, you!

My larger point is when you really understand that you are nothing but pure potential for the future, you will play to the strengths of your personality, intellect and physicality (if it's relevant) and not bang your head against the wall of all the things you are not, but wished to be.

If I haven't stated it this clearly yet, your inner billionaire is your true essence – pure potential – and by aligning with that potential, you are BEing the person you need to BE to DO what you need to do in the world to HAVE the financial wealth you deserve.

This is not a cutesy, pat ending to a chapter on personal finance that you can just nod in agreement to – if you understand that, at your core, you are the true creator of what you want in your world, each and every day, there is no one who can stop you from the life you desire. No one.

Chapter 4: Think Wealthy

Wealth is the product of man's capacity to think.

- Ayn Rand

Here are the facts, Jack and Jackie.

We are the product of our thoughts, for better or for worse, and most definitely for richer or for poorer.

Literally, as the cement dries at the foundation of your belief system from the last chapter, Meet Your Inner Billionaire, your future as a wealthy individual all boils down to HOW YOU THINK.

Just as how you currently think was learned, how you start to think moving forward can be drilled into your noodle just as easily, until it becomes second nature.

If you learned to think working or middle-class (as most of us did growing up), you can also learn to Think Wealthy.

I want to say this again because it's that important:

When you THINK wealthy, you BECOME wealthy.

Wealth can be learned.

I learned it and it turned my life around. For years I couldn't catch my breath because I had so much student loan and credit card debt. Now that we have been debt-free for ten years, it's almost hard to remember that crushing feeling – but I do know I will never go back.

To think wealthy is to pull yourself into financial freedom, whether that means maintaining and protecting your wealth for generations to come or spending what you need and giving the rest away at the end of your days.

The larger point is that our minds are infinitely powerful – it's up to us whether we direct them toward the strongest or weakest results in our lives.

I think I know what choice you've made if you're reading this book.

Let's dive right in...

The Thought Police – From Foe to Flow

It's no great revelation to say that thoughts bubble up in our consciousness constantly, day in and day out. We are all certifiably insane, crazy, cuckoo-headed human beings when it comes to the self-chatter bouncing around between our ears.

If we were able to step back and objectively look at the constant deluge of thoughts jockeying for attention inside our heads, we'd run straight for the state loony bin – the nut house, the funny farm, the booby hatch.

("Todd, that's not very mature or woke of you to call it those names. The people who live there have mental illnesses and deserve our respect and sympathy." See? There was another thought…one *reprimanding* me for an earlier thought – UGH!)

Our minds are so cluttered it's amazing that we get *anything* done, isn't it? All those images (it's called 'image-ination,' after all) and words in the form of affirmations, judgments, opinions, short-term repetitions, superstitions – our minds are a chaotic symphony that has lost its place on the sheet music and refuses to obey the conductor.

But the conductor is YOU!

Sure, you can meditate and learn to bring yourself a moment or two of silence, but the unending barrage of thoughts is a fact of life for all of us. I don't care if you're the Dalai Lama (and if you are, congrats on living on such a low clothing budget), your mind is still going to be an untamed stallion running free across the plains.

Running.

Free across the plains.

(Sorry, I got distracted by the image…)

But we need it! If we didn't have thought, we wouldn't be as civilized a people as we are. Thought is the very cornerstone of our humanity, so I don't have anything against thinking…or thoughts, per se.

What concerns me about thoughts is that most people don't realize how POWERFUL their thoughts are or that they spend most of their time distracted by the shiny-object-ness of inconsequential thoughts, not to mention a constant negative self-talk that so many of us have simply acclimated to over the years.

Most of us have fallen under the spell of our rambling brain chitchat and take it all at face value – we blindly trust the veracity of the chatter in our head without ever asking for proof.

HEY – Are you still with me or are you LOST IN YOUR THOUGHTS AGAIN?

By learning to Think Wealthy we can at least get the money section of the symphony playing in tune and harmonizing.

Yep, I'm saying that by training your thoughts on money, by monitoring and policing them to keep them on the up and up, the positive effects will rub off on other areas of your life. In fact, they HAVE to.

Our Thoughts Pack a Real Punch

The reality is that most of us spend way too much of our mental energy beating ourselves up or placing imaginary obstacles in our own way. It's total bedlam in your head sometimes, isn't it? It is in mine!

Which is okay.

For now.

It's just your ego parroting someone else in your life (probably a parent or other family member) because that's all it knows. It thinks it's protecting you, but once it learns how to actually support you, your life can change practically overnight.

Check out this common phrase I overheard my parents say to themselves while I was growing up:

"You dummy, why did you put the plate back in the dishwasher when it was already clean...[or insert random activity here]?"

They wouldn't talk to me or my sister that way. They talked to themSELVES that way. It was their self-talk.

But it wasn't just one parent. No, my sister and I were the lucky recipients of BOTH of our parents berating themselves when they did any silly thing when they "just should have known better."

So, guess what amusing and destructive self-talk I took out into the world AND guess how many decades it took me to stop thinking that I was an idiot or dumb for not realizing that that plate was already clean when I put it back in the dishwasher, too?

Our thoughts are indicators of our deeper, subconscious beliefs – that thought pattern I inherited from my parents was the tipoff to a belief I had that I was barely smart enough to navigate my own kitchen and that surely everyone else in the world had more common sense than I did.

But wait – this story has a happy ending!

Now I don't call myself an idiot any longer – consciously or unconsciously – I have broken the cycle and it has become my life's mission to make sure our daughter doesn't hear it or internalize it, either – not from us, at least.

It's also my life's mission to ensure that YOU don't do it, either – whether we're talking about a clean plate or your ability to create wealth for you and your family.

Breaking the Cycle of Negative Self-Talk

I now forgive myself for any silly mistakes I make because they simply don't matter against the backdrop of my long-term goals – I also know it's a poor use of the limited time any of us have left on this spinning rock of minerals to replay these inconsequential mental moments ad nauseum.

What helped me past that roadblock was learning to change my thinking and to treat myself with the respect I deserve.

Thinking Wealthy is an expanded and positive way of thinking that will sound alarm bells for you every time you catch yourself thinking this way or hearing someone else verbalize a negative and defeating thought.

When I met my partner, we were both guided by a predominant middle-class mentality of "just surviving" month-to-month because we were saddled with so much consumer debt. By talking about money and setting common goals together, however – by challenging our way of thinking about money – we turned around our financial lives. And best of all, we did it together.

We even turned it into a game – a healthy competition – to see who could get out credit card debt first!

We can all train ourselves to think a certain way, in a way that empowers us in any facet of our lives (financial matters, weight loss, self-esteem, happiness) – we can do this by putting the cart before the horse (or perhaps the cart before the untamed stallion running wild across the plains – wild across the plains...) because with the repetition of powerful thoughts, ever-stronger beliefs form deep within as we saw in the last chapter.

This is the part of the book where I say that if I can do it, you can do it, too. I don't know if you believe that yet, but I stand behind it 100%.

Besides, what better use do you have for your time while you're on the bus or stuck in traffic or standing in line at the bank (do people still go into banks?) or grocery store or Starbucks – use that time for some mental gymnastics just north of your eyeballs.

Financial Cruising Altitude

Before we dig into your brain like a zombie (#nomnom), let me give you a little context for the 10 ways of thinking wealthy that I've created here.

Think of these ten thoughts as your 30,000-foot view of your life and your finances. When you're cruising that high in the sky and looking down on everything, it's easiest to see the big picture. You won't hear all the noise at ground level – all that mental chatter we've been talking about. We're more analytical at cruising altitude, and less emotional.

If you're ever feeling stuck or unmotivated in your life, look back over these ten points and get back into the air at a higher altitude to see if you've strayed from any of these ways of thinking and acting.

Think Wealthy #1: Think Net Worth, Not Salary

This is a great one to start with because we constantly hear which jobs pay the highest salary as if that's the only thing that matters when it comes to our money.

For decades, everyone was told to become a doctor or a lawyer if they wanted to make the big bucks. Then engineering hit the radar screen and, of course, Wall Street bankers and hedge fund managers were added to the mix. And now we're all supposed to be coders and tech entrepreneurs starting private companies that turn into unicorns when they go public – the new American dream.

We are still told that the good jobs are the ones that pay the best. And to get them, we must study hard and go to the right schools.

Sure, we may graduate with over $100,000 in student loan debt that will ultimately cost us $145,000 after we factor in the compounding interest in reverse, but that's the price for a good education so you can make a decent income, right?

Because financial freedom is all about our salary, right? RIGHT?

WRONG!

Back in the day I read that the wealthy measure their money in terms of their NET WORTH and not how much INCOME they bring in in a year.

(Here comes the embarrassing part...)

I actually thought, "Net worth?!? What does THAT have to do with anything?" (As the guy who dreamed of having a zero net worth for years because of his debt, you can see why I might have been a tad confused.)

Now I know, of course, that net worth is the ONLY benchmark the wealthy (and those who write about them) use.

But how ingrained was it in my Midwestern psyche that the only barometer of wealth was a person's SALARY at their JOB?

[If you don't know how to calculate your net worth, you simply take the value of everything you OWN (or all your assets: real estate, cars, bank accounts, retirement accounts) and subtract everything you OWE (or all your debts: mortgages, car loans, credit card balances, student loans). That beautiful remaining number is your net worth.]

Looking at The Money Dam (in Appendix A), your net worth is the water level, or lake of assets, held back by the dam as it rises throughout your life.

For decades I had a negative net worth because in assets I had an average of $2,000 in a checking account and a Honda Civic (of ever decreasing value as that's what cars do best, they lose value or depreciate) that was worth $7,500. So, my assets were $9,500, but the debt of my student loans was $60,000. Take the $9,500 of assets and subtract $60,000 of liabilities and I had a net worth of negative $50,500 (-$50,500).

Negative net worth. For decades. Good times!

It felt crushing. As I've said elsewhere, I felt like I could never catch my breath. No wonder I didn't know the value of tracking my net worth – who would?!?

Before I earned a six-figure salary myself, I erroneously thought the more money a person MADE, the more money they...just...HAD because there was that much more "excess" money in their paycheck.

I soon learned, however, that between higher tax brackets and living a larger, more expansive and expensive lifestyle, most people who make more money don't FEEL any excess coming in from month to month because they've slowly scaled up their living as they've earned more money. In fact, for many people, it's just as easy to live paycheck to paycheck on multiple six figures as it is on the $46,000 lower end of middle class.

What someone makes as INCOME has very little to do with their NET WORTH. As the saying goes...

It's not what you earn, it's what you KEEP.

It is true, however, that the more money you make, the more likely you are to be increasing your net worth by maxing out your retirement accounts and making other healthy financial decisions. If you're making $200,000 a year, for example, there is a baseline financial education that often comes along with that type of salary – it won't be your first job so you'll already know about 401(k)s and the other financial options available to you as an employee. If nothing else, you're working with people at the same income level and them sharing their financial best practices will educate you, too.

This may be news to you, but collecting a SALARY at a JOB makes it near impossible to become wealthy because you lose so much off the top to income taxes.

Add in lifestyle creep that comes with an increase in salary and the nice Instagrammable picture on the outside shows nothing of the financial health on the inside.

How often do you hear of the family that drives a new Mercedes their whole life but have little in retirement – yet a custodian at the local public high school leaves 10 million to his favorite charity when he or she died?

These flipped-script financial stories tend to make the rounds during recessions when the kimono opens on people's otherwise private financial lives.

Ultimately, no one knows what goes on behind closed doors. Your blandly-dressed neighbor (guilty as charged!) may be a millionaire next door while friends who live in the biggest houses lose sleep each night worrying about their finances.

Net worth, everyone's lake of net worth, makes the difference. It is the only metric that can be reliably used to determine an individual or family's financial health and strength.

Forbes magazine ranks the richest Americans and billionaires by their net worth, naturally – if they listed the wealthiest people by salary, the "brand name" billionaire CEOs we all know wouldn't even make the list as so many of them take $1 salary per year. Besides being a savvy political move so shareholders will believe the CEO is more concerned about raising overall stock value than draining cash from the company with a big salary, every CEO knows that taxes paid on income, or salary, will be higher than on other forms of executive compensation like stock options.

One of the best advantages for thinking net worth over salary is that it conditions us to think of money as an asset (something that grows in value) rather than thinking of money as income (something that you spend).

The ENTIRE PURPOSE of this book, in fact, is for you to start thinking of every dollar to your name as an ASSET that can grow in value instead of thinking of your money as income to be spent.

$$$

Wealth Tip: *Think in terms of appreciating assets.*

As our net worth should always be increasing, the primary way to do that is by investing only in appreciating assets.

Yes, a new $45,000 car smells amazeballz, but it should hurt like a punch in the paunch for you to drive it off the lot since it will only lose value over its lifetime, not to mention the additional costs in maintenance and insurance on a higher-priced vehicle.

Of course, we all need to figure out the transportation piece of our lives, but even buying a two-year-old car with a dealership warranty at a fair market price makes stronger financial sense than buying a new car outright.

Wealthy people try not to spend money on things that decrease in value over time – it's that simple. If that sounds topsy-turvy, then you're still confusing wealth with materialism.

When you think of money as an ASSET, you only invest in things that will appreciate and turn into more money later on.

Appreciating assets over the long term tend to be stocks, real estate, currencies, fine art and other collectibles. Even in retirement, a truly wealthy mindset resists the idea of "spending down" the principal of the money they've saved and invested…the real goal is to live off the *interest* of your principal, so your lake of net worth never dips to a lower level.

I've never thought of myself as much of a negotiator, but I bought a smoked glass table that seated 6 for $200 when I moved into my first apartment. I used it for 10 years and after enough friends publicly shamed me into getting rid of it ("smoked glass, dude?!?"), I used a Sharpie to hide all the dings in the cheap metal frame and sold it for $200 on Craigslist.

Not bad, right? Sure, the $200 I spent for it was worth more than the $200 I received for it ten years later given the effects of inflation, but it was one of my first attempts to see what the market would bear. Win-win! Now someone else can be both proud of and shamed by their choice in dining room furniture.

We also bought a new, unused dishwasher from a friend for $100. We used it for 5 years and, before moving into a house that already had one, we sold the 5-year-old dishwasher for $160!

Why did I sell it for more than what I paid for it? Because $160 is what the market (or a couple with a baby about to drop) would pay for a good used dishwasher from someone who took good care of it.

I do not kid myself that these money moves will make us wealthy one day, but the mental machinations behind these sales are already in place and will work on a larger scale, too.

Years ago, I would've just given these items away as if they were worth nothing because I paid so little for them…but now I think of my money as an asset.

Whoever says furniture and appliances always depreciate hasn't been drawn into the tractor beam of my Craigslist marketing prowess!

$$$

Wealth Tip: *Realize your network is your net worth.*

It is said (and there's even a book about it so it must be true!) that your network is your net worth. That means the five people you hang out with the most…their average net worth is going to be about on par with your net worth.

Stop right now and think of the five people you hang out with the most…who you're most real with…ask yourself if you're comfortable in the same net worth zone as them or do you have higher financial aspirations?

Do your closest friends always complain about not having enough money, not knowing where they're going to find the money for x, y, z or never talking about long-term goals and plans?

This makes sense on several levels since we tend to socialize with and even marry people of the same socioeconomic background in which we were raised, but the takeaway is that if you're not connected with people who will push your game even higher, if you're not meeting people who you can emulate and learn financial wisdom from, your financial future is laid out right in front of you.

The financial writing is on the wall.

$$$

Wealth Warning: *Think of consumer debt as an STI to your financial health.*

Consumer debt (credit cards, auto loans, personal loans, even student loans if you don't have a plan or a bankable skillset to show for it) is like a sexually transmitted infection (STI) – it felt good when you got the debt because you weren't really thinking with the smartest parts of your body, but now you feel you may never shake that bug.

And unless you have a plan to get rid of it, it may hang on as long as you do!

For me, I heard Suze Orman's sharp Chicago twang screaming in my ear for years whenever I thought about purchasing something.

For years!

I watched her show every week – with a negative net worth and no retirement accounts to my name, I would always hear her yelling at me to DEEEEEENYYYY myself major purchases so that I could make it to a future day of financial freedom, which arrived much sooner than I thought it would.

Thanks, Suze, for helping me change my world from the inside out! I'll give you a big hug one day, GIRLFRIEND.

The truth is that most people seem to be comfortable with a certain level of consumer debt. They dig themselves out of the hole a little bit and then buy more shtuff because the monthly payments (which are loaded with interest, of course) already fit well into their monthly spending – besides, what the heck is excess money for if not for buying more things you think you need, right?

If it helps, think of revolving debt (anything with monthly installment payments – credit cards, auto loans, student loans) as you setting your hard-earned money on fire and watching it go up in smoke. Gone. Not so much for the thing you bought with that money, but for all the interest being charged month after month until it's paid off.

To be clear, you don't OWN anything that you buy with a credit card until it's fully paid off. It is not "yours" until that balance is zero.

Consumer debt anchors you to the past making it nearly impossible to see a brighter future.

$$\$\$\$$

Money Math: *Daily cost of revolving debt.*

If you want to motivate yourself out of revolving debt, figure out how much you're paying in interest EVERY SINGLE DAY on your debt.

I did this with my student loans at one point and it took me to new depths of financial despair to see that I owed $5 a day just in interest on those loans. I realized that if I wasn't earning at least $5 each day (including weekends), then I wasn't even breaking even on what I owed, and my debt would just continue to snowball UP from there.

Looking at the larger population, if the average American household carries credit card debt of $5,525 at a 16% interest rate, that means their debt is costing them $2.42 a day, or $72.61 a month. And that's not paying down any of the principal, that's just to break even.

When you wake up each morning knowing how much you need to earn JUST to break even with any capitalizing interest you owe, it can either send you back under the covers to sing the blues or motivate you into action – both of which I've experienced over the years.

$$$

Wealth Warning: *Debt résumé.*

As I like to say, if you carry a student loan or credit card balance forward each month, you're really working for the banks because some of the money you earn really belongs to them.

I worked for Capital One and MBNA for YEARS until I made a lateral move and was transferred (via a balance transfer – oh yes, I did!) to work for Discover Card for another few years.

So, who do YOU work for...Amex...Bank of America...Chase? Whoever you owe money to owns a small piece of your soul at the cost of your sense of safety, security and freedom in the world.

Back to The Money Dam™ analogy, there is a hole at the base of your dam that belongs to whoever you owe money to and the only way to shore up that leak is to pay it off as soon as you can.

Think Wealthy #2: Think Long-Term

This is the most crucial piece to thinking wealthy, period.

I feared I may never learn this because I had whiled away most of my life only living and thinking short-term or month-to-month.

Sure, I may have set long-term goals in terms of career, but they were more like dreams floating in between my ears without any real plan of action.

It's said that the middle class thinks month-to-month.

And who could blame them when we all live in a monthly bill cycle? It's perfectly natural to use a month as a financial benchmark because that's what we've all been CONDITIONED to do – get a job that meets our monthly needs and then increase our lifestyle (bigger house, newer car, more lavish vacations) with each promotion or pay raise we receive.

By thinking month-to-month, the middle class creates a lifestyle where whatever money comes in, goes right back out. Pretty logical thinking, actually – it's just too nearsighted for creating actual wealth.

If the middle class thinks month-to-month, then the working class (or working poor as they're sometimes called) thinks week-to-week. They're in survival mode, pure and simple.

Often the working class is not even living week-to-week - they may have been forced into payday loans because it's their only option. With those atrocious interest rates, you could say the working class is stuck in the past, scraping by just to catch up to month-to-month middle-class thinking which is often only one sneeze away from financial ruin, anyway!

How can you move forward with your life when you still haven't paid for the things you bought last week, last month or last year?

If the working poor are bound to the past and the middle class is just keeping their heads above water month-to-month, it stands to reason that the wealthy or upper class is thinking more long-term – in fact, the wealthy think year-to-year. Decade-to-decade even!

To think long-term is to Think Wealthy.

This is why they take smart risks – they have the financial stability today to bet on a bigger payoff or payout down the line.

This is what you see on ABC's hit show *Shark Tank* – a GREAT primer on entrepreneurship if ever there were one. The sharks don't need the investments they make to pay off immediately to keep food on the table, they have a long-term view and can afford to wait years to recoup a healthy return on their investments, all the while creating jobs and contributing cool new products and services to the economy.

If you want to be wealthy, you must think long-term.

$$$

Wealth Tip: *Think of every dollar you earn as a seed of your financial future.*

Then water those financial seeds.

Every dollar you collect has the potential to make many more dollars for you in the future.

This is what motivates the wealthy – they know that every dollar they make today may be worth ten more next year or a thousand more in ten years. They're thinking long-term.

If you remember the difference between cash and money from the first chapter, think of CASH coming in and going right back out, but MONEY growing over time.

Earn more than you spend and invest the rest – dam up your money to raise your lake of net worth!

Keep top of mind that putting $50,000 into a retirement account by the age of 25, earning 8% a year will turn into $1,000,000 by the age of 65.

It's not hard to be a millionaire if that's your highest financial aspiration...

$$$

Wealth Tip: *Figure out cash flow for life.*

Since your only job (and mine…and everyone you know's job) is to figure out how to pay your monthly bills until game over – if you can make a plan for cash flow for life and DO it, a very real version of wealth can be yours.

This is a somewhat modern version of wealth – it's not dependent on amassing a lakeful of net worth (and assets) that will create wealth for generations to come – it involves determining your specific monthly needs and then saving and investing up to a pre-determined amount that you will spend down – or investing in passive income assets that will cover those needs month after month after month. Or some combination of the two.

We'll cover both types of wealth creation in the next chapter, "Create Your Fortune, Big or Small."

This monthly cash flow strategy is the basis behind the FIRE (Financial Independence, Retire Early) Movement which is gaining popularity as Millennials and Gen Zers reach for the rip cord from the rat race.

FIRE is based on choosing your own day of "retirement." In its most basic form, you determine your FIRE number by multiplying your annual expenses by 25 and then you live a substantially frugal lifestyle while saving and investing up to 75% of your take-home income until you hit that number, which you then spend down at a rate of 4% each year.

A FIRE strategy can take the form of traditional tax-advantaged retirement accounts, taxable brokerage accounts for funds needed before reaching 59.5 years of age and income-producing investment properties like single or multi-family homes.

Cash-flow wealth differs from the traditional meaning of wealth in that you won't get a building named after you at your alma mater, but you'll be wealthy in the sense of never running out of money for your monthly bills.

Robert Kiyosaki was the first author and investor I can think of who brought the primacy of cash flow to the fore with his bestselling book *Rich Dad, Poor Dad*. He even created the *CASHFLOW Board Game* in case you weren't sure where he stood on the issue of wealth creation.

I had read Kiyosaki's bestselling book, but it didn't resonate with me until Paul Sullivan, wealth columnist for the New York Times and author of *The Thin Green Line: The Money Secrets of the Super Wealthy*, wrote that you don't need a lot of money in the bank to be considered wealthy – what you need is a solid cash flow plan for the rest of your life.

Figuring out monthly cash flow is very PROACTIVE and IMMEDIATE – you are working to get to financial freedom ASAP as opposed to waiting for an official retirement age (in your 60s or 70s) when Social Security kicks in.

It is based on you determining an exact number that you can comfortably live on whereas traditional wealth creation in the Sara Blakely or Elon Musk entrepreneur model has no real ceiling to their net worth – they're not trying to afford a certain lifestyle – the businesses they created that underpin their wealth have unlimited upside potential.

If you can strategize your own cash flow for life and start implementing that plan today, you'll be in full financial control one day in the future. I'd tell you to go ahead and skip to the end of this book if that's what flops your mop, but then you'd miss all my remaining Dad jokes…and my ego strongly advises against that.

$$$

Wealth Tip: *Bucket!*

This is a mental trick that wealthy people do naturally, and you will, too, once you start beefing up your net worth.

One of the easiest ways to get your synapses to start thinking and planning long-term is to think of your money as being divvied up into separate buckets. If you currently lump all your money together in your mind, start with three buckets, one each for safety, security and freedom.

Here are the three primary buckets:

1) Safety (Saving): The first bucket is a savings account which you maintain to keep you feeling SAFE in the short-term.

If your laptop is about to die or your tooth aches after a bag of Skittles and it's only getting worse…this account is for money that you will need in the relative short-term (within FIVE YEARS).

This bucket sits in a different account than one for monthly living because it's doing something completely different – it's *protecting* you – you're not living in fear of life's little surprises – it makes you feel safe.

If money for monthly living sits in a checking account, the Safety bucket sits in a savings account.

You can think of this as your emergency fund if you want, the goal being that you're never dependent on using a credit card to get you out of a pinch. Only use credit cards if you can pay them off in full at the end of each month while gladly accepting their cashback rewards.

Each month this safety account goes up and up and up with the occasional down for a replacement laptop or dental crown…then up, up, up, down a little, up, up, up, down a little, up, up, up, up…

2) Security (Investing): The second bucket is an investment account (or several of them!) to keep you secure for the future, for the long term.

These are tax-advantaged retirement accounts or taxable investment accounts where you automate money into it from each check and LEAVE IT THERE so that it can grow and grow and grow.

These accounts may be a 401(k) if the company you work for offers one or your own investment accounts easily set up at a TD Ameritrade or Charles Schwab or another online broker. These aren't necessarily accounts for gambling with the latest new crypto craze or whatever is coming around the corner next – these accounts are there to create long-term Security for your future. It's your life and you can invest however you like, but most people ride the market (mostly) up in diversified mutual funds or ETFs.

These accounts may bounce up and down in the short term based on the stock and bond markets or whatever you're invested in, but your long-term interests in this bucket only go up and up and up…

3) Freedom (Your Plan + Your Execution): This third bucket is not as much an account as it is your unique vision for your own future financial freedom.

While the first two buckets work together like gears of a driveshaft to keep your life running smoothly, the freedom bucket is YOUR particular plan for financial independence if you decide to create one.

Your plan may very well involve your current skillsets but with a future payout date if you own your own business…or perhaps it's a separate venture you will invest in, one that provides massive value to others, and for which the market will willingly compensate you in return.

Your freedom plan is as unique as you are.

It's been shown time and time again that the wealthy bucket their finances – they mentally separate their money into different buckets to fulfill the different short and long-term goals they have – "bucketing" your finances is one of the easiest and most effective ways to take control of your financial life.

Other ways to bucket to get your mental juices flowing:

Create a **Vacation Account** where you save up for a big trip or create an ongoing **Investment/Education Account** where you set aside $50 or $100 a month for your continuing education on your way to financial freedom.

When you plan out your buckets, there is no confusion with what your money is supposed to do when it flows in each month because you've said upfront that this is where you want it to go and what you want it to do.

$$$

Wealth Tip: *Plan for the worst, expect the best.*

This is the sign that you're a financial adult in the world. You plan for the worst possible scenario (which is why you carry life, disability and other insurances to mitigate your risks and protect your loved ones and your money - more on that in the final chapter), but you expect the best.

How many more stories must we hear about young parents not surviving a car accident with no living will or trust in place on how to divvy up their assets and protect their newborn child?

With life being the unpredictable fate cauldron that it is, this mantra of planning for the worst but expecting the best will also serve you well in every aspect of life, not just finances.

If something unexpected happens, what's your Plan B? Learn to think in terms of Plans A, B and C – by planning ahead, you can act fast when you need to because you've already done your homework and can course-correct with confidence.

My Broadway singer friend and I watched the YouTube video of Idina Menzel missing her top note in the live finale of the *Frozen* song "Let It Go" one chilly evening. She held onto that missed note for dear life as blood ran out of our ears. My friend yelled at the screen, "Idina, girl! How could you not have a Plan B?!?"

It was cold out (Times Square on New Year's Eve) and her voice was exhausted from doing 8 shows a week of another Broadway show – but she is a professional singer, an expert at her craft – how could she not have a Plan B for that final note?

One would expect that years of training and experience on stage should have instilled in Idina to plan for the worst but expect the best. That missed note probably had its own Twitter account the next day.

$$\$\$\$$$

Wealth Tip: *This is your money! But it's only money!*

Total Contradiction Alert, I realize.

Hear me out.

THIS IS YOUR MONEY. NO ONE WILL TAKE BETTER CARE OF IT THAN YOU.

NO ONE WILL GIVE A BIGGER DAM ABOUT YOUR MONEY THAN YOU WILL.

BUT…

IT'S ONLY MONEY. DON'T TAKE IT ALL SO SERIOUSLY.

YET STILL TAKE IT DEADLY SERIOUSLY – DAM IT!

When you treat yourself with the respect you deserve, you will quickly know WHAT you want to spend money on and WHY. And you will be able to communicate that clearly to whomever you wish. You said yes to that destination wedding because you said yes. You said no to that destination winter ski trip because you said no. End of story.

At the same time, we're only talking about money here. People take it way too seriously as if they'll JUST DIE if they run out of it at any moment. As we've seen, though, money isn't anything more than a tool that provides us with feelings of safety, security or freedom.

And money is ABUNDANT so if you were to lose it all, you just go get more digital commas in your net worth already.

Realize that no one will take better care of your money than you will – but don't put money on a pedestal as it's only good at doing a few things well.

Here again is the quote by P.T. Barnum I used at the top of Chapter 1:

Money is a terrible master but an excellent servant.

Be the master of your money – but create such a big life for yourself that it's nothing more than a piece of the puzzle, not the entire puzzle itself.

$$\$\$\$$$

Wealth Warning: *Hope is not a financial plan.*

If I had a dime for every time my mom confided in me that my parents were dancing on the cusp of financial ruin and not being able to pay their bills, but she cheerfully concluded that "everything always works out in the end," I'd be sipping Mai Thais with Richard Branson on the island I bought next to his.

Hope is not a financial plan.

(And I love you, Mom!)

Unfortunately, for millions of Americans, hope and prayers are the only financial plan many people have in place. Personal finance experts say it's because it's the easiest financial plan to make (which is true), but I think it's equally because no one ever talked openly about money and showed them how to think wealthy for themselves.

If you get on a train, you expect the engineer driving the dern thing to know where he or she is going. Likewise, if you get in your car, you presumably have a destination in mind, you don't just *hope* you'll get where you want to go.

Why is money any different?

The truth is if you expect things to just barely work out, they will ALWAYS just barely work out. As they did for my parents. For decades.

If you want to really live your own life, though, you'll tell your money what you want IT to do and then the world can be your oyster. (Seafood burp.)

$$$

Wealth Warning: *The lottery is not a financial plan.*

Don't get me started.

Hopeful lottery winners think they will just win all that money and every problem will be solved.

Of course, they will be able to get out of debt and buy some shiny things, but if they've never had to manage large amounts of money before, any windfall will slip through their fingers as everyone they know shows up for a piece of the pie – the money zombies shuffle up with outstretched hands – and the newly rich will fritter it away, not knowing what else to do with it except SPEND it, losing all their friends in the process and wishing they'd never won the money in the first place.

If you haven't heard that a lottery is a tax on the poor, it is. You have much better odds of starting a successful business that actually fills a need in the marketplace.

I don't hate the lottery. I have "played" it with friends. To hope for immediate riches and to believe it might happen is a fun diversion for a few minutes, but only if you don't take it too seriously. Or DEPEND on it as an ACTUAL source of revenue.

Would I take the winnings? You betcha!

But I'd also take AMAZING care of that money, too.

Think Wealthy #3: Think Value First

Welcome to the funnest, never-ending game that you already play!

You may not realize you already think in terms of value, but you do. You do it every day when you determine whether the organic bananas are worth the higher price or if the extra wax treatment at the car wash is worth the next tier of pricing – at every corner you look at the price of a good or service and determine whether the underlying value exists for you to buy it.

You may not think of this as a game, but it's a biggie. And it's a fun one!

To think wealthy, you always should be thinking about value within a larger context.

What do I mean by this…

If a larger flat-screen TV goes on sale and is a phenomenal deal, a real steal, even while your current one works just fine, that might look like a great value. In the context of not having any money behind your money dam, either in savings or a retirement account, though, the VALUE of that TV at any price should plummet.

There is little value in putting your future at risk for the sake of another object, another thing, that is not doing anything to help you make more money. A TV is not an investment – it's a depreciating asset just like a car – it provides no long-term return on your money.

Besides, you already have a TV that works just fine, remember?

The wealthy are always thinking of underlying value within that LONG-TERM time horizon we've already talked about.

Let's say you have a 5-year-old car that you just paid off that runs great – what's the value of buying a new car when you don't yet have enough money for health insurance?

Low. An unexpected illness without any insurance in place could saddle you with a hundred thousand dollars of debt overnight.

As already mentioned, in 2021 I had over two million dollars of unexpected health care expenses. If we didn't have health insurance in place, how much of that would I be on the hook for?!? We're still tabulating our out-of-pocket expenses as bills continue rolling in TEN MONTHS after the date of service, but it looks like we're only on the hook for less than .25% of over $2,000,000 – phew!

What's the value of interning or volunteering for free for a few months to check out a possible new career field versus spending all your time at your current job dreaming only about the weekend ahead because you hate it so much?

High. Your passions may be shifting and you will make many valuable connections through volunteering to jumpstart a new career. On the flip side, you may discover that you really don't like performing experiments on chinchillas like you thought you would – but at least now you know!

I took an introductory personal finance course through UCLA Extension years ago because I was fascinated by talking about money. I didn't even make it halfway through the class before I bailed because it was...sooooooo...bloooody...borrrring. I wanted to scream, "This is MONEY we're talking about! Why have you drained it of any excitement? The *time value of boredom* is all I'm learning here!"

Turns out I am more fascinated by the psychology of wealth than the nuts and bolts of personal finance. There are plenty of great financial planners out there who have taken that course and found their calling – turns out my niche is people who want you to "get it," who want you to "get" money because once you get it, you got it, and you'll never forget it.

That UCLA course that I bailed on cost me a few hundred dollars, but the lesson I learned made it worth it – HIGH value, for sure.

Learn to think of everything first in terms of value within a larger timeframe and context.

You can even do this with your current job.

What value do YOU bring to your employer? Rather than ask what value they bring to you, flip it and you'll see where you can improve in your own performance which will only reap more benefits for you.

Grant Cardone wrote something that completely shifted my view on "making money," which I was always told I had to do by my parents, my family, my teachers. They all told me, "You gotta make money *somehow*, Todd!"

Grant says that it's a chore if you think of having to "make money." Instead, see yourself as COLLECTING MONEY because of the value you provide.

"Yes!" I thought to myself. This single shift could do amazing things for this country, not just in terms of work output, but in terms of helping people tap into their own happiness.

This may get a little dark, but what the heck – you can even play the value game in thinking about your friends. What VALUE do they bring to you? Do they lift you up and push you to dream even bigger, to achieve even more out of your life? And do YOU do the same for them? Or do you all just commiserate about how crappy everything is?

Some friends may be great brainstormers – they are great at helping you solve a problem or create something new you want for your life. Other friends seem to know everyone – they can help you meet the right people to get to the next step toward a goal.

Learn to think of everything, even other people in terms of value – not in a creepy "What can you do for me?" way (which is *soooo* Hollywood), but in the sense of achieving goals together. People really do want to help each other out.

By looking at everything through the lens of value, you'll naturally start to seek the things and experiences that bring you the most value in your life, which is completely unique to you.

Case in point...

A friend of mine bought a pen for a thousand dollars.

Then she lost it and decided to buy another one because she felt it was test from the universe and that she needed to proclaim (or reproclaim) her true worth.

I, on the other hand, will never pay more than two dollars for a pen unless it will also magically spring to life and write the Great American Novel for me while I sleep.

What's the value of a pen that (ultimately) cost two thousand dollars in my life which my daughter would probably drop into the toilet tomorrow? L. O. W.

Value is subjective, but that only serves to remind us that we're all unique snowflakes in the snow globe of life.

Needs vs. Wants

Another way you've heard this Think Wealthy point is in the classic Need vs. Want comparison.

Is the thing you're about to spend money on a NEED or a WANT? If you're in consumer debt, simply spend your money on fewer WANTS until you can afford them.

Here my mom has it right whenever I ask her for a Christmas list: "Honey, we're at an age where we don't NEED anything. Besides, that's just one less thing for me to dust!"

(I hate dusting, too.)

That thing you THINK you need may just be one more thing you have to dust – NOW what's the value in it?

Maybe I should change this Think Wealthy point from "Think Value First" to "Think Dust First."

$$$

Wealth Tip: *Know Your 'No'*

Your money is your money. Unless you stole it in which case you suck and you can't hang out with us cool, honest money people any longer.

Your money is your money. You worked hard for it. YOU decide where it goes and where it doesn't go.

How often does a kid selling something at your front door make you fork over your money even if you have no interest in it?

Here's a radical take – that graciously declining to buy whatever they're selling may be an even BETTER lesson for the little scampers in the end. (No, I'm not 80 years old, I don't know where the word 'scampers" came from. This may be the last time it's in print before it finally disappears from the English language.)

It seems like most people don't realize that their money is…well, THEIRS. And I'm not referring to people who say that it's all God's money, anyway. Of course, it's not really yours – you can't take it with you – but while you're here on Earth and not buried in it or scattered on top of it, it IS yours to decide what to do with, when you want to.

If you don't LOVE the new car or new house you're about to spend your hard-earned money on, DON'T do it.

If an investment doesn't feel right, DON'T do it.

"But so-and-so will think…" So-and-so can go fly a kite in a thunderstorm. There's too much guilt surrounding money in these United States of ours.

What you do with your money is your business. You can ask others for advice – and certainly should from time to time, but you then take the advice, or you don't. And you stand behind the decision whether it proves to be weak or strong. No guilt.

We consulted with our financial planner when trying to decide whether I should co-sign for a nephew's college student loan his freshman year. He strongly advised against it because one year would turn into four and, before we knew it, we'd be on the hook for over $40,000 if my nephew didn't pay it back.

I decided to co-sign, anyway, but only for the first year to minimize our financial risk. After two years of on-time payments by said nephew after he graduated, he refinanced it to another provider and no longer needed my John Hancock. I said "yes" for the first year, but knew my "no" for the remaining three and it worked out well for everyone!

To become wealthy, you must develop your "no." Your resolute "no thanks" or "no, thank you" that will stop people in their tracks from trying to "convince" you to buy something you don't want or need or don't understand, whether it's a kid at the front door or the car salesperson with their list of upsells to run you through.

If you WANT the upsells, great! But if you don't, know your no. It's quiet and calm and can stop a bull running right at you in his tracks.

If the bull's first language is English.

Lucky for you, if it's a Spanish bull, "no" sounds about the same in both languages so you should be fine.

Trust me. If you ever come into wealth quickly, people are going to come out of the woodwork asking for money (because everyone knows better than YOU how you should spend it...on THEM). And if you don't "Know Your No," it'll all be gone, and those people will all vanish back into the foggy marshes from whence they crawled.

To the panhandler asking for a dollar if you're not feeling it: "Sorry, buddy."

To the neighborhood do-gooder seeking donations to protect the rights of unborn endangered mosquito larvae: "I appreciate your passion for the cause, but I'm not interested. If you ever switch sides and start selling bug lamps that ensure mosquitoes die a slow and oh, so painful death, I'll be your first sale, though!"

To that adorable, freckled and pig-tailed Girl Scout in front of the grocery store asking you to buy her troop's cookies: "Sorry, not today. But I'm sure you'll sell out real soon!"

You don't have to say yes to everyone who comes around asking for money. For YOUR money.

I have only recently felt comfortable with this thinking wealthy point myself.

Know your 'No.'

Know that you can say 'No' much more often than you realize.

Know that saying no doesn't make you an a-hole simply for saying 'No.' You might be perceived as one if you scream it at everyone in a spray of spittle, but there's a very easy and polite way to do it.

"No, thank you" with a warm smile on your face.

That's all you need to say.

What we're aiming to do with this point is teach you to know the value of a dollar, more specifically the value of YOUR dollars, without having to justify anything to anyone else.

When you know your 'no' you'll also better know your OWN worth and not be afraid to let others know it, too. That's confidence, not ego, my friend. And that is the gift to yourself that will never stop paying dividends.

$$\$\$\$$$

Wealth Warning: *"We can't afford that"*

I heard that phrase so many times growing up that it was etched firmly into the growing folds of my grey matter.

I went out into the world thinking that very few of the things I wanted (even needed, sometimes) I could afford.

We need to shift the conversation to not purchasing something because you don't believe it's of enough VALUE for you at the time, not because you can't afford it. It sounds like a small difference, but it's quite large because it involves you standing firm in making a financial decision.

Declaring that you don't see the VALUE of a purchase puts you in charge of what you do with your money as opposed to being a victim to the scarcity of dollar bills that (you think) exists in the world.

My partner Chris said a few years back, after coming back from the barber, that he loved his haircut so much that he wished he could get one twice a month, but that we couldn't afford it. Because I had been teaching myself to Think Wealthy I said, "Stop right there. Dude, we can AFFORD to do that – in fact," I pulled up the calculator on my phone, punched a few buttons and said, "you can have an extra haircut a month for the next 750 years if you want, but the real question is do you see the *value* in it?"

It might sound like a minor point to call out, but it's a disempowering mindset that we need to hear and catch as soon as it happens.

Before I had a certain level of financial security, I could always deflect a proposed vacation destination by friends – or going out to a restaurant, even – with the excuse that I couldn't afford it. "Maybe next year I can make it to Cabo." Or "Sure, if only I had a million dollars!"

Those are great reasons to give, or they sound like them. But what I later realized was what was really happening is that I was hiding behind my circumstances.

Now that we do have more means, we have to get to the root of what we do and don't want to spend our money on. Which is a much more powerful place to come from because we can't be swayed once we decide.

You can certainly say "it's not in our budget this month" or "this year" which communicates the same message just with you in the driver's seat now.

Don't use the fact that you can't afford something to mask the fact of whether it even holds enough value for you and your family. And don't use "we can't afford it" as an excuse against everything that your kids want because it will teach them that the world is full of lack and scarcity.

If you follow behind me while shopping *anywhere* with my daughter, you'll never hear me respond to her multiple requests to buy things that we can't afford them. "No, honey, we're not getting that today" or "I don't see the value in that" are my go-to lines and that's that.

If the wealthy genuinely can't afford something they want badly enough, they figure out how to afford it and they set a plan in motion.

$$$

Wealth Warning: *"That's How They Getcha!"*

This ties in closely with a money belief I was raised with that everyone is out to get your money. How often did you grow up hearing, "That's where they getcha!" Or "That's how they getcha!"

I'm guilty of this as much as the next feller or lady, but so often we think of a purchase we're about to make as being pure profit going into the immediate business owner's pocket. We get indignant about it, that "they just want to separate me from my cash!" but we forget that every business has its fair share of bills and taxes to pay, too.

"These prices are highway robbery!" we say without knowing anything about the company's financial obligations.

The idea behind this is that you've been duped or had by a company that was just trying to profit off you.

Every company may be trying to get into my wallet, but it's my wallet and I'll let in whoever provides the most value back to me.

But it's not a fight. It's just a company or someone selling a product or service for x number of dollars, and I get to decide whether it's worth it or not.

It's your money. Leave the emotion out of it and simply determine whether it's of value to you. Or not.

$$$

Wealth Warning: *Loaning money to family and friends.*

There are those people in the world who give their money away to family and friends and those who don't. I'm always surprised to hear a friend tell me that so-and-so owes them $1,000 but they don't think they'll ever get it back.

OF COURSE, YOU WON'T.

(Probably.)

If you want to keep the friendship, don't ask for it back. The damage is often already done, though, if the ATM at the Friendship Bank (you!) has opened for business.

I don't think I've ever had a friend ask me for money. And I don't think it's because I've appeared more financially broke than them – though maybe I've looked like it at times. (Have I mentioned how much I hate clothes shopping? And that I have a T-shirt that is 20 years old?)

Maybe it's the energy I've given off. I've also never asked anyone to loan me money in a tough spot, either. (Except for banks in the form of credit cards – and boy did I ask them for "loans" over the years.)

My bottom line is that if you loan money to family or friends, you best never expect it back, so you don't end up resenting whoever hasn't paid it back and who then starts avoiding you.

If you give money away to friends and family without an acknowledgement of any terms and conditions (even if the terms are that you don't expect it back), you may very quickly turn into an ATM in their eyes.

Think Wealthy #4: Think of What's Possible

With anything and everything in your life, there is the current reality and the future possibility.

Today is what today is, and tomorrow is what tomorrow will be.

What most of us do, however, is meld together our current reality and future possibility as if they are one and the same. Yesterday and today have already convinced you that tomorrow is going to be just another helping of what was served on your lunch tray today, right?

We subtract out the possibility of what tomorrow COULD be because we're in a rut or we're scared of change or we have no goals in place...or because we're just plain hopeless and depressed, even.

Or we're just comfortable where we are...simple inertia!

When you start to think of what's possible – and think that way consistently – your entire view of the world changes. In fact, YOUR world changes.

Your imagination is now engaged in problem-solving. You've activated your creativity and the juices are flowing.

You also feel in control because you're taking a stand that things can be better than they are right now. There is hope. Not that today isn't the crappiest day of your life, but can't tomorrow always be a day of new experiences, connections and joy?

The very fact that you start looking at the world through the lens of possibility means that you see the potential in your own capabilities, too.

You see the potential in yourself.

And if you're seeing the potential in yourself, you'll see the potential in others as well.

When you see what's POSSIBLE in the world, life suddenly...comes alive!

The biggest result of this is that you stop complaining about whatever is or isn't happening in your life right now. When you learn to think in terms of what's possible, what just IS right now becomes the fuel you need for tomorrow's accomplishments.

How many years of our lives do we spend looking at a situation or state of affairs and complaining to ourselves and others that it shouldn't be that way?

YEARS!

My grandma shouldn't have died when I was five – I never got to know her.

Why was this POTUS elected? He or she is ruining this country! If they're re-elected...I'm moving to Canada...I swear...but I *mean* it this time!

I'm thirty years old, single and still in massive student loan debt while other friends have families and beautiful homes in the suburbs – why is MY life so hard?

When you complain and live from what's not possible, you FEEL like a victim because your perceived problems make you feel small and powerless.

When you look at the world from what IS possible, your brain gets a zap of electricity like the shock that brought Frankenstein to life.

(Okay, maybe not quite that big of a shock.)

For anyone who has ever created something, it all started with an idea in their head. This can be anything from the creation of an otherworldly literary character like Harry Potter to a completely new innovation or invention such as the Snuggie or iPhone.

How do you know if you're not living in what's possible?

Figure out how much time you spend complaining about the state of your life or listening to others moan about their lives and you validating them.

It might surprise you.

Today is only today.

Tomorrow is what you create it to be.

$$$

Wealth Secret: *Positive people run the world.*

The world is not run by people who think negatively.

The world is not run by people who are hopeless about humanity's ability to change its lot in life.

The world is run by people who believe in a better future and who can share and communicate that vision to others.

The true leaders of our governments and our corporations, of our school systems, they are motivated by a future full of possibilities. They speak in the language of possibility.

You are the leader of your life.

To see what's possible, you need a mindset that is bathed in positive thought. Positive thinking is the backbone of creativity – it's jet fuel for your imagination.

Negative thinking, on the other hand, destroys.

Negative thinking destroys ideas, it destroys morale…it single-handedly stops progress dead in its tracks.

Good leaders, by definition, are positive, future-facing people who consciously steer their minds to what's possible for themselves and others – they don't focus on obstacles.

You would be hard-pressed to find a CEO of any quality that isn't painting a picture of the best of what's ahead for the company as opposed to obsessing about what there is to overcome on the way to that goal.

Are you living in a space of what's possible or are you stuck in a victim mentality where life is a constant struggle?

This should come as no surprise that of the two outlooks on life, positive people are the successful ones.

They are also the much wealthier ones (financially and emotionally) because they see opportunities, engage and inspire others, create their own luck and make things happen.

$$$

Wealth Tip: *See opportunity everywhere you look.*

The only constant in the world is change.

People are born, a litter of puppies pops out of dog bits, flowers bloom…life happens in all its amazing variation and then – spoiler alert – everything dies.

Life is nothing if not CHANGE.

In fact, change is the only thing you can count on. Turns out Buddha was onto something over 2,500 years ago when he said that change was not the problem, it is only RESISTANCE to change that causes suffering.

The catch here is that we're not hardwired to like or accept change – we're not programmed for it. Our amazing, sexy brains are constantly scanning for patterns in our environments to give us the illusion of order, safety and stability.

Your entire life is supported by what you perceive as pillars of unchanging truths.

But ultimately, life is change.

With that acknowledgment, here's a secret that wealthy people know:

With change there is opportunity.

A wealthy mindset welcomes change.

Change means that value is shifting and there is a void where something shiny and new will be ready to provide the value others want or need.

Change?

YAY!!!

So how do we learn to see opportunity?

First, we need to tune our radar for hearing any pain points people have. Where is someone complaining about how difficult something is?

All those people who are negative about the world and can't wait to tell you about it – they may just be your future wealth generators! I wouldn't hang out with them for long since negative cooties are easily caught, but try thinking of them as brainstormers of your rising net worth.

And thank them all the way to the IPO of your company. When you're standing on the floor of the New York Stock Exchange to ring the opening bell, you can publicly thank Bernie in accounting for bitching all day, every day, to you five years ago about his whatchamacallit that you built a company around.

I used to scan the Wall Street Journal that was delivered to my house each day (a "free" subscription from award miles on an airline I no longer flew) and I would see nothing but opportunity for creating better mousetraps for people. That doesn't mean that I'm passionate about any of those areas of opportunity, but I saw them right before my eyes.

Wherever there is a pain point for one person, there is opportunity. The more people who share the pain point, the more financial opportunity that exists.

Opportunities create wealth for those who see and seize them.

Embrace change as the gift it is for wherever there is change, there is opportunity.

It'll also make your life easier as you step into acceptance and flow of the world around you.

$$$

Wealthy Tip: *Always Be Learning*

Only the smartest people know that they know nothing.

In terms of intellect and formal education, the reality is that each of us only knows the tiniest of slivers about our fields of interest.

Yet the world is a FASCINATING place – if you're willing to admit that you don't know much about it.

I was watching a profile of Bill Gates on *60 Minutes* and my jaw dropped when Charlie Rose took their cameras inside Bill's (you know, we're tight like that) private office – and there on the shelf were dozens and dozens of The Great Courses DVDs.

First off, I have ordered a few of those myself so I was comforted to learn I'll soon be wrestling Bill Gates for his on-again, off-again world's wealthiest man title.

Second, it was only a few years ago that I would've thought that someone as wealthy as Bill Gates had a pretty good handle on how much book knowledge he has or needs in his life.

Nope, turns out he understands the power of interdisciplinary thought, how learning about one area can benefit a completely different area, and he knows how to stay CURIOUS and, therefore, stay CREATIVE as he and his (now ex) wife go about giving away billions of dollars toward causes they care about and are working to change.

That *60 Minutes* segment was all the proof I needed that some of the wealthiest people are always learning, always asking questions, staying creative and nimble, always wanting to know how they can help others and improve the world around them. He also had a tote bag full of books he was at various stages of reading…say what?!?

Think about the sharks on *Shark Tank* – they are always listening and learning from the people they meet on the show. They might know the trends of their own industries well, but they don't know anything about how to make beer-flavored ice cream or how large the market for it is.

Always be thinking, "What can I learn from every person I meet?"

Everyone knows something that you don't. Together you might find amazing synergy for your next project or business opportunity. Or perhaps you'll just be able to file away a little piece of information that will help someone else out.

Lest we not forget that the biggest wealth-building tool of all is your BRAIN.

$$\$\$\$$

Wealth Tip: *Embrace obstacles…they ain't going anywhere.*

Of course, you're going to have obstacles.

Everyone has them, including children of super-wealthy parents.

We all have obstacles because life is unpredictable.

But we also need them in our lives. Without obstacles, there is no growth. And without growth, life would be pretty darn boring.

Anyone who has met with success wouldn't trade in all the "failures" that preceded their success because they know the value of those lessons along the way.

Let others help you when you're stuck – doesn't it feel good to help *other* people when the shoe's on the other foot?

Think Wealthy #5: Think Big

No. Bigger!

What you can achieve in this world is only limited by your imagination.

However big of a life you want to live, I want you to dream even bigger!

I'm talking about dreaming with a plan of action to put behind it, of course, not *The Secret* dreaming where you fall asleep every night hugging your tear-soaked vision board wondering where your buxom supermodel girlfriend is or why Hugh Jackman hasn't left his wife for you yet because, yes, that's what would REALLY make your life complete.

One of the biggest obstacles people have on the road to well-rounded wealth is the limit of their own imaginations – instead of dreaming you have a million dollars in the bank, envision ten million or fifty million. I guarantee that when you know you DESERVE it, your brain will get creative on ways of how to bring it to your door.

What you are capable of is only limited by your imagination. I don't care if you're 18 or 80, you have plenty of time left to make a difference in the world.

And you're not going to run out of energy because you'll be passionate about what you're doing and that is its own internal power plant.

$$$

Wealth Tip: *The world is soooooooooooooooo big.*

The world is much bigger than you can ever understand.

Given the phenomenal diversity of human beings, anytime you think you have life figured out, stop and remember that the overwhelming majority of people in the world DON'T think like you. Heck, your neighbors on all sides don't think like you.

Any time I was dreading going into the office of past employment, I would drive past businesses on the morning commute and think how many hundreds of people worked in all those buildings that I drove past, jobs that were not the one that I was headed into (and not liking) and I would dream that they enjoyed what they did and were fulfilled by them.

Just thinking about the phenomenal diversity of jobs and careers in my tiny five-mile commute into the office popped me out of my head and my "woe is me" mentality – it reignited and excited me about how big the world is and that there must be HUNDREDS of jobs out there that were a better fit for me than the current one – I just needed to find it.

To stop and periodically try to grasp the enormity of the world and the vast difference in experiences that people have had should help you see your own problems in a different light, too – it should shrink them down so that YOU, that endless potential you are in each new moment, can become bigger than all your perceived problems pooled together.

You are a gazillion times bigger than your problems. (And that's a lot, as my 7-year-old will tell you.)

All you have to do is watch other people overcome unfathomable odds and circumstances to achieve their goals and you'll soon realize that you have everything within you to do the same.

$$$

Wealth Tip: *Commit to being wealthy.*

Now that you are thinking and dreaming big and that you can overcome any obstacle that stands in your way, what we need is a fire in the belly, the commitment to make a plan for success and to then follow it, one step at a time.

Know you're WORTHY of wealth.

You have every chance of becoming wealthy if you want to.

Most people are ashamed to admit that they want to be wealthy. Money is "bad" or wealthy people are thought to be amoral or greedy or ruthless – whatever the reason, most people WANT to have more money, but they don't want to ADMIT it out loud. Therefore, they don't commit to DOING anything about it because it signifies a break with the herd mentality of the middle class.

Even if you live in BFE, America and for you to leave $100,000 to your heirs when you die would be considered sizeable wealth, commit to it!

Done. And kudos to you in advance!

Make a promise to yourself – do it for your kids, find whatever motivates you to embrace the planning and the work ahead and DO IT.

If money is bad or a taboo topic, go back to the first page of this book and work your way back here. I'll wait.

[whistling *The Muppet Show* theme]

Good…moving right along!

Think Wealthy #6: Think "Why not me?"

The only thing that keeps us from enjoying life and accepting any good fortune that we create for ourselves or that comes our way is our own limited thinking. It stems from a belief that we don't DESERVE the good that we're experiencing or receiving.

How often have you heard people say that they became nervous or scared when things were going "too well for them" in their lives as if the universe always must balance out any good fortune you're experiencing with misfortune?

It doesn't. The universe does not need to balance out you feeling good with you feeling bad.

The underlying belief a person holds here is, "I don't deserve to be this happy or feel this good or this fortunate."

You've probably even thought this yourself at one point, that "all good things must come to an end" or that you don't want to "push your luck" or, God forbid, get used to "too much of a good thing."

That doesn't sound like the self-talk of someone who creates their own life and knows that, if they dream it, they can achieve it, does it?

It stems from thinking that the world is us vs. them where there's a group of people who are lucky or wealthy or happy all the time and who deserve IT ALL...and then there's the rest of us.

So. Many. People. Do. This.

We feel on some cellular level that we don't deserve good fortune or happiness for more than a few fleeting moments.

My partner and I used to think this way and now we stop it dead in its tracks. And you can, too!

For years now, as Chris and I have been invited to exclusive charity events where paddles are flying into the air for $100,000 or even $500,000 donations or to dinner parties with friends who live in beautiful mansions in the Hollywood Hills, or invited out on yachts to sail the waters off of the coast of Los Angeles – whenever we find ourselves in a situation where someone from the outside looking in would think we may very well be wealthy just for being in that environment, one of us will turn to the other and say, "Why NOT us?"

Indeed, why not us?

Why not us to just enjoy this day or night or weekend?

The only thing that would keep us from enjoying life at that level is our own set of limiting beliefs – or guilt – that we were somehow unworthy of having the experience, that we were fooling everyone into thinking that we belonged there, that we were not inherently interesting or smart enough to fit in – whatever the limiting belief is.

Every wealthy person has already made that mental leap at some point in their lives to just accept wherever they are.

So why not us?

There is no reason why not us.

And why not YOU?

There is no reason why not YOU.

None.

When good things happen to you or money falls into your lap or you're gifted something that you've always wanted, stop, say "thank you" and think to yourself, "Of course! Why not me?"

It's that simple.

$$$

Wealth Tip: *"Yes, Please!"*

For years whenever I would receive a check for whatever work I had done, I would stare down at the check and sigh, shoulders slumped carrying the weight of the world because I knew it had already been spent before I'd even cashed it.

That's what debt does to you. After all, where is the joy in making ANY amount of money when it is "already spent."

Or so it felt. Having left college with a liberal arts degree double major in Linguistics and French (that money-printing diploma) and $50,000 of student loans – all I'd known as an adult was deep debt and no clear career path to paying it off.

I had to consciously change my attitude toward money by realizing that any income was MY money to decide what to do with – in that light I started treating every check I received as if it were my new best friend.

I had to become a good RECEIVER – of money, of compliments, of whatever.

I had to consciously reprogram my mind to love money and to respect any money that was coming into my life.

Consciously changing from the thought that I worked only to pay down my debt to the fact that I was in CONTROL of my life and OPEN to money flowing to and through me allowed me to open my eyes and ears to other opportunities where I could earn even more money. It took that literal behavior modification on my part to change the thought process and underlying belief behind it.

By consciously CHOOSING what I wanted to do with my money, I was no longer a victim to my debt or to my life's circumstances, in general.

It's a trap I still fall into sometimes, but by and large, with every check I receive, no matter how small, I get excited as if I had just won it big in Vegas.

A $2 rebate check for paper at Staples? "Awe! Some!"

Annual residuals check of $15 for an episode of Unsolved Mysteries that I shot over 20 years ago? "Bring it on, bishes!"

Sidenote: Those tiny residual checks rolling in each year actually vested me into the SAG/AFTRA pension plan so now when I retire, not only will I have our savings, tax-advantaged retirement accounts and Social Security, but I'll also have a boost of a pension that will only grow larger and larger if I ever do more work under that union's contracts.

"Would you like more money, Todd?!?"

Yes, please!

"Would you like bigger life experiences and meeting new people to find your next opportunities where you can provide value back to the world?"

Yes, please!

This is about saying YES to life, in general, as you never know where your next great idea or opportunity is going to come from, but it will most definitely come from meeting and sharing ideas with other people.

$$$

Wealth Tip: *Imagine yourself in any situation.*

Anytime you think of the life you'd like to lead, whether by seeing other people on TV or reading about them, immediately put yourself in that position.

If you see a beautiful house in Malibu with infinite views of the Pacific Ocean, think about that being YOUR house.

What happens next? Does your chest tighten from fear of living there and everything that comes along with that? Or does it all flow?

Is the house so big that it has any live-in staff there just to maintain it? Who are they and how do you interact with them?

You can imagine yourself into any situation – and if you don't like how you respond in your imagination, you can start working on that right now. As part of our Be – Do – Have equation from the last chapter, BE the person who can HAVE that life first so it has a chance of becoming a reality.

$$$

Wealth Warning: *The Pedestal Effect*

This will either apply to you outright or you won't have any idea what the heck I'm talking about, but this has been a biggie for me.

I always used to put rich people on a pedestal – because my family did. Although my parents always wanted to have more money, they also glorified the idea of being rich and what it must be like to have a great amount of financial breathing room.

My mom would start dragging out her syllables when talking about people that appeared richer than her. Just the fact that they *appeared* to have more than us was enough to get our respect and admiration.

"Did you seeeeee the way they decorated their hoooouuuuuse? Oh, my goooo000dness! We would just never THINK to do ANY of that!"

"Mom, you know the Stronzi family come from a long line of mafioso connections, right?"

"Every party has a pooper, Todd! Now go to bed so the Tooth Fairy can leave you an I.O.U. until your father hits the Powerball."

It's as if anyone who was wealthy was cut from a different cloth. They were not people that we would casually hang out with – they ran in different circles and left a trail of hundred-dollar bills in their path from their overflowing pockets.

Unbeknownst to me, I inherited this belief about how different rich and wealthy people were, from you and me.

As I mentioned in the introduction, living in Los Angeles and projecting 35mm films years ago in the super-posh homes in the wealthiest parts of town, I'd peek out of the porthole, watching "those rich people" rearrange pillows in their private screening rooms, trying to catch a glimpse of how different and more refined and mannered they MUST be – if I could just learn and mimic their wealthy way of fluffing a pillow, it would immediately start beefing up my own bank account.

I was trying to figure out the secrets to their success by observing their behavior so I could become just like them.

The problem with that outlook is I'd constructed a mental wall between who I am and who they are as if the wealthy are a monochromatic group of people operating under one set of rules (which includes the proper way to fluff a couch pillow, apparently) that remains elusive to the rest of us.

When, in fact, they are just people who saw opportunities, perhaps took big risks, who invested in themselves and knew what to do with the money when it came in.

They knew to earn more than they spend and invest the rest – dam it!

The pedestal effect is more Us vs. Them thinking that I have encountered more than a few times in my life.

Now I'd rather know HOW they made and maintain their wealth – there may be things I could learn from their journeys, but not from how they arranged the pillows on their couches or tossed peanut M&M's into their mouths while I started up the film in the projection booth behind them.

The bottom line is to not put people on a pedestal – it means you're looking UP for wisdom and which requires them to look DOWN to share it – and everyone just ends up with pains in their necks.

The difference between a wealthy person's net worth and yours is often just a punctuation mark or two.

What you can learn from them, however, is invaluable. And vice-versa.

See everyone as a peer and you'll be more yourself – more genuine and unguarded – your authenticity will shine through which is what matters most.

You are not in competition with people who are wealthy – you are fellow travelers along the same road looking out for each other and helping each other along. The wealthy are only in competition with themselves, just as YOU are only really in competition with YOUR self.

Think Wealthy #7: Think of yourself as CEO of You, Inc.

No one is going to take better care of your life than you are.

It was your parents' job to make sure you were safe, dry-diapered and fed on time, but at some point, you get to run your own life. You probably kicked and screamed through puberty and adolescence for your freedom – now, here we are – you wanted it you, you got it!

Congrats on the promotion!

You are the CEO of You, Inc. and that has never been more apparent than in this corporation-agnostic, job-hopping, LinkedIn-orgy-of-career-whoredom that we're currently in.

Just as no one is going to take better care of you than YOU, no one is going to take better care of your MONEY than you are. People may ADVISE you on what to do with your money – and at some point, you should let them – but never let go of the reins.

So, let's get down to the very important business of You, Inc.

How are the company's financials? Is it healthy, in general? Will it be around in ten years based on current spending? Does the company have all its risks mitigated via insurance and wills and trusts to ensure as smooth of sailing as possible?

As CEO, how is your integrity – would you want to do business with YOU? Would you trust you in a negotiation? Do you trust you to show up at a meeting on time and prepared or will you just wing it and squeak by? Do you have a vision for the company to help steer it through the exciting, unknown waters of the future? Or are you fixating on the company's past performance, the good, the bad and the ugly?

But hey, you're freakin' CEO now. Whatever you don't like, change it!

No big deal. Companies pivot all the time.

It's very important that you not be critical of the job you're doing as CEO – forgive yourself and move on.

When you know better, you do better.

And as CEOs, we're ALL working to improve ourselves which, in turn, will improve company morale and ensure that we are running a solid business from the CEO on down.

Do you see what's happening as you internalize all these Think Wealthy points?

You're becoming the real leader of your own life.

You always have been, but now you're starting to believe it.

$$$

Wealth Tip: *Pursue Profits, Not Wages*

Wealthy people invest in themselves because they believe in themselves.

They know that whatever they don't know they can learn from someone else or pay someone else to do, so they take chances.

Think of a salesman who doesn't believe in his abilities and so he chooses a salary with a base of $80,000 and a commission of 5% on all sales. If he has a million in sales for the year, he'll make $130,000 ($80,000 base + $50,000 in commissions).

Contrast that with a person who Thinks Wealthy and who negotiates a base salary of $40,000 but a commission structure of 30% on all sales. On that same million in sales for the company as the previous example, they'll take home $340,000 ($40,000 base + $300,000 in commissions). That's over twice as much as our friend who doesn't believe in his or her abilities.

This is a fabricated example as a 30% sales commission is quite high and it must be a product or service with incredible margins like a subscription model or SAAS, but I'm using it to prove a point.

Someone who invests in THEMSELVES is believing 100% in their own ability to drive sales and bring home the bacon.

They create businesses because they believe they can deliver great value to the marketplace and be well-compensated for it.

In general, people who Think Wealthy seek (or create) opportunities where they can make more money than they would with a flat pay structure. They incentivize themselves to work harder and smarter and deliver on their objectives, be they for another company or for their own.

They have a self-confidence that makes them see and accept the opportunities that come their way.

I'll keep hammering away at this until the cows come home because it took me that long to get it.

Wealthy people invest in themselves. They align their compensation with their performance because they know a share of the profits is a much stronger incentive than an hourly wage which, ultimately, puts a cap on what they can earn.

Work for profits and the sky is the limit. Work for hourly wages and you are capped by time to the total income you can earn.

If your compensation isn't linked to a company's profits or earnings, you will always be trading time for money. And there are only so many hours in a day.

MOO.

$$$

Wealth Tip: *Would you hire you?*

As the CEO of You, Inc. your decisions affect the fate of the entire company. If you were to meet you in an interview, does the candidate (you!) seem confident in their abilities? Do you trust them (you!)?

Heck, do you even LIKE them (you!)?

In the real world, for any job that you're going after, put yourself in the interviewer's seat – what qualities in the candidate sitting across from you will make your job SO MUCH easier? The secret is that everyone is looking to hire someone who makes their job that much easier, from your immediate supervisor all the way up to the CEO.

You want the next hire to be the home run for the company.

Be the home run. And, for the love of butter, don't beat yourself if you don't get a second interview. How people do or don't see you is dependent on a million factors, but one of them is never your own underlying worth as a human being.

Bottom line is would you want to hire you in your position? If not, become that person – become the person that sets the bar high and delivers on those goals.

$$\$\$\$$$

Wealth Tip: *Share your vision of the future.*

Share your vision of the future you want for yourself and others to live into.

Life is a team sport. If you have a vision for your own life that you can passionately share with others, you will inspire them.

This is what the best leaders do in their personal or professional lives – they share their bold vision of a better world, and the force of their conviction pulls others in line with it and everyone sets about making it come true. Everyone wants to live in that new world, too!

What do you want for your life? Why not envision it, share it and then create it? No one else will do it for you.

$$\$\$\$$$

Wealth Tip: *Compete with yourself – and love the competition.*

As soon as I say to compete with yourself, a whole chorus of people will chime in and say they do and that when they don't succeed at something, they beat themselves up unmercifully just like they're supposed to.

And they'll say that with a hint of pride, the beating-themselves-up part.

"I mean, I'm just too much of a perfectionist, Todd. It's got to be the best or I'm not happy."

To which I reply, "That's very fascinating, annoying person who reminds me of my former self!"

There's a difference between doing the best job you can and basing your self-worth on your performance.

You are an amazingly complex individual – give yourself a break and do really great work. Save the perfect work for brain surgery on me if I need it (and if you're a brain surgeon). Otherwise, what daily perfectionism does is make you a martyr and a blowhard and most people see right through it.

When I say to compete with yourself, I'm talking about doing the things you want and need to do, striving for wealth, for freedom, for safety, because you are your only REAL competition.

No one is going to know if you did the best job possible except for you.

So do your best work. Always. Because you are your own best benchmark for how you're doing in life.

And if you didn't do your best, ask yourself why, tweak something and move on.

Every time you compare yourself with someone else, you put one person higher than the other and you either judge yourself against them or you judge them against you and that stops the baseball game of life mid-pitch.

When you look around and only see people higher or lower than you, you don't have any peers. Yet the secret is that everyone's a peer when you're confident in who you are.

$$\$\$\$$$

Wealth Tip: *Do what you say.*

Do what you say you're going to do.

If you don't do what you say, no one will trust you. They will lose faith in you and that takes a long time to rebuild.

Be a person of your word – you will stand out among your peers. Guaranteed.

If you say you'll follow up on Tuesday, follow up on Tuesday. Set a reminder – do what you gotta do to keep yourself on top of tasks.

If you know you can't make it to a lunch appointment, cancel it as soon as you can, not an hour beforehand – it shows respect for the other person's time.

That's all keeping your word does – it elicits the highest trust and respect from others. It also shows others that you value THEIR time. Which you do because you know the value of your OWN time.

And if your time is important, so is everyone else's – it's all the same. And if someone doesn't realize their time is important yet, you can lead by example.

You know you're dealing with a class act when someone much wealthier or more powerful than you doesn't keep you waiting.

Do what you say.

$$$

Wealth Tip: *Don't be the smartest person in the room.*

Or don't NEED to be, at least.

No one likes competing for honors. You're already CEO – it's your birthright. Relax and ask questions of people who know more, but YOU then make the decision. And stand behind it.

The wealthiest people consistently and deliberately hire and surround themselves with people who are smarter than them. This is why they're wealthy.

Period.

Think Wealthy #8: Think Thanks

Wealth starts with 'We.'

Always think thanks and GIVE thanks whenever you can.

I honestly thank you for reading this far into this book. No joke, many people won't get this far so you are part of a very select few and I am sincerely grateful that you have decided to spend this much time with me and my goofy humor as it relates to money and life.

Thank you!

See how easy that is? It feels good, too!

I challenge you to show me one wealthy person who did it all alone, who needed absolutely no one's help to reach the heights of their fame and financial glory.

It's an impossible challenge because no one does it all alone, regardless of what the media say.

And winning people over because you're such an awesome and inspiring person starts with gratitude for other people sharing their time and energy with you.

I can't say it enough…

No one becomes wealthy without the help of others. No one.

People, your family, your relationships – they are all assets, not liabilities.

Wealth starts with 'we.'

We have this lone wolf idea in our minds, this idea that people who become exceedingly wealthy are operating all alone in the world as if a company of one could amass millions of dollars in value – at minimum there are clients or customers that you need to think thanks for!

Facebook is a company of over 45,000 employees. You often only see Mark Zuckerberg as the singular – face (Face?) – of the company, but dude is not doing it all alone. No one does.

Wealth starts with 'we.'

Life is a team sport and everyone's time is valuable so be sure to thank them for their help at every step of the way.

$$$

Wealth Tip: *Gift and share randomly.*

Gift things to people because you want to, not to get something back.

Have you ever gifted something to someone anonymously and been able to see their eyes light up or see them break down in tears because they're in shock at the level of thought and generosity?

It's phenomenal. And you can do it at any time you like.

It's one of the greatest joys in life.

It doesn't have to be anonymous if we're talking between friends and it also doesn't need to be that extreme, but why not periodically send your favorite book to a handful of friends who might like it? Or send a bottle of your favorite wine to a new work buddy? Or randomly take a box of donuts or other treats into the office (if/when the global pandemic ends) to kick off or end the workweek?

Everyone loves gracious surprises like these – why should we wait until holiday season each year to revel in the surprise and joy on others' faces?

There are so many ways to show gratitude and be thankful for the people who are in your life, past and present.

It feels great to give.

And that is REALLY the point of creating more wealth for you and your family than you ever could have imagined.

You're going to have to get really good at giving your money away so why not start now with small gifts to those you care about and work with?

Write one email a week to a different person thanking them and letting them know what you've learned from them. In one year, you'll have 52 people who will do ANYTHING they can to help you out, too.

$$\$\$\$$$

Wealth Tip: *Learn people's names.*

I. Still. Suck. At. This.

But I'm getting better.

One of the easiest ways for people to remember YOU is for you to remember THEIR NAME in a five-minute conversation.

It shows you're attentive and that you care about that person, whether you'll ever see them again or not.

It's part of being charismatic.

There is a friend of a friend who used to own famous soundstages out here in Los Angeles. I probably met him ten different times over a couple of years and every single time we were introduced, he acted as if he had never met me before. Distant and disinterested were the words I might use to describe his body language.

It used to infuriate me that he would never remember that we had met before, never mind the fact that he couldn't squeak out my name even if he were being waterboarded.

It made me despise him. If someone mentioned his name, I'd roll my eyes.

This is an extreme case, and it shows my pettier side, but we all have these people in our lives. If he had ever said, "I'm sorry, I know we've met, but I'm horrible with names"...that's one thing.

But to say nothing over the years means that I will gleefully dance on his grave when the Dark Lord of the Underworld comes to retrieve him.

Work hard to remember people's names. Or be gracious enough to admit that you're not good with them.

A trick I've found is to drop a person's name in at the end of a conversation after repeating it silently in my mind while they're talking – it will help you to cement their name even more in your mind and it will give their brain stem a little tickle of fondness for you.

And maybe, just maybe, they won't gleefully anticipate your demise at the hands of the Dark Lord of the Underworld, too.

Think Wealthy #9: Think "I got this!"

Fear will never go away.

And it shouldn't – fear keeps you on your toes and is a loyal talent scout for your hunches and intuition. Treat fear like a babbling toddler – listen to it to see if there's anything of value in its ramblings and then send it on its way.

Life is not supposed to come with an instruction guide. If it did, it would be immeasurably dull and predictable.

On whatever path you now tread and, in the future, think (and know), "I got this!"

You can figure out whatever needs to be figured out by yourself over time or with the help of others because – you got this!

Everything else is noise that can easily distract you from letting your true light and purpose shine out into the world.

$$$

Wealth Tip: *You are bigger than your problems.*

You will have obstacles on the road of life from your first breath to your last. We all will. Even people with more money in the bank than you have them, too.

Problems, obstacles, hurdles, whatever you want to call them, are there for a reason and all you need to remember at the end of the day is that you are not the problem itself and you are not defined by the problem – you are infinitely bigger than the problem.

I'm repeating this point because it bears repeating – we too often associate our worth with the current obstacles staring us in the face, but your inner billionaire knows better.

$$$

Wealth Tip: *See everyone as a survivor. Like you.*

Think of everyone you see out in the world – everyone you previously judged and gossiped about – they're all survivors the same as you.

And they're using all the tricks and potions and voodoo up their sleeve to stay safe in the game of life the same as you – that is how we're all much more alike than we are different.

You're a survivor and you do what you do because it worked for you in the past the same as others do today what has worked for them in the past.

Sympathy and empathy for your fellow man will never go out of style. And if it does…run!

Actually, don't run – stay and be the change we *all* need to see in the world! After years of corrosive political discourse in the U.S., which then carried over into mask and vaccination debates during a once-in-a-century global pandemic, we all need to be reminded of the power of true empathy for your fellow wo(man).

We are all survivors. And most of us are blindly following our invisible rulebooks as if it's the only way to stay safe in the world.

$$$

Wealth Tip: *Forgive yourself.*

Forgive yourself for not having done the ten things you didn't do yet today that would have ensured your success, or for not knowing what your net worth is to the decimal point or how much consumer debt you have.

Forgive yourself and just snicker at the goofy things you do and have done along your journey up to this point, to you reading this sentence right now.

I'm not sure if guilt is the gift that keeps on giving in America from our Mayflower ancestors, but it's time we all stop beating ourselves up.

Forgive yourself.

You are enough.

After you reach adulthood, it's no one's job to tell you this any longer so be sure to remind yourself from time to time.

Just as you were yesterday, just as you are today and just as you will be tomorrow.

Forgive yourself – you are enough.

Think Wealthy #10: Stop Thinking and DO

You are awesome.

Did you forget that already from the introduction? Or did you skip the introduction because you wanted to start creating wealth in your life *that much sooner*?

You are awesome. You have read through all these points and your brain is on fire as new pathways are created for you to Think Wealthy.

That's all great and wonderful and stupendous, but unless you take ACTION toward a goal, no matter how small, and follow it up with another small step, and another, then this is all a big, hot steaming feel-good cup of mental doodoo.

The theory behind this book on how to Think Wealthy is that your thoughts will motivate you to take action, your thoughts will actually PULL you into the habits that will reward you in the form of financial wealth due to all the value you will be providing to the world.

That's how it works.

So, for the love of all that is sacred and holy and blessed with the color green and that smells like sweet, sweet cash, PLEASE stop thinking and go DO something to start on the path to your dreams. And then do one more step. And another and another…

Wealthy people act quickly. It's a muscle like any other that they've trained. They're used to being proactive to a newfound opportunity.

Ethical, wealthy people do what they say they're going to do, and they explore every opportunity with vim and vigor until they know whether it has the potential to be a winner – or they discover it's a dud and they go back to their regular routine of seeing other opportunities and kicking ass.

We have spent the first four chapters working on the internal side of the wealthier you – we have been working on the BE side of our BE – DO – HAVE equation because that is the foundation for all the actions you will DO in your life to HAVE the life of your dreams.

Per this Think Wealthy point #10, however, now it is time to infuse our actions with the underlying beliefs of our inner billionaire and tackle the DO part of the equation.

Action is SO IMPORTANT I'm going to stop this point right–

Summary

You get all that? Good! Now go knock 'em dead, Slugger!

You want to know what we're doing?

We're saying that anything is possible if we believe in ourselves FIRST, are willing to make a plan, work toward our goals and treat others with the respect that they deserve along the way.

You're the leader of your life. And everyone is a peer. And when you can share your passion and purpose with others, you will inspire them to join your cause or company or project or non-profit or whatever it is that lights you up.

Here's a quick recap of our ten ways to Think Wealthy:

1. Think Net Worth, Not Salary.

2. Think Long-Term.

3. Think Value First.

4. Think of What's Possible.

5. Think "Why not me?"

6. Think Big.

7. Think of Yourself as CEO of You, Inc.

8. Think Thanks.

9. Think "I got this!"

10. Stop Thinking and DO.

If you really understand and implement the concepts in this chapter, it will forever change your perspective on how to make money and how to value your time (and everyone else's).

Thinking Wealthy positions you to pull yourself up from wherever you are and take you wherever you want to go.

The secret you may not have realized until now is that life is yours for the taking and the universe will compensate you with financial wealth in exchange for great value that is properly executed.

Chapter 5: Create Your Fortune, Big or Small

We overestimate what we can accomplish in one year - but we grossly underestimate what we can accomplish in a decade.

- Tony Robbins

Do Money and Fortune Really Matter?

I titled this chapter "Create Your Fortune, Big or Small" for two reasons:

First, if you're wondering if I've been placing too much emphasis on money (like what is my ACTUAL deal, right?), all you have to do is ask a random smattering of people if money really matters in the grand scheme of things.

From those who have never had much (or any) money, they will probably say that, no, money doesn't really matter, it's what's inside that counts. Their perspective is one of having lived without "extra" money, perhaps for their entire lives.

They're absolutely right that what's on the inside counts, but that doesn't stand in opposition to the idea of having a very high net worth one day – you can be an incredible person AND be wealthy – those two are not mutually exclusive.

Why you're asking someone withOUT any money about the ultimate value of money is dubious in the first place, but you're statistically more likely to run into someone struggling with money issues rather than people who have managed their finances with confidence and a wink.

Ask a wealthy person if money matters and they'll say, "Oh, hell yeah!"

Money definitely matters.

Money matters because it provides financial breathing room and freedom so you can create the life of your design.

Let's not kid ourselves – money can also provide power, influence, political sway and even serve as a financial barometer for a person's ideas and business savvy in the larger marketplace, which is how most repeat entrepreneurs regard wealth.

BUT, money only matters for the things it's best at – food, shelter, education, travel, entertainment – and feelings of safety, security and freedom – having more or less of it than someone else says NOTHING about the quality of a person or the quality of the life they're living.

Does money matter? You betcha'.

Money matters because you matter.

Your experiences of the world matter.

Your unique perspective matters.

Your ability to create a better future for yourself and others will always matter.

Money matters because YOU matter.

You deserve to feel safe in an uncertain world.

You deserve to feel secure through to the end of your days as you strut and fret upon life's stage.

You deserve to feel free by taking educated risks and testing your ideas within the global economy and being financially rewarded for their success.

Secondly, I titled this chapter "Create Your Fortune, Big or Small" because, now that we've finished talking in the earlier chapters about the more esoteric concepts of money and wealth, your beliefs of abundance and your ability to create your own life, coupled with the idea of thinking wealthy, it's time to get down to some PRACTICAL money matters.

After all, the final point from the last chapter is to "Stop Thinking and DO." So, here we are, getting ready for the DO-ing.

It's time to figure out how MUCH money you'd like or need so we have a destination in mind, specifically WHY you want it and HOW you're going to collect it
All pretty simple what we're talking about – you know, we're just figuring out your ENTIRE financial life.

In one chapter.

The Road to Wealth: How Much Is Enough?

A BIG note here that any specific numbers we discuss are going to be a bit arbitrary because a) the cost of living varies greatly depending on where you live in the U.S. or within the larger world and b) your financial aspirations are particular to you and you alone, but we can chat ballpark numbers without summoning the trolls. (Oh, who are we kidding?)

As I'll say until I'm blue in the face...

The only three things money does well is grant a person a feeling of short-term safety, long-term security and, ultimately, financial freedom.

Now let's use The Money Dam to help drive it all home!

The Money Dam

Here again, on the next page, is The Money Dam™ (found in Appendix A) which I created as a visual representation of the road to wealth. I use this, too, for checking in with my family's financial progress and to remind myself, from time to time, of what's truly important on our journey together.

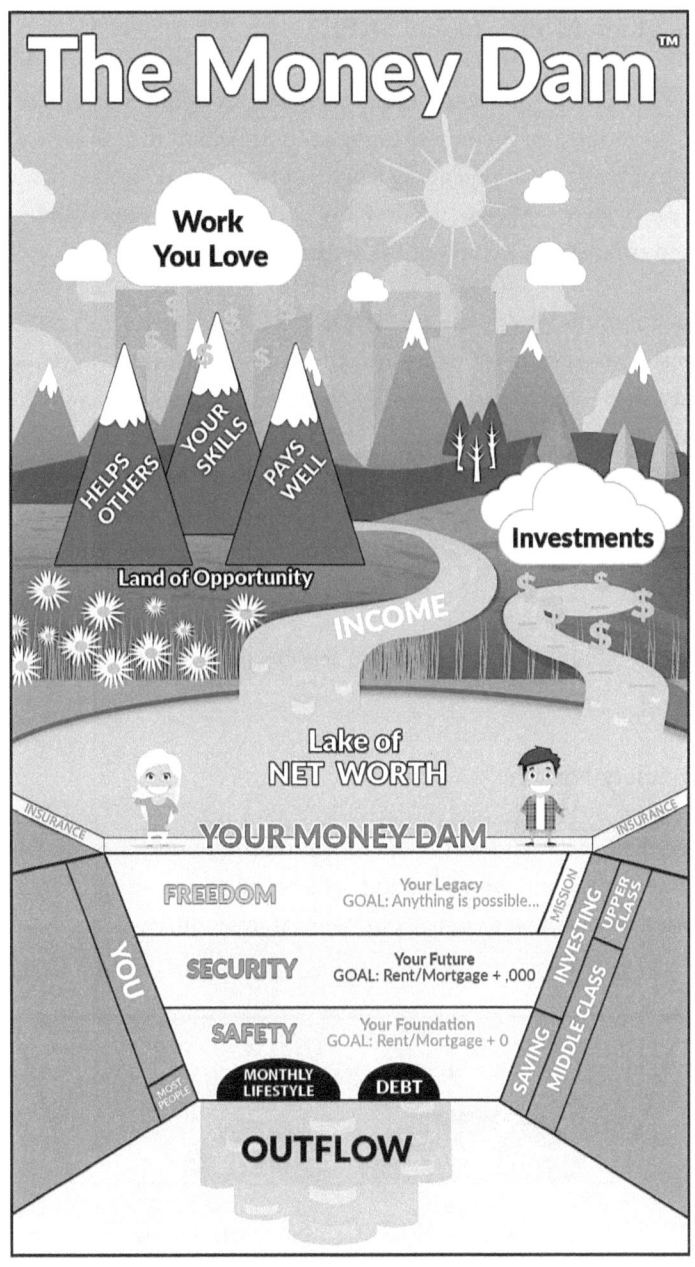

How Much Money to feel SAFE?

To get to a point of feeling financially safe, everyone agrees that you need 3-6 months of income sloshing around behind that dam of yours. At that point you can practically laugh at the car breaking down, a small fire destroying your prized Hello Kitty collection, a dropped and (now) cracked smartphone or any of life's other little surprises.

Just 3-6 months of income for SHORT-TERM SAFETY. You'll hear financial gurus espouse one or the other – for someone just getting out of debt they'll tend to set three (3) months of expenses as a goal, so it doesn't feel too overwhelming. For people with more established or higher-paying careers, they tend to emphasize saving a minimum of six (6) months' worth of expenses, the rationale being that if you lose a high-paying job, it may take you longer to find another one with a similar salary.

So, 3 to 6 months is what it takes to feel financially SAFE.

Your Safety Number

Rather than the traditional route of figuring out your monthly budget (which can vary and which I find a wee bit mind-numbing), I've found an easier way for you to figure out your safety number…

SAFETY: Take the amount you spend each month on rent or a mortgage and add ONE zero (0) to the end of it.

For example, we pay $3,000 in rent each month. I add a '0' at the end and that comes out to $30,000. ($3,000 a month in rent + one zero = $30,000.)

Our family should have $30,000 in relatively liquid accounts if we want to feel safe.

Fortunately, we do have that in place. The first third of our Money Dam wall is accounted for and, indeed, we feel SAFE for having that in place.

Like our own personal umpire that greets us when we wake up in the morning to start the day, "Safe!" And as we go to sleep each night, "Safe!"

That's the price you pay to know you're safe…some random dude in an umpire mask moves into your place and screams at you at least twice a day.

We had a flat tire last week and it was not stressful knowing that we could easily cover the cost of it. Turns out it was easily repaired at a shop for $24! Did you honestly think any car repair could cost so little in 2022? Neither did we!

As I mentioned before, I had over two million dollars in health care treatment in 2021 – thanks, incurable blood cancer! As the bills continue rolling in after insurance has paid their share, we have little stress knowing that we can cover a large bill if and when we need to.

For you to feel SAFE, now you know how much money you need behind your dam, YOUR rent or mortgage plus one zero (0).

This safety number SHOULD NOT INCLUDE any big-ticket items you're planning on buying within the next five years: if you want a next-generation TV because you've always wanted to count Judge Judy's pores or a down payment for a tiny house because you're a big fan of the Tiny House Movement (is that still a thing? I know I still want one!), separate out any of these big-ticket items from your safety number.

It may be a new concept to think of money just sitting there in an account that doesn't "do" anything, that isn't being "saved up" to be spent on something specific, but it's giving you the room to BREATHE and THINK more clearly throughout your days and nights.

Many people don't understand this, but you DESERVE to feel this way. It will provide you with more options and opportunities in life.

You keep this money in very "liquid" (or easily accessible) accounts like a savings account or online money market account, ideally with a reputable online bank that can return a base level of interest on your money to hedge a bit against inflation.

If you've already checked this box and are feeling SAFE, this is a great start. Congrats! You are in the financial minority in the…world.

You are earning more than you spend and have the luxury of savings chilling behind your financial dam to remove the sting from any of life's short-term financial surprises.

SAFETY Number: Anywhere from $5,000 to $100,000 in liquid savings depending on your lifestyle and where you live.

Wealth Equation: Earn > Spend

Your Turn: To feel truly safe, I need _____ dollars in a savings account.

How Much Money to feel SECURE?

Here we're talking about long-term SECURITY so you can pay your bills for the rest of your life after you're done clocking in and out of the 9-to-5 or whatever working path(s) you choose.

One of the main goals of any professional financial planning is to ensure that you have accumulated this LONG-TERM SECURITY of assets by the time you retire so you can live a financially worry-free life for decades after you stop working.

Long-term security is why we invest our money and why everyone is always yakking on and on about tax-advantaged retirement accounts – we're all going to die, but we don't know when, so we need to keep our money invested and GROWING as long as we can. You may be in the workforce for 40 years (ages 22-62) but need to live off your investments for another 30 (62-92) – the only way to do that is for your money to always be growing in the background of your life.

If you work for a company that still offers a solid, sturdy and dependable pension, then that will inform this segment of the money dam wall for you – but hopefully you've heard enough horror stories of pensions being gutted when people are already in retirement and dependent on that income [coughs "GM" and "United Airlines" and "almost any major corporation"] that you will not rely SOLELY on a company pension in retirement. Or if you do, you better have a plan B, C, and D sketched out in the event that your pension payments keep getting raided and reduced because of mismanagement.

For people without company pensions (which is most of us), the responsibility for feeling secure rests squarely on our shoulders.

So, let's find the number that will make you feel SECURE.

Remember that your time horizon for achieving this number may be decades and, to accumulate a million dollars in a lifetime is not that difficult if you get a head start on it: $50,000 invested by age 25 with an 8% annual return becomes more than a million dollars by age 65. Likewise, $100,000 invested by the age of 35 with the same rate of return becomes a million dollars by age 65.

How *incredible* that the simple passing of time can make you a millionaire even with relatively low-risk investments of market-tracking index funds.

It's not hard to be worth a million dollars if that's what will make you feel secure, amigo. The things they don't tell you in school!

Your Security Number

To feel SECURE let's dust off our handy-dandy Money Dam and…

SECURITY   Your Future
GOAL: Rent/Mortgage + ,000

SECURITY: Take the amount you spend each month on rent or a mortgage and add THREE (3) zeroes to the end of it.

Again, using me as an example, we pay $3,000 a month in rent. For retirement we should have $3,000,000 of net worth between our savings and retirement accounts. ($3,000 a month in rent + three zeroes = $3,000,000.)

That may seem like an astronomical number, but with decades of an investment horizon, you'd be surprised at how quickly it can add up through the power of compounding interest. It'd be impossible to save up this kind of money dollar for dollar, but it's achievable with investing.

If you retire with this kind of money AND still have Social Security, that's just icing on the cake!

To show you that the Money Dam security number is comparable to standard financial planning, we'll use the most common method out there...

We're going to back into "the 4% rule" that many financial planners use which basically says that you need enough money in savings and investments by the time you retire that you can live off 4% of your total nest egg each year until game over.

The pack-thinking here (woof! woof!) is that if you can live off a 4% drawdown of your financial assets in retirement, then you will be financially secure.

I just read an article (in November of 2021) that Morningstar is advising a 3.3% drawdown now (as opposed to 4%) based on projected future market trends, but that is a blip on the radar screen. They may be right – they may be wrong. The minutiae of your own spending will come into focus as you near retirement age and work with a trusted financial planner to hammer this all out.

It should go without saying that no one can predict what the financial markets will do leading up to your retirement or the length of your lifespan. Another wild card is no one knows what will be left in the U.S. government's Social Security coffers by then – so our Security Number is more of a benchmark goal for financial self-reliance – after all, you don't want to be dependent on the federal government to keep the kitchen cabinets stocked full of Cheez-Its and cheap rosé. (What? It's retirement – you can eat and drink whatever you want.)

Your Security Number with the 4% Rule

To get to your SECURITY number based on the 4% rule…

SECURITY with 4% rule: Multiply your annual salary by 25

If you make $75,000 a year, multiply that by 25. This number, $1,875,000, is what you need sitting behind your dam to get you through retirement if we follow the 4% rule.

With 1.8M dollars, you should be able to draw it down 4% each year for over 25 years and live the same lifestyle in retirement that you did during your working years. In theory, your home is paid off and the kids are out of the house so your bills decrease as you age, although health care costs will increase.

When I made an even $100,000 a year (which is not a massive salary by any modern standard), using the 4% rule would require that I have $2,500,000 by the age of retirement ($100,000 x 25 = $2,500,000). You can see we're in the same ballpark ($2.5M with 4% Rule vs. $3M with The Money Dam), but the easier method is to use The Money Dam to arrive at our long-term Security Number.

Remember our rule of thumb for our financial lives – we're planning for the WORST (U.S. Social Security disappears and there's a major economic recession right as you retire) and hoping for the BEST (you retire with plenty of money to live on from your retirement accounts AND Social Security AND an astronomically high sale of your Hello Kitty collection and you can leave a few million extra dollars to your heirs or to a charity or bury it in on an island and leave a treasure map).

If you are on track for meeting this SECURITY number, you have lived by this core principle of Thinking Wealthy:

EARN > SPEND + Invest the Rest – Dam it!

Congrats, you have given a dam about your financial future!

SECURITY Number: $500,000 to a $5,000,000 by the age of 65 to 70.

Wealth Equation: Earn > Spend + Invest the Rest

Your Turn: To feel secure for the rest of my life, I need _____ dollars in net worth by the time I retire, not including the value of my home and cars.

How Much Money to Feel Financially FREE?

Well, now. We've finally arrived at THE CONVERSATION.

We've discussed our SAFETY and SECURITY numbers, but now we're at the level of a Hoover Dam with millions or billions of gallons of water/dollars sloshing around behind them. This requires solid financial engineering from the first concrete slab to the last…the pinnacle in building true wealth that can last for generations down the line if you so choose.

If you don't plan to leave a family financial legacy, you can always join the Buffett-Gates Giving Pledge (givingpledge.org) and donate most of your wealth to philanthropy before or at your death. It's all the rage these days. Why not jump on that train, you crazy billionaire, you?

In any event, at this level you have funded all your tax-advantaged retirement accounts, not because you needed to, but because you understood how powerful they are for preserving and protecting the money you've stored there and as vehicles for passing along money to your heirs.

Speaking of tax-advantaged vehicles, there's been a lot of digital ink spilled recently as confidential IRS records were released and it was revealed that billionaire tech entrepreneur Peter Thiel (pronounced 'teel') has amassed over five billion dollars in a Roth account! Of course, Roth accounts are typically reserved for middle-class families and have a rather low annual contribution limit. So, how did he do it?

Apparently, Thiel originally placed 1.7 million shares of PayPal into this Roth account when PayPal was still an early, private company back in 1999. Over the years those shares increased in value, from their original $0.001 per share (a total of $1,700 placed into the Roth at the time) through the company's IPO to when the company was acquired by eBay. Thiel then sold those shares and invested in other early companies (including Facebook) still within that Roth IRA that brought ever more gains (by which I mean BILLIONS).

Did Thiel make a lucky bet? Those initial shares could have just as easily been worthless if PayPal had gone under.

In any event, it was completely legal and now he has a Roth IRA worth over five billion tax-free dollars. The fact that he can't touch it until he turns 59.5 years of age without a 10% penalty doesn't sound like much of a concession for those of us watching from the sidelines. In fact, he already crossed that early penalty bridge when he withdrew from the Roth some $254 million over the course of five years starting in 2010.

The financial nerd in me salivates at his situation because Roth IRAs are a great vehicle for passing along an inheritance to family members – there are quite a few considerations and pitfalls to be aware of if the beneficiary of the Roth IRA isn't set up correctly, so the advice of a professional tax planner should be sought if you're headed down this path.

But I progress (getting ahead of myself) again…back to our talk of financial freedom.

Your Freedom Number

We can assume that anything above ten million dollars ($10,000,000) will provide most middle-class families with the feeling of financial FREEDOM.

Of course, you can easily squander it away as lottery winners and pro sports athletes have shown us over and over (and over) again, but if that were to happen you've broken more than one of our ten ways of Thinking Wealthy.

It is said that a millionaire can lose his wealth in one lifetime if they're not careful, but it's nearly impossible for a billionaire to do so.

As I wrote in an earlier chapter, if you spent one dollar every second, as a millionaire you'd run out of money in 11 and a half days. But as a billionaire you wouldn't run out of money for 31 and half YEARS.

Incredible difference between one million and one billion dollars.

FREEDOM Number: $10,000,000 (ten million) up to billions of

dollars.

Wealth Equation: Earn > Spend + Always Invest Your Time and Money in Appreciating Assets

Your Turn: Not so fast…

If Your Goal Is Total Financial Freedom…

If your goal is to amass more money than you could possibly spend in your lifetime, if your goal is total financial freedom above and beyond feeling SAFE and SECURE, let's stretch your brain a little bit and play with some numbers.

First, reach for a number where you can easily live off the interest ALONE from your investments. For example, if you have a million dollars that kicks off 5% each year in interest, that's $50,000 pre-tax income for you to live on.

That's not a lot of money, but you're not drawing down any of the principal, the original million dollars, so you could consider that "free" money. It's also why being a millionaire doesn't mean what it used to – everyone should be a millionaire in their lifetime because it's a baseline level for feeling SECURE, it's just not nearly enough to feel FREE unless you live an exceedingly frugal lifestyle or have very few expenses.

Two million dollars generates $100,000 a year, five million would give you $250,000 a year and on and on. How dreamy is that? You're able to live off the simple interest that those sums of money are kicking off.

If you want to REALLY Think Wealthy, aim to live off the interest of the INTEREST of your investments.

In that case, 100 million dollars kicking off 5% interest is five (5) million dollars a year, relatively risk-free. That five (5) million dollars of interest, in turn, kicks off $250,000 in interest even as your money continues to grow year after year – this is quite a financial empire you're going to leave behind!

And since we've been talking about the difference between millionaires and billionaires, let it sink in that 1 billion dollars kicking off 5% annually amounts to $50 million. You would have to spend 50 million dollars a year before you'd even touch the principal. At this level, one would hope you'd have a private foundation set up to help disburse the money to organizations that are in alignment with your personal giving objectives.

For a dose of perspective, in early 2022 the world's wealthiest individual is currently Elon Musk of Tesla and SpaceX fame at 278 billion ($278,000,000,000). It bounces between him, Jeff Bezos, Bernard Arnault and Bill Gates based on the value of their underlying assets, but as I write this it's Herr Musk.

Most billionaires keep the majority of their wealth in their company's stock so there is no scenario where their full net worth would be kicking off a flat 5% interest, but since we've been running the numbers, Elon's reported 278 billion dollars would return $13.9 BILLION dollars each year if it were sitting in some sort of low-risk investment vehicle.

These figures are unfathomable, but not out of the scope of conversation since they belong to the real world.

(As I write this, Christmas presents ordered through Amazon for the 2021 holiday season keep dropping onto my front porch – you're welcome, Jeff! For that trip to space, too! We're working hard over here to put you back in the #1 spot!)

If you want to be the first trillionaire ($1,000,000,000,000 - a million millions or a thousand billions), I think you'll have to freeze yourself before you die and come back at a future point when inflation and market forces have made a trillion dollars not as stratospheric a number as it looks in 2022 against our current financial landscape.

But I told you to dream big, so I'll take partial credit for inspiring the world's first trillionaire when you unfreeze your body and find that The Rolling Stones are still on tour.

By the way, it may feel like we're pulling numbers out of thin air here because they sound good, but it's important to think about the lifestyle that you desire and how big of a life you want to live.

It helps to define wealth for yourself and start with a specific number in mind so your imagination can start running in the background and open up to the possibilities and opportunities that are available all around you.

A specific number acts as a destination before you even start the trip. You can't call Uber and ask them to drive you aimlessly around town, the app needs to know exactly where you're going first so you can get there in the shortest amount of time possible.

Likewise, you need to know where YOU'RE headed first in terms of wealth even if we're starting out in Happy, Happy Make-Believe Land so we can get you there in the shortest amount of time, too.

What's your number?

No one you know will probably ever ask you this, but I'm happy to do it as it could be the most important number you'll ever think about.

How wealthy do you want to be one day?

Your number will tell you how driven you are to succeed in the money game. No judgment one way or the other, of course. The honest pursuit of financial wealth and the ambition and sacrifice it requires is not for everyone.

Besides, if you set a number of $10 million and only end up with $5 million – and that's $5 million more than you ever dreamed of growing up as you did in a family living paycheck-to-paycheck – well, congratu-freaking-lations!

Now it's time for you to figure out your FREEDOM number.

Think of your number as the amount of water sloshing around behind your financial dam. The bigger the number, the higher and stronger the dam needs to be is all.

How do we build the highest and strongest quality money dam possible?

We're already doing it!

We do that by building and reinforcing our beliefs in abundance and in our own abilities and by letting the concrete set in the dam by Thinking Wealthy. If the concrete in the Hoover Dam is still curing and setting some 86 years later, you can see how important it is to continue reinforcing your belief in yourself and to stay in the conversation wherever possible by reading books and articles about wealth creation and sharing your ideas with supportive friends and family.

To even be having this conversation is quite extraordinary, if you think about it, as most Americans don't even have a dam – you could say they don't give a dam about their finances or their financial future.

But not you, amigo and amiga, you're already defining what wealth means to you and you're forging your own path to get there.

The bigger you dream, the more you engage the biggest wealth-building tool at your disposal – your own *mind*.

In talking with people, one thing I've discovered is that people don't dream large enough.

Many people think that $500,000 in the bank is a big juicy number and is more than enough to see them through 30 years of retirement, but when you look at the lifestyle they live (and that they presumably want to continue to support in retirement), you realize they're going to be burping cat food as they travel toward the white light.

So, let's dream big. You're worth it. You deserve it.

If You Need Help Setting Your FREEDOM Number...

Let's head on back over to The Money Dam to see what it says:

To feel **Safe**, we added ONE zero (0) to our rent or mortgage.

To feel **Secure**, we added THREE zeroes (,000) to our rent or mortgage.

To feel financially **Free**, let's add FOUR zeroes (0,000) to your rent or mortgage.

Again, using my family as an example, we pay $3,000 in rent each month so to feel SAFE we need $30,000 behind our dam, to retire and feel SECURE we need at least $3,000,000 and to feel financially FREE we can set our sights on $30,000,000 in assets.

Thirty million dollars kicking off 5% a year would give us $1,500,000 before taxes. I don't know about you, but a million dollars a year feels sufficient for a retirement lifestyle and donating a chunk of change to organizations that are close to our hearts.

Of course, we would never have our entire net worth liquidated into one account that kicks off interest like that – it would be invested across different asset classes with varying degrees of accessibility. Real estate and fine art would be harder to turn into cash if we needed it whereas stocks and bonds would be much more liquid unless there's been a dip in the market and we're waiting for a rebound first.

Again, we're just talking ballpark figures here…

The Bigger Why of Financial Freedom

If you're just looking for financial safety and security by creating a solid nest egg, the first two levels of the Money Dam, then your why is completely personal – you are building your financial dam to protect yourself and your family.

It's that simple.

No one can argue with your desire to protect yourself and your loved ones – they may not understand some of the decisions you make if they're not yet prioritizing their own family's protection, but who doesn't want to feel financially safe and secure in their lives…SHEESH!

But that's a reasonable and completely defensible motivation for shoring up money behind your dam, to protect you and your loved ones.

However, if you have your eye on financial freedom, on wanting to bring in the big money, on pushing the American Dream to its limits – if you want to stand up and say, "Yes, please!" to collecting all that life has to offer – then you need to have a bigger Why.

The why behind your freedom number is more important than the number itself because your why will actually PULL you forward into this biggest life possible.

Your bigger why will get you out of bed even on those mornings when you just want to pull the covers back over your head and chase some missing z's.

That big why will also no longer just be personal like wanting to protect your family, it will be a mission that compels you into action each day. Think of it like a motto or a personal vision that you set for yourself.

Look at these company mission statements – they could just as easily be a mission statement for an individual:

- Give people the power to share and make the world more open and connected. (Facebook)
- Bringing clean and safe drinking water to people in developing nations. (charity: water)
- Provide a free, world-class education for anyone, anywhere. (Khan Academy)
- We inspire, educate and outfit for a lifetime of outdoor adventure and stewardship. (REI)

Think of the obstacles in everyone's daily life, too, if you want to find a mission. You could set out to:

- Ensure no kid goes hungry in America.
- Eradicate malaria.
- Provide no or low-cost loans to help single parents earn a career-advancing degree.
- End cyber-bullying so tweens stop killing themselves.

You can see how a mission statement, a big personal Why, can quickly become emotional and keep you motivated for months and years ahead.

To achieve your financial freedom number, you will need a larger mission and vision for your time here on this spinning globe – larger than the protection of you and your family – and one that ideally makes the world a better place.

Of course, you can just start out to make a lot of money without much regard for the betterment of the world at this stage in your life, but you run the risk of doing little more than playing Monopoly – you may end up the winner, but you may lose all your friends in the end because you pissed everyone off in your quest to "win" the game.

(Was it just me or did everyone else hold grudges against their family and friends, too, after a traumatic and eternal game of Monopoly?)

Think about your Why, a Why of a better world, a Why that motivates you to work harder and smarter than you ever thought was possible, a Why that hundreds or thousands of employees can get behind in your quest to dominate your market.

What will you do, as one person but ultimately with the help of many others, to affect the lives of millions or billions of people?

What is your Why that pushes you through the fears you will inevitably face on the road to financial freedom?

Think of this as your personal elevator pitch – something you might have to communicate to others, including investors, at some point.

A Word on Financial Wealth – Who You Become

You as you are right now reading this and you with a hundred million dollars in your various accounts...or two billion dollars...are two different people.

We may not want to think that's true, but it is.

I have been saying throughout this books that you today and you with one or two or ten million dollars in your bank accounts are basically the same person. Nothing would necessarily change, but you would have more flexibility or opportunities available to you.

With larger amounts of money, with extreme wealth in the tens of millions of dollars or more, however, comes an ever-greater amount of responsibility than you may be accustomed to. You are now working with wealth advisors who may offer competing ideas of how to invest your money for the biggest return. You will be consulting and coordinating with various legal teams and tax professionals to ensure you're not running afoul of any regulations while taking legal advantage of every line of the tax code.

Your life requires a team of professionals and specialists – and you must lead them. You are now being asked to lead others as the CEO of You, Inc. (Think Wealthy point #7) as your company grows.

WHO you become along the way toward our goal of well-rounded wealth is a more confident, self-realized, powerful and (we hope) compassionate you.

Staring at the additional commas in your net worth will be exciting for awhile, I'll give you that, but then you will sober up that life is still happening and that YOUR life needs someone at the helm.

And since we're not chasing money itself, which is neutral and a terrible master but a brilliant servant (h/t again to P.T. Barnum), becoming wealthy must be about YOU and who you BECOME and the you who improves the world around you in some way because of all the value you bring to it.

That's the goal here. And it's also why wealthy people are often religious about improving themselves and continuing their education.

A wealthier you is a more responsible you on most every level. That or you won't be wealthy for long. Or you won't be a very likable wealthy person and you'll be surrounded by sycophants and others that make you continuously doubt the inherent good of humanity.

Geez, Todd, way to end it on a dark note...

Define Wealth for YOU

Now that we've thrown around some benchmark numbers, let's recap what financial wealth means to you as of today based on The Money Dam™ and what you pay each month in rent or mortgage.

It will change in the future as you move and increase or decrease that core rent/mortgage number, but doing this right now is extremely relevant for the commitment you're acknowledging within yourself.

Fill in the blanks and finish these statements, thinking in present tense as if it's already happened. Say it out loud to make it even more concrete of a commitment to yourself.

Financial Safety:

To feel truly safe, I have _____ dollars in liquid bank accounts so I can sleep soundly at night and think clearly during the day.

Financial Security:

For long-term security, I have _____ dollars in net worth by the time I retire so I can live as long as I want, however I want.

Financial Freedom:

I have a total net worth of _____ because I feel a deep calling to (insert your life's mission statement) _____.

Great! I can already smell those greenbacks lining your woobie blanket of net worth.

This may feel like a silly exercise, but you should honestly congratulate yourself for even THINKING about your finances in this way – you are now part of an elite club of people who are finally "getting" money.

We're well on our way, my friend!

The Only Two Ways to Wealth

Of course, it's all fine and dandy to fantasize and visualize our financial goals, but just how do we achieve them?

How do we make our financial dreams a reality?

There are only two ways to create and maintain financial wealth:

1) Appreciating Assets

After we collect our money – as Grant Cardone would say – we protect it and ensure our lake of net worth never lowers by investing in appreciating assets.

We *remain* wealthy by investing in appreciating assets.

That's a fancy way of saying that we think of everything we own in terms of whether its value is going to go up and up and up over time.

Whatever asset (or thing of value) we're talking about needs to have the potential to INCREASE in value with the passing of time.

If you own a company, its limitless revenue potential is an appreciating asset. The employees of that company are assets, too, that you treat with the respect (one hopes), so they continue to contribute to its overall (and upward) success.

The mutual funds, target date funds or ETFs that you own in your retirement accounts are financial assets that you expect to go up and up as the stock market, historically speaking, always has.

Any real estate that you own, whether a property that you live in or any investment properties, may well go up in value. In fact, real estate is favored by the wealthy as an asset class that, at minimum, maintains its value when properly vetted and, at maximum, has no upside in its ability to appreciate in value.

That's really it, folks. That is the only rule for creating and maintaining wealth – always be investing in appreciating assets.

I'm going to write that again (as I do) because it's so important:

To become and stay wealthy, always be investing in appreciating assets.

If you did not start out wealthy from a family inheritance, you will initially be trading your time for money to buy and invest in appreciating assets, but at some future point, those assets will appreciate enough where your money can make money.

Think of what you currently spend your money on, especially the big-ticket items - are you in the habit of purchasing appreciating or depreciating assets?

New cars are notorious depreciating assets. Classic cars are a different story, but the dime-a-dozen luxury vehicles on car lots across America are the poster children of a depreciating asset, as we've been told for years now.

What about the American Dream of buying a single-family home with a white-picket fence? There are many professional points of view (economists, mainly) out there backed up by data that show that a primary residence can be considered a somewhat stagnant asset (depending on where you live) whose value only rises at the pace of inflation after you factor in property taxes, insurance(s), costly upkeep, utilities, etc.

Yes, I did just say that the wealthy will often invest in real estate, but it must be real estate that checks certain boxes in the due diligence process, such as kicking off an income stream like multi-family housing or commercial real estate or high-end property like high-rise condos and beach homes on the coasts whose underlying value has historically only appreciated.

Of course, the goal is to own property that kicks off income AND appreciates in value so you can have your cake and eat it, too.

Single family homes of the American middle-class, however, should not be viewed as significant wealth vehicles unless they generate tax-advantaged income or are in areas with historical appreciation that beat inflation once all costs are factored in.

This is a game-changer, though, when you learn to look at everything you spend your money on as an asset that will either depreciate, stay the same...or appreciate into ever more value.

The real kicker here, if it hasn't crossed your mind yet, is another non-secret secret of the wealthy which is:

You are the biggest asset you will ever own.

You!

Your brain. Your intellect. Your brawn. Your ability to learn more, to accomplish more, to meet the right people who you can help and who can help you, to be more efficient, to lead, to effectively communicate your vision to others – you.

YOU!

You are the biggest, most unbounded appreciating asset because you are the only asset you have complete control over.

The more you invest in yourself to make YOU appreciate in value, the more you will grow your financial assets, too.

It sounds like common sense...and it is. But sometimes we have to throw the switch from a different breaker for the light bulb to illuminate.

You are in control of you. And you can create whatever life and whatever financial situation you want because no one can do it better than you.

If you want to take charge of your life, think of everything you DO as an investment of your time and everything you BUY as an investment of your money.

You're reading this book because, presumably, you feel it's a good investment of your time – you want to hear a different perspective on financial matters or finally "get" money – or because your commute is a slog (again) as the pandemic seems to be subsiding and someone told you to listen to this on audiobook.

Start waking up to how you're spending your time and energy and ask yourself, "Does what I'm doing with my TIME get me closer in any way to my financial goals? Does what I'm about to spend my MONEY on get me closer in any way to my financial goals?"

If it doesn't, do something that DOES get you closer.

Bam – that's it.

And no, I'm not oversimplifying here without having lived it myself.

When this really hits home, you'll see that we are always investing our time (in developing the asset that is ourselves) to become the best we can be and creating assets (starting businesses, helping other businesses succeed, writing books, creating music and art) or investing our money by buying assets low (stocks, bonds, real estate, art) and selling them high(er) at some future point in time.

This is not rocket science and this is why millionaires and even billionaires aren't any smarter than you.

[Todd raises his choir baton and leads the congregation in the wealth hymn…]

The only way to create and maintain wealth is by always earning more than you spend and thinking how you can invest your time and your money to create and own appreciating assets.

[Sung together] Amen.

Now that we've covered appreciating assets as a path to wealth, let's take a look at…

2) Income Stream for Life

I have a confession – when I started writing this book a few years back, I thought of wealth as the simple accumulation of ever more appreciating assets.

You save and invest for several decades before retirement and then you live off the interest, but you never touch the principal and then you pass that on as inheritance or dissolve your estate upon your death and give it to charity. (Or bury it and leave behind a treasure map – this idea is really gaining steam with me lately…)

The wealthiest men and women in the world keep increasing their net worth, after all. The richest person in the world used to be worth 50 billion and now the bar is up to 278 billion – most of us think about wealth as having more and more money, or more assets of ever higher value whether that be investments in company stock, the stock market, or real estate holdings, etc.

And this fits like a glove with my primary definition of wealth where you have a *higher net worth tomorrow than you do today*, a higher net worth next month than this month, higher net worth next year than this year, and on and on.

But there does come a point for many people when their net worth starts to go down – in retirement.

If you only saved and invested enough to get you through 30 years of retirement, for example, you must start spending down your net worth to support your lifestyle.

The ever-increasing net worth model of Appreciating Assets is logical and easily digestible because it shows you how easy it is to start feeling financially safe, secure and free starting at any age.

But the first approach of Appreciating Assets might best be viewed as a legacy approach – knowing that your net worth will only grow higher over time – your lake of net worth will only keep rising as long as you don't drawdown any of the principal means you can leave it to your heirs to continue the investments and growth.

It is also what was happening in our own retirement accounts – they have gone up and up, thereby increasing our family's net worth.

However, as I've said since the beginning of this journey together, our ONLY JOB in this lifetime is to make sure our monthly bills are paid.

Therefore, there is ANOTHER way, this secondary approach, to be considered wealthy:

You are also wealthy, by all accounts, when you have figured out **monthly cash flow for life**.

If our only job is to pay our monthly bills until we're hugging grandma at the end of the tunnel, then you can consider yourself wealthy as soon as you have enough cash flowing in each month to cover your expenses until THE END.

You may not be able to rent a private jet to fly your friends to Napa for a getaway weekend, but you won't have to trade your precious time for money – you will be able to lead a *self-directed* life.

Nowadays, this is called being financially free – you are FREE from the rat race of a daily job or career you may or may not like as soon as you no longer need it because your savings and investments more than cover the earned income generated by that job.

In a way, it's an acknowledgment of the REAL value of your time that we discussed – "Hey, life is short, how can I spend what time I have left doing the things I WANT to do instead of grinding away my best years for this heartless corporation?"

It's a different definition than I've been using for financial freedom, that of a net worth higher than you ever thought possible, so we need to acknowledge two different meanings of Financial Freedom, as either:

- A monstrous net worth (the Appreciating Assets approach) or…

- Having enough cash or cash-producing assets that you can replace your monthly income from a job/career

Of course, these two ways to wealth are not exclusive the one from the other, as we'll soon see. But first let's look at how you might generate an **Income Stream for Life**.

As an example, let's say you live in Denver, CO and your bills are $4,000 a month. If you purchased six properties (residential or commercial) over time that each kicked off $700 net revenue a month and always would, you would have $4,200 a month coming in. Forever.

This is hypothetical because there'd be times when you didn't have full occupancy of your buildings and once you paid off those mortgages, you'd have higher net revenue, not to mention how your own expenses fluctuate month by month and healthcare costs go up as you age, but the IDEA behind this scenario is completely achievable – people have done it all over the world.

Or perhaps you have saved and invested JUST enough money that you can declare early retirement and live off those savings and investments for 40-50 years by spending them down as you need them using the 4% rule (or some derivation thereof).

In either scenario, you have figured out your **Income Stream for Life**.

As mentioned earlier, most of us first heard about this definition of wealth by reading Robert Kiyosaki's *Rich Dad, Poor Dad*. In that book, he rattled everyone's brains by saying that a house you lived in, which most people considered an asset, was actually a *liability* because you pay a mortgage each month to live in it, not to mention all the expenses you pay in property taxes and maintenance, etc.

For a house to be an asset, it must generate revenue. His poor dad bought a house for the family because that's what everyone "is supposed to do" whereas his rich dad bought investment properties that kicked off an income stream that helped to fund his lifestyle using all the tax advantages of owning real estate, to boot.

The house you live in is a liability – only real estate that generates income is an asset. The formula was simple: if you wanted to live a bigger, more lavish life, you only needed to buy more income-generating properties.

A total game-changer for those of us who grew up with the middle-class American Dream of one day owning a house with a healthy, green front lawn and white-picket fence.

From Robert Kiyosaki's work to today's financial landscape, this second path to wealth has morphed into the **FIRE Movement** (Financially Independent, Retire Early).

It follows a similar path to his book – live frugally so you can save up and invest all your extra money into savings and retirement accounts OR into income-generating real estate, either through flipping them or living off the revenue stream generated from tenants of those properties.

Those properties don't even need to be APPRECIATING assets – the real estate market goes up and down, and in many places in the country (and in the world), it can remain relatively flat for decades.

Having lived in Los Angeles for so long where an outhouse with a coat of paint is worth a million dollars, I was shocked when I started looking at real estate back in Ohio (where I grew up) for investment properties – the real estate there didn't appreciate much over time. Not much of a house-flippers paradise, perhaps, but certainly a lot of income-generating multi-family properties to be found.

Which is all you would need for this second way to wealth – your wealth doesn't come from appreciating assets, it comes from a strategic acquisition of assets that churn out the monthly income you need.

You don't need a 9-to-5 job at that point and you don't need to have amassed millions of dollars in assets...you just have 6 properties that take care of all your financial needs (in our Denver example).

That sounds like wealth to me!

I've hardly dedicated two pages to this concept, but I want you to be aware of it. This is the path that many people are taking right now when they buy investment properties in strong real estate markets and plan to hold onto them for consistent cash flow vs. flipping them for a quick profit.

Or where they live an EXTREMELY frugal life so they can sock away up to 75% of their income for an early retirement.

It's worth knowing and understanding this second way to wealth as it could easily be a plan that fits into your financial sensibilities.

The Iceberg of Retirement

The traditional path to middle-class wealth, of only funding your tax-advantaged retirement accounts over decades of a career to spend it down in retirement when you turn 62 or 65 or 70, has one very large and considerable drawback – that pool of appreciating assets you've accumulated, of mutual funds, stocks and bonds, etc., is locked away within those accounts and you will be penalized if you take any money out of them before 59.5 years of age.

There are exceptions – for example, contributions to a Roth IRA can generally be withdrawn because those are post-tax dollars, but any *earnings* withdrawn will be penalized. (Consult with a financial planner or tax advisor, of course, before tapping any retirement accounts.)

All that money you've socked away, that capital that has grown through compounding interest over the years, is essentially frozen in those accounts and you can only access it in your latter years. So, although you have been diligent and faithfully funded your 401(k) and other accounts, you can't drawdown or generate any INCOME from those accounts until you reach almost 60 years of age.

This is one of the main differences between the two paths to wealth, appreciating assets (within retirement-specific accounts) and income stream for life.

Let's say you are 35 years old and have $500,000 in your company's 401(k). If an incredible opportunity arises for you to invest in an income-generating property across town, you will have to come up with the down payment from savings or another avenue as that $500,000 is basically frozen and untouchable.

I bring this up because our own net worth is locked away in retirement accounts. That's great for us for the future days of retirement, but it means we have don't have free cashflow within reach for any investing opportunities NOW without generating it through our jobs (earned income) or through borrowing. It also means our current net worth isn't kicking off any monthly cash flow for us – that is 100% on us to generate through a job or any other revenue streams we can create.

That's a big difference to note between the traditional model of funding retirement accounts in the pursuit of a large net worth of appreciating assets (how most Americans do it and what we've done so far) where all that capital is locked away in an iceberg…and figuring out monthly cash flow for life, the more modern approach to financial freedom.

Two Sides of the Same Coin

Let's not get too far into this conversation before we acknowledge that the two paths to wealth, Appreciating Assets and Income Stream for Life, are two sides of the same coin.

You can invest extra money each month, let's say, into dividend stocks in a simple brokerage account, outside of a retirement vehicle, and have the dividends reinvest and buy more shares of the stock. You start with a hill which will become a mountain of **Appreciating Assets**. At some point in the future, you can turn off the dividends from reinvesting and take them as cash distributions which you can use to support **Income Stream for Life**. You flipped the coin, using one path to wealth to support the other one.

By the same token, if you bought those six properties in Denver which provided you with enough FIRE income to quit your job and declare early retirement and those six properties rose in value by almost 9% each year as the Denver housing market has, then those properties that are fulfilling your **Income Stream for Life** are also **Appreciating Assets** that are raising your underlying net worth. You will be able to sell those at a profit in the future, if you choose. Or your heirs will.

Each path to wealth is inter-connected to the other so it really depends on the life you want to create for yourself.

Do you love your career and look forward to working up to retirement and possibly beyond? Maybe Appreciating Assets is the primary path to pursue because working week after week for earned income is a joy.

Do you lean more toward creating your own schedule and pursuing passion projects outside of the more rigid structure of a 9-to-5 workday? Perhaps Income Stream for Life suits your personality and disposition best.

There is no right or wrong way, only options!

The Billionaire Balance

Speaking of two sides of the same coin, let's peek behind closed doors of what the ultra-wealthy do with their money to see both paths to wealth in action.

When you are a multi-billionaire, how would YOU invest your money?

As we've already noted, most billionaires keep most of their wealth invested in company stock. Elon Musk, Bill Gates, Bernard Arnault, Shari Arison, Warren Buffet, Jeff Bezos (and on and on) – each of these billionaires walk the path of Appreciating Assets – the bulk of their wealth comes from paper assets, the limitless ceiling of company stock that THEY have a hand in raising.

So how do they pay their bills each month?

They keep a certain percentage of their net worth in cash. (Not literal cash, of course. Remember how much I prattled on about this to drive the point home in the first chapter?) They use a small percentage of their net worth to create an Income Stream for Life. Their vast net worth remains in Appreciating Assets, but a sliver has been shaved off to sit in cash to create Income Stream for Life and to invest in other ventures.

Many multi-billionaires keep a billion or two sitting in cash. Keep in mind that if they're getting a 5% return on that cash, the interest alone is $50 million a year. Can you spend $50 million a year in "free" cash even as your net worth reaches ever higher for the heavens?

Of course, you don't have to be a billionaire to engage in this two-sided strategy – multi-millionaires do it, too, all the way down to you and me, as we've seen.

When your net worth starts to climb to heights you had never expected (or so soon, at least), you start strategizing the mix of Appreciating Assets vs. Income Stream for Life based on your age, your investing horizon and, truly, what you want out of life.

When my partner and I retire, we will look for ways to turn our iceberg of net worth into Income Stream for Life without touching the principal of Appreciating Assets. That is the current thought, at least, as we hope to provide for our daughter and her family after we're gone. Our daughter seems to have quite a few character traits of a no-nonsense entrepreneur, too, so our money might be in good hands for the next generation of exponential wealth creation.

Now that we've explored the only two ways to wealth there are, both of which ultimately require OWNERSHIP of assets with room to appreciate, let's look at creating our fortunes.

Create Your Fortune, Big or Small

Let's use the specific numbers we came up with from The Money Dam™ to reinforce the foundation of our dam. Between those concrete numbers and learning how to think wealthy, you are fortifying your financial future from this day forward.

We're in our financial Uber now – we have a financial destination – so now HOW do we get there?

It's time to talk about a bit about investing. Not the nitty-gritty of where to put your money to grow your lake of net worth ever higher, but writ large.

You create a fortune by owning appreciating assets. Whether you fill up your lake of net worth first before switching from the earned income stream (job/career) to the investment stream is ultimately your choice, but the underlying ownership of assets will always remain true.

This is an obvious non-starter – you will never be safe, secure or free without owning appreciating assets.

In terms of investing, most people only think of *money* and how they want to invest it, but they're overlooking an even more powerful investment angle.

Investing Your Time and Your Money

At the end of the day, all you have to invest is your *time* and your *money*.

It's really that simple. You can always boil your life down to those two core investing ingredients.

Am I maximizing the best use of my TIME to lead me toward my goals?

Am I maximizing the best use of my MONEY to lead me toward my goals?

What the wealthy already know and what you may be clicking into is that time is the only thing you can never get back once it's gone.

You can always earn more money if you lose it all as a high-risk investment tanks gloriously across the home page of The Wall Street Journal. There will never be a shortage of opportunity out in the world to earn and collect more money, but the one thing you will never get back is your time.

Money is abundant but your time is not.

This has never been clearer to me, personally, than in May 2021 when I was told in an emergency room that the MRI showed that my bones were riddled with tumors, too many for the radiologist to count. Did I only have a week to live? A month? Your priorities can shift within a single conversation.

It is for this reason that the wealthy choose how they spend their TIME with more care and attention than others do – from this vantage point, it's easy to see how most people who don't yet think wealthy seem to devalue their time with the choices they make by assuming it's in endless supply.

It's also why it's HIGHLY unlikely that you will ever become a billionaire if you spend evenings and weekends on the couch catching up on your top 20 favorite streaming shows on Netflix, Hulu, Amazon Prime, Disney+ (and on and on…) or playing video games for months or years on end.

The road to well-rounded wealth involves both a strategic and thoughtful use of the only two things you have to invest: your time and your money.

When you understand on a gut level that money is always in abundance in the world, the most precious thing that remains is how you spend your time.

(Did you get a chill reading that? I did…and I'm freaking writing it!)

When is the last time you thought of your time as being THAT valuable?

Perhaps this is the first time ever.

Giving a Dam About Your Fortune

Now that we're seeing the true value of how you invest your time and, to a lesser degree, your money, let's look back at the different levels of The Money Dam and start putting the pieces together to solve the puzzle of how you will create your fortune.

$$\$\$\$$$

Wealth Tip: *Safety + Security + Freedom All at Once*

I have structured The Money Dam to show you how to THINK about your finances, by first talking about Safety, THEN Security and FINALLY Freedom.

But they NEED NOT happen in sequence.

If you are starting at the very beginning of your financial journey, you do not need to reach your Safety Number FIRST before starting to invest for your Security Number. If you have $500 surplus each month, for example, you can put $250 toward your Safety and $250 toward your Security.

I'm calling this out because if you spend a few years saving everything you have just to get to your Safety Number, you might have sacrificed valuable compounding interest time toward your Security Number by not yet being invested in the markets.

Don't think "first → then" with The Money Dam, think how you can simultaneously fund EVERY level of the dam so that you're growing all three levels concurrently.

The Money Dam works best when it's not being funded as "either/or" but as "yes/and" to all your accounts simultaneously.

$$\$\$\$$$

With that being said, let's dive into your lake of net worth!

Your Safety Number (Rent/Mortgage + One Zero)

This is not yet at the level of creating a fortune as this is a simple savings account, but it's the first step toward financial freedom and I'm confident that if you can get to this point, you will continue checking off the boxes to keep leveling up.

A secret to achieving this goal is to AUTOMATE a portion of each paycheck into a savings account with an online bank as they will have an interest rate higher than any brick-and-mortar bank chain with all their overhead expenses.

You're not investing this money, you just want it to kick off a bit of interest to hedge against inflation. This money needs to be very liquid so you can get to it quickly if you need it.

You don't even have to like your job or your co-workers or anyone in your life, really, to make it to this goal. I'm not saying you *should* be, but you *can* be pretty miserable in life and still get to this safety goal – just don't be so miserable you lose your job, capisce?

The point is that you can phone it in for this one since we're just talking about basic savings – simply earn more than you spend.

Your Security Number (Rent/Mortgage + Three Zeroes)

This is how you create a small fortune.

You can easily become a millionaire at this level if you have several decades of a time horizon to do it and the discipline to fully fund your retirement accounts while in the workforce – the earlier you start, the better.

Remember that $50,000 invested at the age of 25 becomes $1,000,000 by age 65 with no additional contributions at an annual rate of return of 8%. Boom – you just became a millionaire!

Or $100,000 invested at the age of 35 turns into $1,000,000 by age 65 with no additional contributions and the same 8% rate of return.

This traditional approach to retirement Security is to amass this money within tax-advantaged retirement accounts.

Armed with your Security Number from The Money Dam™, Google "Compound Savings Calculator InvestingAnswers.com".

The website, InvestingAnswers.com, calls it a Compound Savings Calculator, but we're going to use it for investment returns. This was the easiest online calculator I could find that lets you input your Security Number (called the "Goal Amount" on the site).

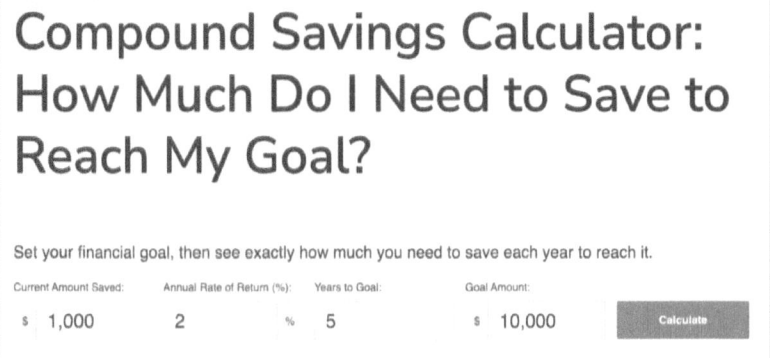

Compound Savings Calculator: How Much Do I Need to Save to Reach My Goal?

Set your financial goal, then see exactly how much you need to save each year to reach it.

Current Amount Saved:	Annual Rate of Return (%):	Years to Goal:	Goal Amount:	
$ 1,000	2 %	5	$ 10,000	Calculate

Credit: InvestingAnswers.com

Start plugging in your numbers: "Current Amount Saved" is any money you've already invested toward retirement and your Security Number. "Annual Rate of Return (%)" should be 8%. "Years to Goal" is how many total years you have to invest before you retire at 62, 65 or 70. And, of course, your "Goal Number" is your Security Number.

Hit "Calculate" and it will tell you how much you need to invest each year to get to your Security Number.

As you can see, you're clearly not socking away your full Security Number dollar for dollar, you're investing the minimum amount and, with as long a time horizon as possible, you're allowing it to grow with the stock and bond markets or wherever you have it invested.

Keep using the secret of automation and AUTOMATE a certain amount of money from each paycheck into your 401(k) if you work for a company that offers one or into whatever tax-advantaged retirement accounts you've set up.

This is NOT investment advice: most company 401(k)s nowadays offer target-date funds which work just fine for most people. You choose the date closest to your retirement year and the mutual fund will rebalance a higher percentage toward the historical safety of bonds over time, away from the historical volatility of stocks.

Again, not investment advice: for any other retirement accounts, there is a mountain of data showing that low-cost market index funds are all you need to capture the gains of the stock market's historical upward trend. Yes, you'll grab all its losses, too, but if you don't need to sell low, recessions are a phenomenal time for BUYING more. And there *will be* recessions during your investment lifetime.

Even Warren Buffett, investing GOD in the eyes of much of humanity, advises people to simply invest in low-cost index funds, specifically an S&P 500 index fund. It's what he has advised the trustee of his estate to do with his money for his wife after he dies – to invest 90% of his money into the S&P 500 and 10% in treasury bills.

One of the best books that covers the absolute simplicity of investing for future wealth is *The Simple Path to Wealth* by JL Collins – a personal finance classic for your bookshelf or Kindle library. NOT one of the snoozefests I mentioned in the preface – JL has a great voice and writes in a very down-home and conversational tone.

I remember during the 2008-2009 recession – when, again, my partner and I practically laughed at people who were freaking out about the markets crashing because we had nothing yet invested for retirement (oof!) – Suze Orman was on Oprah Winfrey's TV show and she said that a lot of people were going to make a LOT of money off of the recession. That perked up Oprah's ears (and mine, even though I had no dinero at the time to invest).

Suze's point was that smart investors who had cash sitting on the side were going to buy into the stock market at bargain basement prices and ride it up and up and up, watching their investments grow wildly with the simple market rebound.

It sounded like magic at the time – now I know it best as Warren Buffett's seminal advice on being greedy when others are fearful.

Here on the home front, our money is invested in a mix of target-date funds, low-cost index funds and a basket of stocks, the latter actively managed by our financial planner. Truth be told, everything rises pretty much in lockstep so there is no obvious winner-winner-chicken-dinner to our different investment strategies – no glaringly obvious winning or losing investment strategy as we reach for our Security Number.

INCOME STREAM FOR LIFE ALTERNATIVES: If you are alternately looking to create Income Stream for Life through investing in real estate or through the FIRE approach of frugal living and saving and investing upwards of 75% of your earned income for an earlier day of retirement, those approaches demand a very detailed analysis of your monthly and annual expenditures.

For the FIRE approach, specifically, you take your annual expenses and multiply by 25 to determine your FIRE number. Once you get to that number, you raise your fist (or middle finger) to a 9-to-5 career and basically declare yourself retired because you can drawdown your nest egg at a rate of 4% a year.

Although you may use tax-advantaged retirement accounts to help you get there, you will also need to save and invest using taxable brokerage accounts as you work toward your FIRE number so you have income in the years between declaring your early retirement and when you can access your traditional retirement accounts starting at 59.5 years of age.

You may also have a mix of investment properties in your asset pool – there are many creative variations within the FIRE movement, but its principal goal is to put you in the driver's seat of your life – you save and invest as much as you can, as fast as you can, to get you to your early retirement goal.

I get the sense that the FIRE movement is only going to expand from this point on as current and future generations refute the 9-to-5, 40-hour workweek holdover from the Industrial Age. The pandemic only added fuel to the…I have to say it…fire by showing millions of people a different perspective on their lives as they learned to balance the new reality of working from home.

Already there is LeanFire if you plan to *reduce* your expenses in retirement and FatFIRE if you need more of a financial cushion to fit your lifestyle – this latter approach is used more by doctors and lawyers who have a higher income stream and net worth, in general.

Any way you slice it, regardless of your approach (The Money Dam, determining Income Stream for Life or a FIRE variation), your Security Number is the amount of money you will need to live out the rest of your days on this spinning spheroid of a planet in total financial independence.

Your Freedom Number (Rent/Mortgage + Four Zeroes)

This is how you create a big fortune.

If you don't know where to start, determine your personal Freedom Number based on the largesse of the life you want to live or by using The Money Dam to get you started.

Again, our Freedom Number based on The Money Dam is $30,000,000. We are not going to get anywhere near that number relying on the investments we've made on the road to our Security Number. There we want to capture the strength of the American (and international) economy with a diversified portfolio, but with relatively little risk.

We will only get to our Freedom Number by angel investing early in companies that go public, in creating a business or businesses that we can later sell for big payout, by leading a corporation at the C-suite level and being compensated with stock options, etc.

You simply can't attain the level of a Freedom Number by investing in vanilla index funds. It's highly unlikely you'll get there even if you have a flair for picking individual stocks – the secret most people don't know about Warren Buffett and his stock-picking prowess is that he doesn't pick stocks passively and wait for his gains – he is an active investor (and always has been), often acquiring a controlling interest in the companies he invests in or joining the board of directors where he can help push the businesses to ever higher profits. He is also known for buying companies outright with plans on how to integrate and maximize these investments for himself and his investors.

There are almost 22 million millionaires in the United States as of November 2021, just over 100,000 multi-millionaires (those with a net worth north of $30 million) and 724 billionaires (just in the U.S.). Obviously, the numbers drop off as the net worth climbs into the stratosphere and touches the weightlessness of space.

As I've said, it's not hard to be a millionaire if you have the time horizon and discipline to invest your money – 22 million others have done it before you. To get to a net worth of $30,000,000 and above, however, the numbers drop off significantly, but it still makes you feel good, doesn't it, to know that over 100,000 people have gone before you to hit those heights?

What is the difference between the millionaires, multi-millionaires and billionaires?

Two requirements we have yet to talk about on the way to a big fortune and hitting your Freedom Number are: **Risk** and **Commitment**.

Risk

Fortunes are most often made with an increased appetite for risk.

George Soros betting so heavily on the fall of the British pound was a big risk – he didn't know how that would turn out.

John Paulson betting so heavily on the implosion of the U.S. housing market – he didn't know for sure that it would happen or, even more importantly, WHEN.

Those were two HUGE investing risks they made with their own and other people's money.

Felix Dennis slipping a piece of paper across the table asking for 10 million dollars for the sale of one of his first companies, not knowing if he'd be laughed out of the room, was a monumental risk for him. He tried to hide that his hands were trembling as he did it, he wrote in his wry *How to Get Rich*.

In general, if you're going for the BIG net worth, you need to have a strong appetite for risk. Not blind risk, mind you – educated risk. At some point you make the leap from educated guess to following your gut on the timing or the asking price and you just. Go. For. It.

To build a massive net worth, you know that you are worthy of that level of wealth and that the time you're putting into it will pay off.

One, two, three failed companies in your past do not define you when you have a higher appetite for risk than the rest of society who yearns for the relative security of a steady paycheck or who thinks of "work" as a necessary evil to afford a middle-class lifestyle.

There will be setbacks along the way, but for the truly wealthy, they learn from them and get right back on the horse because they all have an ironclad commitment to achieving their goals.

To become a billionaire, you must become risk-friendly as opposed to the masses who are decidedly risk-AVERSE.

Commitment

Commitment may be the biggest reason that people, who otherwise have no reason NOT to succeed, don't make it across the finish line to the level of wealth that they desire.

Commitment means putting in the hours to get your business off the ground.

Commitment means weighing vacations and "time off" against that nagging desire to accomplish more, moving ever closer toward your goals.

Commitment means not shrinking from so-called failures along the way, but learning objectively from those losses and dusting yourself off for the next adventure.

Commitment means keeping your eye on the prize with a tenacity unlike anyone else you know.

Commitment means more sacrifice from what others your age are doing – it doesn't require total sacrifice, necessarily, but sacrifices (plural), nonetheless.

Commitment is the container that holds your unstoppable ambition and desire for independence.

If you learn of a high-millionaire or billionaire (besides someone in line for inheritance) that achieved it with, meh, an average amount of work, I am all ears and would love to hear about it.

Otherwise, it's relevant to note that both risk and commitment are fellow journeymen on your road to not just the 1% of the U.S. (or those with a net worth of $10 million which is not completely unachievable through low-risk investing), but the 0.01% of the U.S. with a net worth in the hundreds of millions.

Of course, when we Think Wealthy, both risk and commitment are by-products of that core mindset – any fear associated with risk is viewed as a motivator and not a debilitator toward our goals and we believe in ourselves and our ability to figure things out (with the help of others) so deeply that our commitment to success is practically inherent in the air we breathe.

Positive people run the world. People who believe in a better future for themselves and others collect the most money in the game of life.

You can feel SAFE with a healthy savings account and you can feel SECURE for the long-term with the small fortune borne of the luxury of time and a relatively low-risk pool of investments, but to feel truly FREE, that big fortune requires that the dials in your brain labeled risk and commitment default to higher levels than, perhaps, most everyone you know.

How the Wealthy Do It – Three Wealth Strategies

The good news is that there are not that many broad strategies to becoming wealthy from a personal perspective. With YOU as the biggest asset you will ever own, there are not that many lenses through which you can create your future fortune.

The majority of us have been told to get a good education so we can get a well-paying job and save up enough money so that we can happily die

30 years into retirement after our souls have withered to dust from sheer boredom.

(Okay, I added in that last part. But I've witnessed it firsthand.)

Our education system is still geared toward the Industrial Era model of creating a smart and hardworking labor force. We walk into kindergarten with our backs to our teary-eyed parents and pop out the top of the education tower treating our diplomas as boarding passes to a cookie-cutter future.

There is nothing wrong with it, of course. You can be an amazing child, parent, employee, employer, local and national citizen, all the while impacting the lives of thousands and thousands of people for the better by clocking in and out of a 9-to-5, earning more than you spend and smartly investing the rest in retirement accounts.

That's a brilliant life if it's the life you want and CHOOSE for yourself and for your family.

What the American educational system doesn't do well, at its foundation, is teach students responsible entrepreneurship, the fundamentals of a successful business, how to invest money and the risk/reward relationship that underpins it or how to spot and size up potential opportunities for personal and professional growth.

If all you want is to be a millionaire by the time you retire, that's not hard to do. It's just a basic numbers game that will get you there.

If we have our hearts and minds set on a lifestyle of financial independence that only the wealth of appreciating assets or income for life can provide, however, there are only three core strategies for achieving it:

1. **Develop and Excel**
2. **Create and Sell**
3. **Buy Low / Sell High**

You'll see that these strategies can be used at any stage in your life and in any career.

I'll highlight this later, but the more you can mix and match these strategies, the better chance you have at achieving any financial goal.

Let's look at each individually:

1. Develop and Excel

This is the realm of becoming the best that you can be, ever an improving work in progress, reaching for the summit in your chosen field so that you can command top dollar for what you do.

Professional athletes develop and excel a particular physical talent and then parlay that into endorsement deals and lucrative player contracts.

Develop and excel.

A singer who has a natural vocal talent can reach for the zenith of his or her abilities and mesmerize audiences the world over. By working with a respected vocal coach, they can find nuances in tone and timbre that will send chills down their audiences' spines and bring tears to their eyes.

Develop and excel.

CEOs and anyone bouncing around the C-suite of American corporations, both private and public, have honed their abilities of vision and leadership…and political savvy…to rise to the upper echelons of business. They have the confidence and foresight that propels their companies forward into greatness and they are compensated handsomely based on their performance.

Develop and excel.

Notice that no one is chasing money, per se, they're pushing themselves as far as they can to learn and achieve the heights of their profession.

This can be sports-related, arts-related (writing, singing, acting, filmmaking and on and on), business-related…or the path you're already ON-related. The top performers in most any field always command top-dollar because of the value they bring to the table day after day, week after week, month after month.

Look in any field at those who are performing at the top of their game and you'll notice that they work ten times harder than anyone else. Does it FEEL like work or are they simply driven to be the best they can be?

When they are interviewed and asked if the sacrifices they made were worth it, they will most likely respond, "What sacrifices – I did what anyone would do, didn't I?"

They develop and excel the biggest asset they have – themselves.

Always be thinking of the value you provide and how you can increase your value by developing and excelling. To an employer. To a board of directors. To society. To your community. To your friends and family.

To be an effective CEO requires a recipe of great leadership, strong business savvy and the charisma and vision to incent people to work toward the same goal. You are developing your workforce into their own level of excellence.

You carry within you the same abilities as any CEO you see being interviewed in the financial news media.

Develop and excel.

What are you good at that you could become truly GREAT at while always be getting better at?

What do you love to do where there is a market for being an expert with that skillset?

Can you become a strong and respected leader where you currently are? Those skills will practically print money anywhere you go from there.

What can you develop and excel at to stand out from the rest of the crowd because you understand that your biggest asset is YOU?

Develop and Excel in Business

As we know by now, the ultra-wealthy are often titans of enterprise within their respective business fields.

They have created or run companies that dominate the marketplace (by design and by force, many times).

They have envisioned new ways to ply their trade in older, lethargic industries.

They have bought up and consolidated a particular vertical of commerce and have capitalized on economies of scale.

Heck, have you ever heard of Mohed Altrad? He started his billionaire empire by taking over a bankrupt scaffolding company. It was the first time he had ever heard the word "scaffolding." He grew up as an orphaned Bedouin in the Syrian desert who was expected to become a shepherd, but he knew that he wanted something different for his life and, for that, he had to take control of his destiny – and, Boy, did he ever!

Too often we think only of the CEOs because they are the ones who appear on magazine covers or are interviewed on CNBC and Fox Business, but many fortunes have been made just a step or two behind or to the side, as well.

Charlie Munger, Warren Buffett's right-hand man, is worth an estimated $2.2 billion himself. The two men have run Berkshire Hathaway for decades, and in 62 years of business partnership, have never once had an argument, they declare.

There are many opportunities for wealth creation right next to the person in the spotlight – the more value you can provide to any rising stars, the more your own fortune can be made, too.

$$$

Wealth Warning: *Neither developing nor excelling*

When I was casting reality shows on MTV, the one response that I'd hear day in and day out from applicants was, "I just want to be famous! I want everyone to know who I am."

But when I'd ask them HOW they wanted to be famous…did they want to act or rap or be funny or dance…what talent did they want to share…what value did they want to add to the airwaves…they'd stare back at me blankly…"No, I'm going to be famous for being me."

That was usually the end of the interview (in our minds, at least) because someone who just wants to be famous for fame's sake is someone with no real voice, no point of view, no thought on how they're going to develop and excel – in essence, their egos are so fragile that they're looking for recognition and accolades for just being, for just breathing…with no thought of doing or contributing value on any level. "Next!"

They thought the shining gift-to-the-world of their personality was enough. But rarely, if ever, does personality alone, without a context or structure or talent to back it up, create wealth. Anyone with any lasting power has a business plan they're implementing to turn raw fame they've achieved into a scalable, profitable and valuable brand name.

Think Michelle Phan and Ryan Kaji (of Ryan's Toys Review) all the way up to Kim Kardashian…any celebrity who has developed a successful brand of their own likeness and lifestyle and then leveraged that into a diversity of successful businesses.

This includes athletes, actors, anyone whose talent is leagues beyond everyone else's because of their innate ability and consistent practice, coaching and refinement.

Keep in mind that, as your personal brand grows, you need the support and advice of a team of experts, legal and otherwise, whose own livelihood is in part dependent on YOU continuing to develop and excel in your field – proof that no man or woman is an island on the road to wealth and everyone needs to learn to become an effective leader of their own lives.

If you are dead set against developing and excelling, you might want to stop reading right here.

$$$

2. Create and Sell

The second wealth strategy is to create something...create an asset of value for others...a product or a service or both...and sell it.

Start a business that solves a problem...the bigger the problem, the better! Or the more people that can benefit from your solution, the better!

This is the path you hear about most often. It's the "easiest" and most common route to extreme wealth in America and around the world.

It's the Facebooks and the Microsofts all the way back to the Hearsts and the industrial giants like the (Andrew) Carnegie Steel Company and the others that espoused and promoted the United States' brand of capitalism the world over.

Start a business that solves a problem for a lot of people and leads its category so strongly (develop and excel) that competitors find it impossible to catch up.

Technically, you could just knit kitten-faced beer koozies and if all your friends clamor for them (indicating the potential size of your market), you can sell them on Etsy – with either a high profit margin or through sheer volume – and set your family up with a nice nest egg. Stranger things have happened.

To back up this Create and Sell strategy with some data, most of the wealthiest one percent created or grew a valuable business in which they held onto a sizeable equity stake. (It's not always for the faint of heart to hold onto as much equity as you can, but you MUST – the late Felix Dennis hammers this home in *How to Get Rich*.)

Note that this doesn't mean that they were necessarily the only major shareholder of the company, just that when the company's revenue went through the roof, their own net worth went along for the ride.

They created something and sold the product or service to the height of their abilities within their particular markets.

This is the path for anyone with a mind for business or the desire to learn it and the chutzpah to ask for the sale because they believe in the value of their offering.

Then, once you have consistent revenue, you hire a sales team to do the heavy lifting so you can concentrate on scaling and diversifying.

Create and sell.

Keep in mind that many of the world's wealthiest businessmen and businesswomen didn't come up with the original idea or core product or service that they then sold. They may have copied the idea from others where there was no patent to infringe upon (or even when there was!) or they may have licensed the core product or service – the difference is that they saw THE way to market and sell it to as wide an audience as possible.

Create (or copy or license) and sell.

Write a book about a boy wizard on a journey of self-discovery.

Or dominate any of dozens of niche book markets. Be prolific to hone your talent (develop and excel) and market wisely to turn it into a viable business and revenue stream and pat yourself on the back as the royalty checks roll in and you see your words spoken by beautiful, talented people on a screen at your nearby multiplex.

Create and sell.

Write music for the world's top performers and collect the royalties indefinitely.

"Create, let THEM sell…and collect" we might call that.

The opportunities for improving people's lives where they will gladly pay you to fix their pain points or make an aggravation go away or to even ignore all their problems through entertainment are limitless.

There has also never been an easier time in the history of humanity for you to start a global, scalable business online from your own home as inexpensively as you can in this hyper-connected, tech-obsessed world.

Create and sell a product or service, build up your customer base, listen to and respect them, keep adding value and then ultimately sell the business for what it will fetch in the marketplace.

You created a viable and successful business which generated great cash flow for you while you ran it and then you converted that into a big payday with a transfer of ownership.

Or hold onto the company and take it public, if you can, for the biggest jump in wealth anyone you know has ever seen.

Start looking around at all the businesses you interact with day in and day out and peek behind the scenes to understand their business models, their possible profit margins and how scalable they may be.

3. Buy Low and Sell High

The third strategy is to buy low and sell high.

You always hear this mentioned in reference to the stock market. Buy stocks when they're low and sell them when they're high.

Unfortunately, most people buy high when everyone else has already joined the party, thereby leaving no room left for growth, and then get scared when the markets dip and they sell low.

My friend's parents were just about to enter retirement when the Great Recession tanked the stock market in 2008-2009. They lost a million dollars, about half of their total net worth, in the market crash. Given their age and their jitters that it was never going to come back, they cashed out at the bottom and decided they had to keep working to bring in a steady income. Worst of all – you guessed it – they missed ALL the gains of the market recovery.

They certainly weren't alone in selling low – millions of other investors felt the same gripping fear and sold, too.

Yet that's fortunate for the disciplined investor who keeps Warren Buffett's investment strategy top of mind, to "Be fearful when others are greedy, and be greedy when others are fearful."

Buy low and sell high.

Buy a piece of land that will one day be more valuable than it is today and sell it later for the highest asking price.

Buy low and sell high.

Or create a business out of real estate by flipping houses. You're combining Develop and Excel with Buy Low and Sell High because you're buying properties low, adding value to them and then selling them higher.

Buy low and sell high.

Are you seeing yet why the house you may live in for ten or twenty years or that you plan to die in...or the car you drove off the lot high on the new-car smell of the interior...are assets that are either illiquid or are depreciating assets?

This is why the millionaire next door drives an economically-sensible car that is dependable and holds its value the longest.

What can you buy today…what can you exchange your time and money for today…with the hope and intent of selling it later at a profit?

Remember the examples I gave of making money off of furniture and appliances by buying low (or receiving for free) and selling higher?

I told my friend Melissa that I usually make money on any furniture I sell, even after a decade of use, and she shook her head as if I was swiping money out of little old ladies' hands.

"What?" I said, "I'm merely asking for and receiving what the market will bear for these things. I keep them in great condition, y'know?"

She wasn't having any of it. To her I was a heartless thief.

What I should've asked her in the moment was if she had planned to sell her house for less than she paid for it. And if she had (obviously) hoped to realize some appreciation of the asset of her house, how was furniture any different?

Buy low and sell high.

Listen, I'm not going to become a multi-millionaire hawking used goods with a small profit margin on an individual basis, but a chain of stores along the West Coast that does just that might get me there.

These three strategies are all straightforward, right?

Everything you own should go up and up and up, including your own skills and talents. They should only get stronger because that's where you invest your time…in yourself.

The more you can mix and match these three strategies and are always thinking in terms of your time and your money being investments in your future financial awesomeness, and the more you view your life through the lens of appreciating assets, the faster you will feel financially safe, secure and...free.

The Passion Trap

If I hear one more time how you're supposed to follow your passion or your bliss because, when you do, the world will rise up to welcome you to heaven on earth and faeries will toot glitter dust of happiness out of their sparkling little hineys onto you...I will scream.

It's what I call The Passion Trap and it held me captive for too long.

I thought there was ONE thing out there – ONE primary passion or interest of mine – that if I could just discover it, I'd be happy for the rest of my years.

Now I know that is all a bunch of horse hooey.

For me, at least.

My sister is an interpreter for the deaf and she has loved her work from the day she discovered it. Yes, she gets exhausted like anyone else and perhaps dreams of a different life from time to time, but she's always helping others and is providing for her family. And at the end of the day, she leaves the office at the office, too.

Other friends have found their thing and they just love, love, love it.

Good for them.

My problem was that the first-world mantra of "Follow Your Bliss" stopped me from taking ANY action in my life. I was waiting for my One Big Passion to show up and give me a big sloppy wet kiss, yet when I finally stopped searching and seeking…and simply thought back to previous times in my life when I was really happy, it was when I was running multiple clubs and organizations in high school (and then again in college) – it was me in a leadership role within MULTIPLE organizations of varied interests.

My passion, it turns out, was to be a hyphenate – to have multiple roles across different organizations.

I realized I was happiest when I was stretching my brain to work with all different types of people toward a larger common vision and always learning, learning and learning more. I was in the moment much of the time, never knowing what the next problem to solve was going to be. And it was awesome.

Once I realized that, I snapped into action: I wanted to write comedy so I reached out to my good buddy where I worked and we started collaborating on an animated TV series.

I wanted to develop an app that would solve my neighborhood's problem of barking dogs and other unwanted noises, so I created a company to test out its viability.

And, of course, I also wanted to share what I'd learned about money and wealth over the years, so I started what has become this *Think Wealthy* book.

And I loved all these things equally!

Add being the father of a now eight-year-old into the mix and things did get hectic some days, but when I feel like I'm firing on all cylinders, THAT makes me happy. Feeling productive every day and inching ever closer to my many goals makes me happy.

The problem with FOLLOW YOUR BLISS or FIND YOUR PASSION is that it arrested me from doing anything. I take full responsibility for that, but I'd like to propose a new way of thinking of it if you have had the same problem...

Follow Your Bliss RIGHT NOW.

ADD PASSION TO WHATEVER YOU'RE DOING RIGHT NOW.

HELP OTHERS TO THE BEST OF YOUR ABILITY IN WHATEVER YOU'RE DOING RIGHT NOW.

Or if you feel stuck waiting for your passion to smack you in the face, listen to Elizabeth Gilbert's great line to FOLLOW YOUR CURIOSITY.

Do something. Do anything. Maybe you can find joy as a barista in helping others get their morning coffee fix. You can drive old people around on errands and laugh with them about the folly of life. Do SOMETHING right now that feels fun and joyful because when you throw yourself into something with abandon like that, doors will open to greet you.

When I was doing nothing but clocking in and clocking out, I wasn't creating or sharing or giving back to the world – I most looked forward to IM'ing with people in the office and saying inappropriate things to get a few giggles out of them in what felt like a hushed library of a work environment – and this was a six-figure job!

I didn't realize that I would only find what I liked to do by getting back on the court of life, as opposed to just observing from the stands.

You never know. Your next passion may just be discovered over coffee with a good friend because of something that they blurt out that they need help with and where you are willing and able to lend a hand.

Please don't let this idea of ONE, MAGICAL PASSION slow you down like it did me…do something right now. Always do something with joy in your eyes…right now…and you may just find your faerie-farting passion that much sooner.

I once received advice from Jess Jackson, lawyer turned wine entrepreneur and founder of Kendall-Jackson wines. I was up for a marketing position at one of his companies and he sat with me for fifteen minutes outside one of his tasting rooms to share with me some of his life lessons.

I knew at that time that he was a billionaire and an epic figure in the American wine scene for popularizing California Chardonnay under the Kendall-Jackson brand. If I had only known then what I know now about the dogged pursuit of wealth, I might have asked a follow-up question or ten, but the single piece of advice that he gave me was to approach everything with passion. He had been an ambulance driver, lumberjack and policeman in his early days and even a successful civil lawyer until he turned his interests to wine-making – and wine-promoting – in retirement. He was also a very successful owner and breeder of thoroughbred racing horses.

Whatever work he was doing at various points throughout his life, he attributed his great success – and the amassing of a financial empire – to finding the passion in everything he did. On days when you don't feel the passion, he said, your job is to *find* it.

If I'd have asked him in the moment, I'm sure he'd have admitted that his path to financial success was not a straight line, nor one that he had envisioned from the very beginning – but that by finding the passion in everything he did, he excelled in every line of work that interested him and, to those on the outside looking in, his eventual success in ANY field should have come as no surprise.

There's a famous story of his early wine-making days, which was supposed to be his retirement hobby, where a batch of white wine "stuck" in the fermentation phase, rendering it much too sweet. Experts were called in who suggested dumping it on the bulk market, bankruptcy was discussed, but Jess decided to mix it in with the other batches of the same grape (he liked it, after all!) and sell it at a price point that hadn't yet existed in the U.S. wine market, just under $5. That is how the Kendall-Jackson Vintner's Reserve Chardonnay was born – it won awards and introduced California Chardonnay to a very thirsty American palate. His business bravado, tenacity and hard work single-handedly changed the wine industry.

Even though he was 80 when we met, he probably saw that I was rudderless, staring off the back of my boat thinking that the wake drove the boat.

From my current work with nonprofits and my years in entertainment marketing, I now know exactly what he was saying. Whenever I can FIND or GENERATE the passion for a particular project or for the larger mission of an organization, doors fly open and I'm practically tripping over new opportunities.

According to Jess, instead of following your passion, FIND your passion in the work you're currently doing and keep your eyes peeled for other opening doors.

"But, Todd…"

I know. For some of you, there are just too many options for what you CAN do in the world that you're overwhelmed by the choices.

I get it.

At the end of this book in Appendix C is a bonus called The Game of Wealth. This will be particularly relevant for you because the game asks you to spend mongo amounts of virtual money.

When you spend millions of (virtual) dollars, you'll see where your interests and values lie. You'll see what companies or charities or religious organizations you care about most.

Spending millions of dollars before you have them can show you HOW you might create a net worth you'd only ever dreamed of through your *current* interests and passions!

$$$

Wealth Tip: *Ask and Ye Shall Receive?*

At two recent times in my life, I have creepily set my mind to achieving a specific financial goal and then, as if by request, an opportunity has presented itself for that precise amount.

First, after being endlessly frustrated at my remaining $30,000 in student loans, I told myself that I was going to knock that debt out by the end of the year. I knew that, before taxes, I needed about $50,000 of additional income.

Along came a much-hyped opportunity via the Murphy-Goode Winery up in Sonoma County, CA. (This is how I met Jess Jackson whom I just referenced.) The winery was looking for a social media specialist who was going to be given a house to live in for free and be paid $10,000 a month for six months – all the person had to do was drink and talk about wine, most specifically Murphy-Goode wine, across a multitude of social media channels.

There it was! My opportunity! $60,000 pre-tax would easily knock out my remaining $30,000 of debt to Sallie Mae.

I went for it. I made a video, branded myself as A Goode Guy and submitted it. Out of 1,000 or 2,000 people (there was debate), I made it into the top ten! I was flown up to Healdsburg, CA with the other nine top applicants from all over the country and we spent an extended weekend going through various wine-world challenges so the powers-that-be could choose their social media maven.

I didn't get that gig – it went to a candidate who already had a die-hard wine following – it could be argued from a marketing perspective that the most bankable candidate won – but I didn't care at that point. I had seen the power of choosing what I wanted for my life. That and we were all SO DIFFERENT and all got along so famously that we knew we weren't really in competition with each other.

The second time wish-granting happened was the year following the Murphy-Goode competition. I told myself that I was going to make $100,000 a year. For some reason that nice, round number was calling to me. It wasn't but a few months later that the president of the company that I had been freelancing for invited me out to lunch to see if I wanted to come onboard full-time as they were in a pinch with an open position and thought I'd do a great job. The base salary? $100,000

Two times in two years? My head started spinning because I felt so powerful.

Wow – anything I want I can ask for?

And anything YOU want you can just ask for?

What if, eh? What…freakin'…if?

(Note to self: Why haven't I done that voodoo again, now asking the universe for a billion dollars?!? I'll be right back…)

How Will You Create Your Fortune?

I know every person who has made it to this page is looking for THE ANSWER to how they will easily create wealth in their own lifetime. I would skip ahead to this page, too!

They want to find out which new cryptocurrency will soar beyond all expectations.

They expect to find a relevant piece of information that they can leverage into a financial pot of gold.

Those may exist out there – maybe in a Medium article or in a subreddit – and you can certainly create a small fortune by getting in early on the…Next. Big. Thing. Or the next big thing for right now, at least.

But for the big fortunes, it is going to take time, hard work, tenacity, the taking of big risks, undying commitment and a deep-seated joy for the journey itself that will precede the collecting of financial wealth.

Even an ability to SPOT the next big thing and be number two or three in line can render you wealthier than you'd ever even dreamed.

Else, marry someone wealthy. Or win the lottery.

The incredible opportunity that you have before you in 2022 and in the foreseeable future is the great access to new ideas and the people who are leading the charge in their respective fields. In this age of information, you can follow Elon Musk, the world's wealthiest individual, on social media, reach out directly to business leaders and innovators on LinkedIn, offer your services (volunteer or otherwise) to fledgling startups and future unicorns on AngelList.

It has never been easier to capitalize on opportunities that others have missed or have failed to execute properly on or to hitch your wagon to a rising star. Create value, provide value – wake up every day excited for what it may hold and how you may leave the world a better place than you found it.

The world's billionaires tend to work in high-growth industries where the upside in terms of scalability and financial potential is limitless. Are you already working in one? Or can you see the next high-growth industry just around the corner? Is there a scaffolding company about to go bankrupt down the street that you can turn into a billion-dollar construction empire?

The scope of this book is on the psychology of wealth and opening your eyes to a different financial future than you may have previously thought or dreamed of for yourself. With that as my goal, I literally don't have the word count left to deep dive into the unique paths that the world's billionaires have taken to get there, including the mix and match of strategies they may have employed.

If you're looking for a deeper analysis of actual billionaires and the tools and key principles they used to land on the Forbes 500 list, you must check out *How to Be a Billionaire: Proven Strategies from the Titans of Wealth* by Martin Fridson.

Another solid billionaire-based book based on face-to-face interviews with international billionaires (most of whom I've never heard of) is *The Billion Dollar Secret: 20 Principles of Billionaire Wealth and Success* by Rafael Badziag.

If you're not sure how to maximize the investment of your time, unclear on the options even open to you, or the industries or avenues that inherently create the most financial gain, a wealth-creation classic for you to read is Ken Fisher's *The Ten Roads to Riches: The Ways the Wealthy Got There (and How You Can Too!).*

Follow the Money

Throughout this book, I've been asking you to examine your current mindset around money and see if there aren't ways to empower yourself so that the accumulation of money behind your dam and the short and long-term safety and security of your life starts to fall into place because you CHOOSE for it to.

The truth is that nothing is new under the sun. If you want to become the world's next wealthiest person, there are plenty of people who have gone before you and who you can study and emulate.

That's a nice way of saying that there are plenty of wealthy men and women in the world who you can COPY.

You don't have to reinvent the wheel to become wealthy. As we've seen, you don't even need to come up with an original idea that will change the world – in fact, you're setting yourself up for disappointment if you're waiting for THAT ONE WORLD-CHANGING IDEA to arrive. You're more likely to become wealthy by simply executing BETTER than the next guy or gal.

Summary

In this penultimate chapter (you gotta squeeze in a few SAT words wherever you can – even if colleges no longer care about the exam), we started to assign actual dollar amounts to the three ways in which money matters in our lives by taking what you pay in rent or a mortgage each month and adding zeroes to the end of that to determine what you should have in savings to feel SAFE and what your goal should be for retirement to feel SECURE. We also toyed around with a big enough number to grant you financial FREEDOM.

We boiled this quest for financial freedom down to:

- Money matters because you matter.

- To feel SAFE, you need 3-6 months of money sloshing around behind your dam…in addition to money for upcoming big-ticket items. Add ONE zero (0) to your rent or mortgage payment to determine that goal.

- To feel SECURE at retirement age, you should have a net worth equal to your salary multiplied by 25 (the traditional approach), or add THREE zeroes (,000) to your rent or mortgage payment for your Security Number.

- To feel financially FREE, you need to set a wealth goal in step with the size of life you want to live and back it up with a personal mission statement that literally pulls you into action each day. If you have no idea where to start, add FOUR zeroes (0,000) to your rent or mortgage payment as a target and let your mind work in the background to figure out how to get you there.

- You are the biggest asset you will ever own because you are the only asset you have complete control over.

- The only two things you have to invest are your time and your money.

- Money is abundant in the world, but your time is not.

- The only way to create and maintain wealth is to always be earning more than you spend and always be thinking how you can invest your time and your money in appreciating assets.

- The only two paths to wealth are Appreciating Assets and Income Stream for Life.

- The only three strategies for creating wealth are:

  ✓ Develop and Excel

  ✓ Create and Sell

  ✓ Buy Low / Sell High

- You don't need to reinvent the wheel on your road to wealth – find someone you respect and admire who has gone before you and model your approach after them.

Before we fully push you off the edge of the nest, though, let's take a look in the last chapter at what it means to have mastered your money, at what a life of Well-Rounded Wealth looks like in action.

It's true, we're almost done with learning how to Think Wealthy and we only have a few nuts and bolts left to cover. Yippee! And yet #sadface at the same time.

Chapter 6: Master Your Money for Life

*The real measure of our wealth is how much
we'd be worth if we lost all our money.*

- Benjamin Jowett

Oh no! I feel like we just got started talking about the most exciting thing in the world...MONEY...err, the two most exciting things in the world...MONEY AND WEALTH...and here we are at the top of the final chapter already.

This totally harshes my mellow.

The cool news is that the money talk we've been having is not a one-time conversation just between you and me – it is an ongoing dialogue between you and the people in your life, be it with your partner for the daily decisions you make toward your goals, with your children as they grow up and need to understand the difference between value and price and to view money as an asset, not income…with your parents as they navigate retirement…and, of course, with your friends as you bounce ideas off of and help out one another on the road to wealth.

And that's just the tip of the iceberg in terms of talking about money. (And gnarly run-on sentences, apparently.)

Wealthy people talk about money a lot. They know what their money is doing (or not doing) and you should, too!

So, Thinking Wealthy is an ongoing conversation – the six chapters in this personal finance book are really just the beginning – you talk about money because you care about feeling safe now and ensuring future security for you and your family, your friends, your pets and on down the food chain.

We have a Betta fish that my daughter has managed to not yet kill – it might just be time to ring up our estate attorney to add Banji to all the relevant paperwork.

In this final book, we're wrapping it all up to cement your financial future – by making sure you give a dam about your money – so that it continues growing to make ever more money.

Before you give it all away.

Or not.

It's your choice – after all, you're the one in charge of all the commas in your bank accounts, you powerful money guru.

This is also where the rubber meets the road and we learn about the four pillars of **Well-Rounded Wealth**.

We're going to see what Thinking Wealthy looks like in action –

everything your parents never told you because they didn't know, or they never shared with you.

Or maybe they DID try to share it, but you had already stopped listening to them as a teenager and never opened your ears again. (It happens.)

But I progress (getting ahead of myself) one final time...

Let's recap what we've talked over so far. We know that:

- The only reason for building a financial dam and amassing a fortune, big or small, is to feel safe and secure and free to be who we want to be. The higher we build our dam, the more we get to help others now and further down the line.
- We invest our money to grow (free money!) because we're going to die one day (bummer!) and we don't know when (stop stressing me out already!).
- There is only one wealth equation anyone has ever used to attain wealth: Earn > Spend and Always Invest Your Time and Money in Appreciating Assets.
- Money just makes you more of who you already are as a person – good or bad. Who you show up as in the world is always YOUR choice.
- Wealth is abundance in whatever form it takes. There is no shortage of money in the world or value being provided to earn it. The ceiling for personal wealth has no limit to it.
- There is no financial $uperman who is going to fly in and figure out your finances for you. We are all responsible for building our financial dams as high as we can and it is never too late to get started.
- The only thing all wealthy people have in common is that they know they are worthy of or deserve financial wealth and that they will take good care of their money. They are not smarter,

more educated, more blessed, luckier or greedier than anyone else – they view money as an asset (for investing), not as income (for spending), that can grow into more and more money over time.

- The true order of manifesting the life we want is Be → Do → Have. When we ARE (and feel) wealthy/abundant on the inside, we DO the things in our lives we need to do to HAVE financial wealth on the outside.

- We first become wealthy on the inside by knowing and living the three core beliefs of our inner billionaire:

  ✓ I create my own life.

  ✓ I am worthy of wealth.

  ✓ I can handle any situation.

- There are ten points to Thinking Wealthy that we use to keep tabs on our underlying, subconscious beliefs and to make sure they're aligned with the abundance of the world around us. They are:

  1. Think Net Worth, Not Salary.

  2. Think Long-Term.

  3. Think Value First.

  4. Think of What's Possible.

  5. Think "Why not me?"

  6. Think Big.

  7. Think of Yourself as CEO of You, Inc.

8. Think Thanks.

9. Think "I got this!"

10. Stop Thinking and DO.

- The Money Dam is a great tool for checking in on our financial progress. By using what we pay each month in rent or a mortgage and adding zeroes to that number, The Money Dam gives us a goal for feeling Safe in the short-term (rent/mortgage + 1 zero), Secure in the long-term (rent/mortgage + 3 zeroes) and ultimately financially Free (rent/mortgage + 4 zeroes).
- There are two ways to wealth, though they're actually two sides of the same coin: Appreciating Assets and Income Stream for Life.

I hope there isn't anything you don't agree with in this list.

I kinda gotta have you on board with these points because a) they're TRUE and b) this isn't a book about Todd putting words next to each other to create warm and fuzzy feelings just for his own pleasure. (Eh, maybe a little bit of that.)

THIS IS YOUR LIFE.

Okay. So now what?

Mastering Your Money

To master your money is to operate from a level of confidence in how you handle and control all aspects of your growing net worth.

To master your money means approaching every dollar you earn through income or investments with a LONG-TERM view of how each dollar can best be used to keep you feeling SAFE, SECURE and FREE in your life.

It doesn't mean you won't make mistakes along the way if an investment decision doesn't pan out (who knew Americans weren't ready for a fast-food chain based on kangaroo meat pies?), but that you'll make financial decisions with the height of confidence based on the facts you had at the time.

As my 2021 cancer diagnosis and eventual remission have shown our family, you never know what's around the corner, medically, emotionally and, without a doubt, financially – what surprises, good and bad, that life might have in store for you.

Mastering your money involves the five following stages:

1. Collect Your Money

2. Respect Your Money

3. Protect Your Money

4. Grow Your Money

5. Share Your Money

You don't need to memorize these as they flow organically when you Think Wealthy – they are firmly grounded in your desire and ability to create whatever financial future you want for yourself.

1. Collect Your Money – Provide Value

First, we need to shift the phrase in our minds from "making money" to "collecting money." When we provide value to the world, have integrity in our interactions with ourselves and others, act out of service to helping others and solving problems (big and small) and generally are efficient with our time, money is just waiting for us to collect it.

So, let's collect our money!

Looking at The Money Dam™ (Appendix A), collecting your money starts in the Land of Opportunity with Work You Love. When you're firing on all cylinders and fully committed to the work/career side of the equation, you use your Skills to Help Others (be they fellow workers, management, your employees, clients, customers/consumers, etc.) in a position that Pays Well.

That may sound easier said than done, but think of this as an evolution of our relationship with a job or a career. If you go to college and graduate, this may not be your first job out of school – but it just might be!

In whatever job you're in or currently seeking, how can you provide more value than what is being asked?

As a Board Member and Archive Director for a nonprofit (Hollywood In Pixels), I recently produced an in-person awards show for Hollywood's best and brightest digital movie marketers. The key award went to a Senior Vice President at Sony Pictures who is universally loved for being a nice guy and all-around great human being. His advice to anyone just starting out was the path that he followed – to always provide more value, take on increasing amounts of responsibility and to keep asking, "How can I help?"

His professional guidance and own journey confirm that it works – it's also a common success strategy, or way of being in the world, that practically guarantees results, both personal and professional.

Of course, now that the pandemic is easing up a bit, America is in the midst of the Great Resignation as workers are fed up with working conditions and the stagnation of salaries that haven't kept up with the rising cost of living over the past few decades.

If you are in a job that is not quite doing it for you and you're just itching to join the Great Quit, perhaps try following billionaire Jess Jackson's advice first to find the passion in what you're doing RIGHT NOW and see where that takes you.

As I recounted in the last chapter, I met Jackson while I was interviewing for a marketing and social media position at one of his wineries. He had many successful careers and acknowledged that his own interests had changed over the decades he was in the workforce, but that the one secret he had from one career to the next was that he always found and maintained the passion in whatever he was doing at the time.

Of course, this first step of COLLECTING MONEY, is predominantly aimed at those working as employees for someone else or for a large corporation. Collect your money by knowing your worth and always providing value in both the workplace and the marketplace.

If you simply must hand in your resignation without another job waiting in the wings, however, or if you just need a breather to collect your thoughts and figure out next steps – if you ever get stuck on HOW to collect money – start by asking yourself, "How Can I Help?"

How can I help others?

How can you help your friends with any obstacles they have in their lives?

How can you help a local business?

How can you be of service to others or be of service to the marketplace at large?

If you want to be an entrepreneur, where are your own frustrations in life? Do others share them, too, and are there solutions you can execute on better than anyone else, or in partnership with them?

You know that many of the most successful entrepreneurs and businesspeople took a shared frustration and turned it into an innovative and market-dominating product or service. They turned their pain into their gain because they helped not only themselves, but thousands (or millions or even billions) of others.

To lead your life with an attitude of "How can I help?" is the hallmark of a compassionate and optimistic leader, too.

This one simple phrase can practically transform your life overnight – it is the secret to creating your own Land of Opportunity and collecting money to send it flowing downstream to your Lake of Net Worth.

2. Respect Your Money – Give a Dam about Your Worth

You are an exceptional host and show the money you collect all the respect it deserves by giving it a good home. You do that by structuring your financial accounts so each and every dollar that comes in has a clear and distinct job to do against your short and long-term goals.

You know that this is one of the key reasons (having no account hierarchy in place) that people who win the lottery or get a surprise windfall see it slip so quickly through their financial fingers – the money doesn't know where to go or what to do and so it just...floats... away...downstream past their dam of good intentions.

By thinking of your money in terms of different "buckets" (as we discussed in the fourth chapter), you know that as you amass more and more financial wealth, that money will know where to go and what to do once it flows in.

Respecting your money builds the highest walls for your financial dam.

Bank Accounts

Providing a good home for your money breaks down into two key categories, bank accounts for Short-Term Safety and investment accounts for Long-Term Security or Growth.

These accounts flow up – that is, if you're starting with no money (or water) in your lake of net worth, you first start by plugging any holes of debt in your dam while simultaneously providing yourself short-term safety (the first level).

If you've ever read or listened to Dave Ramsey, this level of short-term safety is akin to his classic Baby Step #1 of saving $1,000 for a starter emergency fund.

As you plug the holes on any consumer debt, you do not need to have met your Safety Number BEFORE you start working on your Security Number – you can work on all three at the same time.

Some people buried under consumer debt (myself included, back in the day) want to start investing FIRST with the hope of making a fast return that will then pay off their debt and fund their savings account. It rarely works out this way in real life, unfortunately, as the risks associated with a high return on an investment are too great and the inexperienced investor often loses what little spare money they have.

The silver lining in that desire, though, is that a person is finally seeing how important INVESTING is for creating their future of an ever-increasing net worth.

1) Short-Term Safety

You give the money you collect a safe haven to keep it and you feeling safe.

You keep your money safe and relatively liquid by putting it in a savings or money market account that is kicking off a very safe rate of return. As of December 2021, Synchrony Bank is returning 0.5%, which is a lot more than your big-chain brick-and-mortar banks can provide.

You know that this money is an investment in YOU – it's an investment in providing you with options in your life starting with feeling financially SAFE.

GOBankingRates conducted a survey in 2019 and determined that 69% of Americans didn't have even $1,000 in a savings account. Practically reading these words puts you in the wealthiest minority of the country – now all you have to do is crest the $1,000 mark of a savings account to be in the top 31% of the wealthiest nation known to mankind – scary and unbelievable.

Automate a withdrawal from each paycheck into this savings account and you'll be surprised at how quickly it adds up as you PAY YOURSELF FIRST.

If it's not obvious, feeling financially SAFE is the first step toward mastering your money.

2) Long-Term Security

While keeping your short-term cash-flow Safe, you also have long-term growth accounts where you ask your money to multiply like rabbits and make even more money.

You know that a company 401(k) match is one of the few times in life where you can receive free money, so you take full advantage of it.

You LOVE your long-term investment accounts (401ks, IRAs, anything Roth, 529 plans) because they offer tax-deferred or tax-free growth which can make a difference of hundreds of thousands of dollars to your net worth depending on your time horizon. You would marry these accounts if you could because of the tax benefits they provide.

You know that Roth accounts can actually serve as great vehicles for passing money tax-free to your heirs because Roths have no required distributions based on age like traditional IRAs and 401(k)s do – you've already paid the tax on the money, so the IRS doesn't care much about them (it's not often that you read that!).

Again, entrepreneur and venture capitalist Peter Thiel (pronounced 'teel') amassed a staggering 5 billion (!) dollars in a tax-free Roth IRA...legally. I don't know if the IRS cares much about that Roth and its 96 sub-accounts, but a whole cacophony of other people who are decrying an abuse of the system sure do.

You know one of the easiest ways to grow your tax-advantaged accounts is the same as growing your savings, by *automating* money to be taken from each paycheck and put into them.

With all your long-term financial accounts being consistently and automatically funded, with the goal of reaching your Security Number (your rent or mortgage payment + three zeroes), you are setting yourself up in the strongest financial position to always be in total control of your life, now and well into the future.

You are confident that you are doing everything you can to ensure a lifetime of financial security and it feels gooooooooood.

$$$

Wealth Warning: *Bad Debt*

You've probably heard that there are two kinds of debt – bad debt and good debt – but if you grew up working or middle class, you most likely only understand bad debt.

Bad debt is paying 20% interest or more on a credit card you can't or don't pay off each month for a shirt that you wore once and it didn't fit quite right or a new $500 smoothie blender when your old one works just fine.

Bad debt is paying interest to someone else (the bank behind the credit card) for things that you may not have needed in the first place.

When you hear that the average American carries over $5,000 of revolving credit card debt, you know that means they're effectively paying $1,000 each year in interest to the credit card companies just for the privilege of that loan. And that $1,000 is in after-tax dollars from W-2 income so they are really paying close to $1,500 from their total salary just for that "privilege."

(My left arm just went numb from typing that. Someone call 911.)

You understand the evil of bad debt – it's not an investment that will ever pay off – it's consumer debt, pure and simple. Bad debt anchors you to your past and prevents you from living in the present, let alone planning for the future.

Bad debt is quicksand on your path to financial freedom and wealth.

Or more apt for The Money Dam, bad debt is a glaring hole at the base of your dam always draining away any money flowing into your lake of net worth until it is paid off and sealed up once and for all.

$$$

Wealth Secret: *Good debt*

You have probably also heard that debt can be a good thing if used properly.

For example, you might choose a car loan even if you have the cash to pay for it outright if you know that that your money can make MORE money, a higher return, that is, in a safe investment than the interest rate on the loan.

We just did this. We didn't pay for our "new" used car outright because the loan was so cheap (near 0% based on our credit scores and down payment) that our money would make MORE money sitting in a money market account with an online bank. This is an example of good debt via a relatively small financial transaction, but it works the same as it scales up.

Another example of good debt is when you leverage bank debt for investment properties.

Let's say you want to buy an apartment complex as an investment property to generate cash flow. For a $1,000,000 apartment complex, you pay $250,000 (or 25% down). If you sell it two years later for $2,000,000 (twice the money – this must be New York or San Francisco...or almost anywhere in America, it seems!), you pay back the bank the $750,000 you owe them on the mortgage and you walk away with $1,250,000.

You used the bank's money to leverage a gain of $1,000,000! Yes, you paid interest on that mortgage, on the debt, for two years while you had it and you will be taxed on your gain of a million dollars, but you made a handsome profit by investing only 25% of your own capital. The bank held most of the risk in the deal yet only asked for their original loan back.

This is why you hear of wealthy people carrying debt. Debt can be used to your distinct advantage when you LEVERAGE it as opposed to being sucked into the past by it, such as with consumer debt.

Good debt is part of an overall investment strategy, often with distinct tax advantages (especially with real estate), whereas bad debt is months, if not years, of indentured servitude to a creditor with no return on investment.

Many of the world's wealthiest people use their significant stock or equity holdings as collateral against a low-interest loan – in effect, creating a credit line – it saves them from having to sell their company stock (which can often spook investors and affect a stock's price) and it also saves them from having to pay much higher capital gains taxes on those shares than any interest on the loan itself.

Good debt comes from a place of planning and forecasting, bad debt comes from a place of helplessness, and often, impulsive purchasing.

3. Protect Your Money – Defend Your Future

Now that we're collecting, and even more importantly, respecting our money, we need to talk about a few inevitables of being the CEO of You, Inc. – how to protect your money from the what-the-truck moments of life.

As you rocket your way to financial security with an ever-increasing net worth, you need to protect as much of it as you can from any of life's surprises that may be waiting just around the corner.

Of course, we all know about health and auto insurance. That's not to say that we all have the best coverage, but we know WHY we pay for them and, in many cases, it's illegal NOT to have those forms of insurance in place.

But as your net worth rises, so do your insurance coverage and legal needs.

Did a neighbor just trip on your uneven sidewalk and break their leg in multiple places? Were you recently diagnosed with cancer and the emergency surgery and all the side-effects-heavy immunotherapy treatments are preventing you from bringing home any bacon? (Hey, this sounds familiar.)

When you grow up middle class, it can really hurt to pay your insurance premiums – after all, you're paying for nothing tangible (or what feels like nothing) month after month, year after year.

And don't get me started on legal fees – to someone in the working or middle class, attorney hourly fee schedules seem downright sadistic.

What anyone with any semblance of wealth knows, however, is that insurance and legal costs are not a waste of money at all – it is a core tactic of your overall financial strategy – to always plan for the worst but hope for the best.

With an increasing net worth, you need various forms of insurance and a solid legal team to protect you and your family at every turn.

Insurance

When you have a growing net worth, to protect yourself and your loved ones you simply must carry the necessary types of insurance.

Reflecting on The Money Dam – you've spent years building your dam as high as you can and filled the reservoir with water/money – now here comes a stick or two of dynamite floating downstream about to blow your dam to smithereens!

In a world where anyone can sue anyone else for just about anything, there are ways to protect our fortunes, fortunately.

The Non-Negotiables for the Middle Class – Auto and Health Insurance

You carry **health insurance** because you know most people are only one medical emergency away from financial ruin.

We KNEW this already, of course, but really saw it come into action this past year. Because of health insurance, we should only be on the hook for the max out-of-pocket costs of around $7,000-$8,000. That's…umm…a big difference from the $2.2 million dollars of services. Thanks, health insurance!

You understand how important it is to factor in any health insurance offered as part of a job offer as that company may well be kicking in over $10,000 on your behalf – a sizable number that doesn't show up in your salary number, but can be a considerable financial benefit.

For a bit of perspective, we currently pay $2,400 a month out of pocket for our family of three for health insurance premiums because my partner runs a small business and that's the best they can find with a broker. That's almost $30,000 a year we pay out-of-pocket for something we RARELY use – until last year [ahem].

A good friend recently started her own company after being furloughed by her employer at the height of the pandemic. She has worked for different corporations her entire career and is only now seeing the real cost of health-care coverage for her family of four. As her COBRA coverage is coming to an end and she is searching for ways to keep her family covered, she is horrified at a) how much health insurance costs and b) how little coverage she will be getting compared to the employer(s)-sponsored plans she has always been on.

I know everyone is working on fixing the American health care system – figure it out and you DESERVE to be the world's first trillionaire – I'll be FIRST in line to tell you what a freaking genius you are.

Auto insurance goes without saying – U.S. federal law requires it of all drivers. Vehicles injure millions and kill thousands of people each year, not to mention all the damage to property they cause. If you drive a car, you already have this insurance in place. Or should!

The Non-Negotiables for the Wealthy – Life, Disability, LTC and Umbrella

We all know that **life insurance** is income replacement for anyone who is financially dependent on your income at the time of your death, whereas disability insurance takes care of them AND YOU while you're still here and recovering from face-planting into the sidewalk off a scooter while you were texting a selfie to your peeps. (It's happened.)

Our financial advisor convinced us to get **disability insurance** over ten years ago. He said you're much more likely to be disabled through health issues or injury during your working years than you are to die during them. I'd be lying if I said we didn't wince at those annual premium payments during lean years, but I can now safely report back that it has provided us valuable financial wiggle room when my cancer was misdiagnosed and I physically deteriorated for several months at home, hardly able to stand some days, let alone work.

What many people might not yet know are all the ways that life insurance can be used as an *investment tool* to build family wealth, well beyond the income replacement we so often hear about.

Here is where I admit that I am not intimately familiar with the ins and outs of upper-end life insurance investment strategies. Of course, I understand that if I buy a universal or whole life policy on myself for $400,000 that pays out $2 million tax-free to the beneficiary at my death – that is a significant way to build wealth as long as it falls under the estate tax threshold.

Some of the more arcane and specific uses of life insurance, however, such as to pay for estate taxes for your heirs or to use as a tax-free investment tool on the cash value side while you're living or even using the cash value as collateral while making an interest-free loan to yourself – these strategies are the purview of a qualified wealth management advisor and specialized insurance broker.

Of course, there are many business applications for life insurance, too – if you own a business with someone else, you often buy life insurance on each other to fulfill a buy/sell agreement in the event that one of the owners dies prematurely.

Another use of life insurance is to tap it for expenses related to end-of-life care, which can be significant and can destroy a family's blossoming generational wealth. The actual long-term care insurance industry still seems to be figuring out whether the products they've been offering for only 30 years now are ultimately going to pay off for their bottom lines, so using life insurance for those needs is a wise financial decision if you have the extra capital to do so.

Once your house is paid off and the kids are out of college and surviving on their own (fingers crossed), chronic or terminal health care costs are the biggest threat to your nest egg. To protect your net worth as best you can, proper **long-term care insurance** or earmarking a life insurance vehicle for those expenses is invaluable.

One of the final insurance products available to anyone with a rising lake of net worth is **umbrella insurance** that piggybacks on your auto or home policy and protects your assets in million-dollar increments.

That neighbor who broke their leg in multiple places? Your homeowners policy may only cover a portion of their medical bills (or, God forbid, the lawsuit they won in court) – this is where umbrella insurance opens up to provide you with the supplemental coverage you need to be done with them once and for all without the garnishment of your wages or some other assault on your personal net worth.

With the addition of more commas in your net worth, there are all types of insurance you can purchase: **deposit and securities insurance** to supplement the FDIC's relatively low $250,000 per bank guarantee, **kidnapping and ransom insurance** (things just got real, right?), **jewelry insurance, directors and officers insurance** and on and on…

The fact of the matter is you can find a company to insure just about any asset you want to protect….yes, maybe even that prized Hello Kitty collection you swear is going to make you rich one day.

You understand that the more money you have, the more you may need to spend to protect it.

Legal Support

If you thought you could get through life without the help of a wicked smart lawyer (or a gaggle of them), you may be putting your money and other assets at great risk.

A great lawyer or team of lawyers is exactly who you need in your camp to not only protect and help you keep as much of your money as possible while you're alive, but also to ensure that your loved ones and heirs have easy access to your estate once you're vaping all the clouds you want in the Great Beyond.

Remember that you are hiring them and that they are on your side – they are there to provide you with the very best legal advice they can. They are your legal bodyguards.

Of course, you ask questions about their counsel to ensure you understand every angle to a situation and all the ramifications because – what? – lawyers make mistakes, too.

At a certain level of wealth, you have a target on your back for anyone who believes they deserve a slice of your financial assets…because you have MORE than enough, right? The very best legal team in your corner is invaluable.

Just as you have worked hard to collect your enviable net worth, the proper amount of insurance and legal protection is what truly solidifies your dam so that no stick of dynamite (or ten) can ever bring it down.

4. Grow Your Money – Turn Those Soldiers into Armies

You beautiful human being, you – you're collecting your money, respecting every cent and dollar that has your name on it and protecting it from as many of life's pitfalls as you can, but so far everything has been pretty cut and dried.

After all, there aren't that many types of bank accounts to stash your different buckets of cash in.

The landscape of insurance products is pretty well settled and not growing.

Attorneys specialize in established areas of practice.

It's not too difficult to figure out these pieces of the puzzle.

On the subject of GROWING your money, however, the playing field of potential investments is practically infinite.

For investment options, you have thousands of individual companies listed on the various stock exchanges at your fingertips, not to mention mutual funds, ETFs, bonds (corporate, municipal, government), REITs, commodities, currencies, penny stocks, precious metals, private equity, hedge funds, cryptocurrencies, art, collectibles (everything from NFTs to baseball cards, coins, magazines and alcohol on up to classic cars), angel investing in startups, real estate (residential, commercial, industrial) and just about anything else where you invest your money and hope (and pray) it will turn into more money down the line.

INVESTING PYRAMID

The Investing Pyramid shows how higher gains correlate to higher risk across different investment vehicles.

Just as your path to wealth will be uniquely yours, so will your path to *staying* wealthy which has everything to do with how you invest your money against your risk tolerance since the biggest investment returns require ever higher degrees of risk of your capital.

Our family's net worth, as I've discussed before, is pretty much all locked up in the Retirement Iceberg of accounts that we can't touch without penalties before turning 59 and a half. We are riding the market up to our Security Number through a low-risk portfolio of balanced index fund ETFs, target-date mutual funds and individual stocks actively managed by our financial planner.

We are not invested in any penny stocks or cryptocurrencies or kangaroo meat pie fast food chain franchises. Yet.

We may venture into riskier waters one day, but our investment strategy thus far has done the trick with little demand of our time. And with little risk of mental daytime and nighttime anxiety.

Some might say that being so heavily weighted in the stock market is actually higher-risk than if we had put it all in real estate, but to each his own – there are pros and cons on both sides of this, and ANY, investment debate.

Truth be told, we are leaning toward real estate to a) own something tangible and b) diversify into an asset class that we can use and enjoy as a family.

In terms of GROWING your money, personal judgment plays a fundamental role in when and where you choose to invest, of course.

You know the difference between your Cousin Earl who asks you for $5,000 to open a bait and tackle shop although he knows little more about fishing than taking a 24-pack of Miller Lite out on the lake once a month and your Cousin Ellen who runs two successful local restaurants and is looking for $5,000 to help open a third.

Or maybe you don't want to invest (or loan) your money to family at all! That is totally up to you.

A wealthy friend of mine is always being pitched for seed stage money – he is not an investor, per se, but a media personality that has lived well below his means for many years now. He has a great system in place where he will listen to pitches that interest him and read over the business plans but then pass them onto his business manager who can play "bad cop" for the final say. That's my friend's choice to begin with – even entertaining the pitches at all.

You get to decide as you come into increasing amounts of wealth (and as people KNOW it) how you want to handle the Cousin Earls and Cousin Ellens of the world.

Oh, I may dream about sitting in a chair as the week's latest *Shark Tank* investor, but we are not at the level of wealth where we have highly disposable buckets or ancillary net worth to invest in high-risk ventures like DrumPants.

In terms of getting started and testing the waters with investing, it has never been easier to set up an online brokerage account and dive right into the stock markets, if that's your thing. Most deep discount online firms even provide you with hundreds of commission-free ETF (love), most of which also have low expense ratios (double love!).

Or you can set up a crypto account and learn the ins and outs of the blossoming NFT (non-fungible token) markets. How much Bored Ape Yacht Club will YOU invest in? (P.S. This is definitely NOT investment advice.)

The only real rule of thumb to investing is to not risk more than you're willing to lose. You worked so hard to collect, respect and protect your money, why would you so easily risk the loss of it?

Lest we lean on Warren Buffett to get his thoughts on the preservation of capital, he has famously stated:

Rule number 1: Never lose money.

Rule number 2: Don't forget rule number 1.

If you can't stand to lose any money, keep your money in the bevy of safer investment options near the base of the Investing Pyramid.

5. Share Your Money – You Can't Take It with You, Start NOW

Why do we even WANT to create the largest lake of net worth we can in our lifetime?

The only reasons to become wealthy are to a) be financially free so you can live life on your own terms, b) ensure financial security for you and your family for generations to come, c) use the free markets as a barometer to validate the execution of your ideas and d) to give as much of it away as you want to the people and causes that you care about most.

There are only so many THINGS you can buy and invest in. At a certain level, you have maxed out your power and political sway, too. (Who are we kidding – there will always be MORE politicians to take your political contributions.)

Wealthy people don't just give to charities because of a potential tax write-off (though I'm sure they know all the tax implications of their giving), they share their wealth because they want to leave the world just a little bit better than they found it.

With wealth comes great responsibility – and part of that responsibility is to give back. To give IT back.

When it's game over for you on planet Earth, your financial dam will crumble and all the money you've collected will flow downstream...somewhere...and you get to decide WHERE it goes and who benefits from it.

Leona Helmsley, the famous hotel owner and real estate investor who was worth around $4 billion at her death famously left $12 million to a trust solely established for the care of her 8-year-old white Maltese dog.

The world is your oyster in terms of sharing your wealth, that's for sure.

How creative will YOU be?

Family & Friends

When you come into money, it's important to set ground rules with your family and friends in terms of any financial gift-giving because everyone needs to know the financial boundaries – first and foremost, YOU.

Since money can do strange things to your relationships with family and friends (when they know you have more than them!), you might consider being totally transparent and upfront about what you will and won't pay for and the why behind it, if necessary. Of course, most people don't want to have everything paid for by you, anyway – and if they do, RUN in the opposite direction. Also, try not to marry them! (Well, certainly don't marry your family, but *other*, non-family members who want everything to be paid for by you, I mean.)

We used to let my grandpa pay for family meals out (and then one of us would run back in to leave a real tip because he never quite figured that part out), but I would never let a friend pay for all my meals out. Occasionally, friends will surprise a group of us by picking up the tab, but it's an exception to the rule.

You know now that money is nothing more than safety, security and freedom and you want your family to feel the same breathing room that you do, but you also know the value of teaching a man to fish versus feeding him all the fish he can eat.

You also know that love has no price tag but that family members and friends who have never had financial wealth may confuse love with monetary value so you want to be as clear as you can about why you do the things you do. If that doesn't work, gift them a copy of *Think Wealthy!*

Philanthropy

If the world is your oyster in terms of investment opportunities and places to GROW your money, you will be happy to know that there are equally as many opportunities and places to DONATE your money.

Our daughter receives an allowance each week and puts $1 into savings and $1 into charity. When she had saved up $7 in her charity box, we went online and found a local bunny rabbit foundation for her to donate that money to because that was where her heart led her that day.

Bunny rabbit rescue and rehabilitation, folks.

The donation world is yours for the taking.

The options available to ALL of us are truly mind-boggling. And why shouldn't they be in a world of over 7 billion people?

Still, even as we would all love to support every organization that needs it, this is where a bit of soul-searching early on can help you greatly narrow the field of philanthropy to areas that interest and speak to you emotionally.

At the end of the book, I included The Game of Wealth (Appendix C), a mental exercise in spending vast sums of virtual money. You simply HAVE to spend it all and, by doing so, you come to realize what you care about in terms of giving back to the world. Here again, we are completely individual snowflakes in what is important to each of us.

After going through the cancer journey this past year, the Make-A-Wish Foundation held more meaning for us than it had in years past and so we donated to them. As a parent, St. Jude has always held a special place in my heart as you simply can't imagine how gut-wrenching and taxing it must be to support your own young child through a battle with cancer.

There are many different approaches to finding your convictions and there are even services out there to help you determine how much and where you want to direct your charitable giving. (Of *course* there are.)

Are you drawn to a particular region of the country or the world? Do you want to help eradicate a global disease like The Gates Foundation did with polio? Maybe you'd rather help the working class in Chile develop financial literacy? Or have a state-of-the-art performing arts center named after you on your college campus?

The sky's the limit when it comes to philanthropy and the impact you can make on the world.

In terms of how much you should give, I will not wade into those waters – that is a very personal choice. Christian churches have asked for a 10% tithe for centuries and Muslims have a 2.5% tithe request of surplus wealth.

Every family needs to determine the level of giving with which they're comfortable. Some families dedicate all their financial gifts to one organization while others spread the financial love, as it were.

I am not of the mindset that a person MUST donate anything, really – that is, I don't believe it should be mandated or required, but I also don't think I'd want to spend much time with someone who was a multi-millionaire and who didn't understand the moral pull to help others with their affluence.

And lest we forget that there are two ways to donate to charity – both with time and money.

I find it so odd, looking back as an adult, that my family never prioritized donating money or time to charities. If you met my mother, you would immediately be struck by her level of compassion and obvious mission to help other people in any way she could, but there was a block in my parents' minds with charity, that there was just "never enough to go around." That is, the family never had any "extra" money to donate to charities. And donating our time was never considered, either. That was the narrative, at least. Perhaps it was just a muscle that was never flexed, or a habit never formed.

My partner's family also never volunteered time or money for causes so it has been a hurdle for both of us to integrate giving into a regular financial cycle. Even changing the monthly rent reminder on the calendar to "Rent + Donation" has not turned it into a habit for us, yet we want to raise our daughter with the idea that it is our duty, the same as the next family's, to help others with our time and money as we best see fit.

Here's to 2022, the year of rehabilitating rabbits!

We are a work in progress in this area.

Maybe you already know what causes are near and dear to you. If so, great! If not, keep your eyes and ears open for organizations that grab your attention for the work they're doing and see if you can't start donating something starting today or this month. You won't be able to donate a million dollars one day if you're not comfortable donating $10 or $100 now.

As I mentioned, you could always join the Giving Pledge (givingpledge.org), "a promise by the world's wealthiest individuals and families to dedicate the majority of their wealth to charitable causes." The Gates, The Buffetts…so far 225 wealthy individuals and families have taken the pledge. Do I hear 226?

Well-Rounded Wealth

I set well-rounded wealth as the goal at the beginning of Chapter 2 when we looked at wealth being nothing more than abundance.

Well-rounded wealth is a well-rounded life.

It means striking the balance between career, family and friends. It's being passionate about whatever work you're doing and having the vision to create more for yourself and live as big of a life as you want with plenty of money in the bank to cover it.

And then some.

Well-rounded wealth is a mindset that puts you squarely on the path to financial freedom.

Well-rounded wealth, at its core, is personal freedom – freedom to discover who you are and to pursue that full-steam ahead because you're "choosing" your version of life every step of the way.

It is also the freedom to be a work in progress whose interests and passions have the flexibility to change throughout the stages of your life, just as they did with billionaire Jess Jackson.

The reality is that you can have most any version of your life that you want if you a) know what that is and know that you deserve it, b) have a plan on how to get there and c) DO something every day, no matter how small, toward your goals.

That's the big secret of success – attack your *future wealth plan* day after day to bring it closer within your grasp. Sounds simple, doesn't it?

Wealthy people are no different from you and me.

I'm going to keep writing that until my fingers turn blue and fall off my hands.

Wealthy people are no different from you and me – they have simply set goals and achieved enough of the right ones in the right sequence to catapult them into a wealthier realm.

What IS true about having incredible financial means, however, is that it requires you to lead a bigger life. The bigger your life, the more processes or systems (and people) you will have in place to support it, be that a staff that helps maintain any properties you own, a group of money managers to advise you on investments and who help you run the numbers on prospective deals, specialized lawyers who can set up intricate estate planning, and on and on.

Perhaps you want a life that is so big that you need a driver to take you into the office and back home every evening. If you live in Los Angeles and have anything close to an hour commute each way (which is true again now that the pandemic is waning – but is it?), think of what you could ACCOMPLISH in those TWO HOURS if it were someone else's sole job to get you safely from Point A to Point B and back again.

Hollywood producer Jason Blum of *Paranormal Activity* franchise fame has a rigged-up office minivan in which he is driven to and from work each day. He leads a big life with all the films he has in various stages of development, production and release and has determined that driving himself around town is not the best use of his time. He understands that money is in abundance, but his time is not. Maybe you will reach that point, too.

He also mitigates his company's risk by developing a handful of films at any time with the hope that even one or two will break out to larger success – he's operating like a venture capitalist in that sense.

Of course, you don't have to live THAT big of a life or hire any fulltime staff to help you manage it all. You can be wealthy and keep your life very simple and low-key just like all those Millionaires Next Door. You're a master problem-solver as CEO of You, Inc., remember? You'll figure it out.

The best news of all is that if one of your many choices or decisions isn't working out, you can change course and try another route. Every successful person has pivoted at some point in their journey. You are THAT in control of your life. We all are, whether we realize it or not.

But what does well-rounded wealth look like in real life?

How do we know if we're on track and setting ourselves up for success, to BE wealthy on the inside so that we DO the things that will lead us to HAVE wealth on the outside?

My only goal is to inspire within you a wealthier version of yourself, that you believe in enough to pursue and achieve using the principles of well-rounded wealth.

Here we go!

The Four Pillars of Well-Rounded Wealth

I designed these four pillars to always remind mySELF of what's important, too.

With the belief firmly in hand that every book needs an acronym, I've turned the four pillars of Well-Rounded Wealth into LIFE.

The four pillars of Well-Rounded Wealth are:

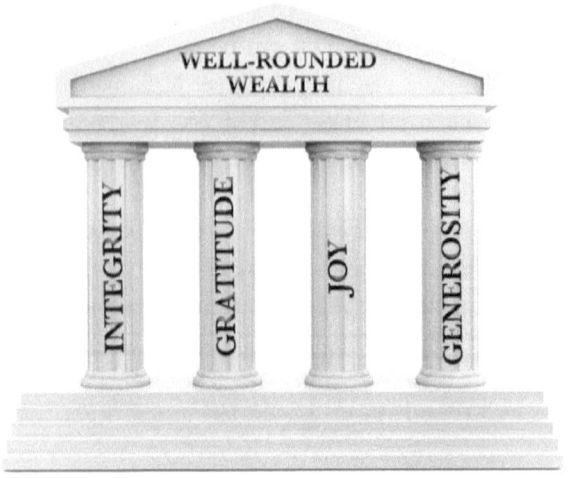

1. **Lead w/INTEGRITY**

2. **Invest in GRATITUDE**

3. **Find JOY Daily**

4. **Express GENEROSITY**

Let's look at each of them individually...

1) Lead with Integrity

Integrity sounds like a high-minded noble concept, something discussed by the Knights of the Round Table. But it's much simpler than that.

You DO what you say you're going to do, always acting from a strong moral compass. Pure and simple.

And you do it WHEN you say you are going to do it.

A life of integrity is a life led in search of the TRUTH.

Perhaps the most visible example of integrity in our daily lives is showing up somewhere when you say you will.

You show up to work on time – you show up to business meetings, Zoom calls and important social engagements on time.

We tend to treat our personal lives as if they are more casual than business life – but true integrity means showing up on time for our personal meetups as well.

This might be a particularly American ideal as when I lived in Europe in college (Italy, Spain and France), there was an almost whimsical "oh so European" flair to using a meeting time as more of a guidepost than a hard and fast rule. Unless you were meeting for a movie, you could show up 20-30 minutes late without anyone batting an eye. This was also before the era of smartphone addiction so perhaps those countries are more cognizant of meeting times nowadays.

As someone who leads with integrity, you know that when you respect your time, you respect yourself. And when you respect yourself, you treat everyone as a peer whose time is just as valuable as yours – whether they know it yet or not.

You have proof that you are awesome and living with integrity when you also show up on time for the meetings you DON'T want to attend.

Part of integrity is only committing to something new when you know you can deliver results on time or earlier. If it pushes you even closer to your goals, financial and otherwise, then you find a way to fit it in.

There's an old saying that "if you want something done, ask a busy person." We don't know that that busy person leads with integrity, but for sure they've managed their time well to be able to accomplish so much and they wouldn't have been asked to do so much already if they continually failed to deliver results!

I'm not referring here to the people we all know who are only too happy to tell you JUST HOW BUSY they already are – that is the busyness of martyrdom, of someone decidedly NOT in control of their lives.

To avoid that fate, you graciously reply to requests that do NOT inch you closer to your goals with a "No, thank you."

Since you do what you say, you quickly become known as someone who can be trusted. Being trusted by your family, friends and business associates is akin to having a bank vault stuffed to the ceiling with gold. It means you are a person of the strongest character, one who everyone will go to the mat for without you even knowing it.

Due to your honesty, a key component of integrity, people know where they stand with you. You don't beat around the bush or play unnecessary passive-aggressive games.

Because of your own strong character and moral center, you have learned to only do business with people who exhibit similar integrity – if potential business partners are habitually late, if they change the agreed-upon terms between a verbal agreement and the legal contract, you know that this is only a precursor to bigger headaches down the line. If someone can't be fully trusted at a first deal together, why would they be any different the next time around?

You are an adult and you only want to work with other adults – honest, confident, big-hearted adults – not grown children who play games with your time and your money.

As an adult, you take responsibility for your actions. You are quick to apologize and make amends, if and when necessary. Then you move forward because you are not your past, you are the possibility of the future that you create with others.

You know that your reputation is all a person has at the end of the day and that trust is not easily gained, but quickly lost.

You are a class act all around whether you run a company with thousands of employees, are a budding entrepreneur or, perhaps the hardest job of all, are a stay-at-home parent with a brood of any size.

A Note on Honesty and Business Deals

Leading with integrity means living a life in the pursuit of Truth with a capital 'T' and that includes operating out of honesty with others. Not playing games. Letting people know where they stand and why.

I'd be remiss if I didn't mention that some high-stakes business deals, the ones that may slingshot you into the upper echelon of financial wealth, often come down to information that one party has that the other does not.

A business deal may well involve a sizable win for your side if you hold information back from the negotiation table.

And that is a part of business and the negotiation game.

You can chalk it up to playing the game to win – the love of the deal – ruthlessness around the conference table – it's not personal, it's just business, right?

There is a sliding scale of truthfulness here, from being an outright lie to being a savvy negotiation tactic. I feel the need to call this out because a) this is how the real world works when there are millions or billions of dollars at stake and b) it doesn't mean that you aren't leading your life with integrity if you're not fully transparent with information at the negotiation table.

Where you fall on that sliding scale and what you are comfortable with is up to you and those that you do business with on your side.

If you are a leader who habitually lies (the far end of the spectrum) to get the best terms out of every deal, I believe that that will eventually catch up to you – you'll have a stained reputation that will keep you out of future deal flow or enough associates will find the game you play too toxic for them to be able to sleep at night.

But, again, it is a grey scale and everyone must determine what shade they're most comfortable with.

$$$

Well-Rounded Wealth Warning: *People Who Don't Do What They Say*

Who doesn't do what they say they're going to do? Who doesn't habitually honor their agreements?

Turns out many, many people don't do what they say they're going to do.

Many, many people.

This can be everything from not showing up to a meeting on time, not calling at the agreed-upon time, habitually showing up to restaurants late, not returning an email when they said they would, bailing on an agreed-upon contract, etc.

I have run into this on LinkedIn too many times to count. Someone at a company has pursued me for an open role within their organization –

very flowery language about my accomplishments and what a great company they are to work for, but after I thank them and politely decline – ghosted – no thanks for my time, no let's keep the door open.

Similar experience to dealing with HR execs. You jump through an ever-increasing number of hoops in terms of calls and interviews only to have your outreach ignored with no resolution.

We could call these two examples a lack of inherent integrity – people who should know better than to thumb their nose up at Business Communication 101.

It's an epidemic in our modern times, this inability to deliver on what we say we're going to do and lack of integrity, in general.

I had seven rounds of interviews with a company that specializes in teaching financial literacy to thousands of corporate employees. On the final Zoom interview with over five department heads, the CEO was the only person who didn't turn on his camera. He never made mention of that fact, either – to me it felt like a weird power play and, honestly, turned me off from how the company was run from the top down. I had already read between the lines that employees were expected to walk on eggshells around him. When I wasn't offered a position with the company, I felt like I had personally DODGED A BULLET. Like Keanu Reeves in *The Matrix*. Phew!

Did you know that being on time has been noted by several authors as the singular necessary trait of successful people? Let's hear it for punctuality!

Is this one a total shocker to you? It was for me.

I started watching *Inside Bill's Brain: Decoding Bill Gates* on Netflix and I was struck by something one of his assistants said about him: Bill Gates is on time for every meeting. One of the wealthiest men in the entire world is always on time!

Yes, he probably has a lot of support staff in his life. And perhaps his brain processes information faster than the average bear so he makes efficient use of the meetings he DOES have, but that man is ON TIME. Can you say the same for all the meetings and Zoom calls you're on?

Of course, we may miss the mark from time to time, but you're in the Danger Zone if you become KNOWN to people as the person who is never on time or who never gets things done on time – you are cutting yourself off from a whole world of opportunity – and it only takes a few times before you earn that reputation.

Doing what you say you're going to do is a foundational building block of trust. And without trust, you can have no true relationship with another human being, be that in a professional setting or a personal one.

Being punctual used to be a real doozy for me. I grew up working in the family business which was a miniature golf course and video game room called Putt-Putt Golf & Games. I worked there from my earliest memory where my sister and I picked up cigarette butts once a week for a quarter.

However, when I was in high school, there were many times I didn't want to go to work in the afternoon and relieve my dad who'd been there since he opened the place in the morning. If my shift started at 3p, I'd routinely roll in between 3:05p and 3:15p. Half the time when I pulled up, I'd see him look at his watch and shake his head in frustration.

I know now that it felt like it was my only way of pushing back against not wanting to work so much in my teenage years. It was a family business and I loved having my own cash flow, but that one habit I took out into the world as if there were no other way to express myself. If I was at the point of no longer liking a job, you could count on me to never arrive early and to rarely arrive on time.

Passive-aggressive much, Herr Havens?

Being late to work was the only tool I had in my toolbelt for pushing back against something I didn't want to do. Or so I thought.

$$\$\$\$$$

If you don't do what you say, people have no reason to trust you. They're not going to help you with your big passion project, they're not going to fund your startup with any seed money and you will probably end up banging your head against the wall wondering why the world is so unfair.

Do financially successful people not honor their commitments or not do what they say they're going to do, too? Of course! But I sure as heck don't want to work with them once I find that out – my time and YOUR time are too valuable for that.

On a fundamental level, if you're not in control of your time, you're not in control of your life.

The funny thing about integrity is that it's a silent weapon for good in the world – you won't hear people speak very often about whether someone HAS integrity, you'll only hear its opposite, their bad manners or disappointing behavior, referenced.

At the end of the day, if you don't spend your waking hours operating from a strong moral compass, honoring your commitments and agreements, you're just playing games with yourself and others.

As a pillar of Well-Rounded Wealth, leading with integrity is foundational to showing up as the very best version of yourself.

2) Invest in Gratitude

We talked about this in Chapter 4 under Think Thanks, point #8.

I bring it up again because making gratitude a central tenet of your life will help you move literal and figurative mountains.

You'll notice I also phrase it as INVESTing in gratitude because it will always pay dividends and return a strong ROI (return on investment) for everything you do.

There is simply no bad that can come from appreciating all aspects of your own life and celebrating everyone who is a part of it, at home and in the office (when and if we ever fully go back to offices — and maybe we shouldn't — discuss amongst yourselves).

As an employer, you should have an infinite well of gratitude for the work others do in pursuit of your vision and mission. Yes, you pay them, but they're not there just for the paycheck — everyone appreciates kind words and gestures to let them know that they are seen and acknowledged beyond the list of job duties they were hired for.

Being able to communicate your sincere gratitude to others makes you a leader of high emotional intelligence, a high EQ.

I was recently working with a top-tier American business school who was looking to skate where the puck is headed in terms of training America's future C-suite. We had the opportunity to interview a dozen current CEO and CMOs of Fortune 100 companies, including the consultants who advise them, and over and over, it kept coming up that tomorrow's leaders need to lead with EMPATHY and have a high EQ.

Without a doubt the word "empathy" is the new executive buzzword to emerge from the COVID pandemic – my buddy and I were astounded at how often it came up in our conversations and interviews. We thought the joke was on us each time "empathy" was uttered, as if all the executives had joined forces behind our backs in some sort of hidden-camera show.

Are you known as an empathetic person? Are you able to put yourself in other people's shoes and still drive home your vision with passion, all the while making it relevant to who you're talking to?

Bob Iger, who led The Walt Disney Company as CEO for 15 years, recently "told CNBC he began thinking about stepping down as chief executive after feeling he was becoming too dismissive of other people's opinions."

In his own words: "Over time, I started listening less and maybe with a little less tolerance of other people's opinions, maybe because of getting a little bit more overconfident in my own, which is sometimes what happens when you get built up."

Bob Iger is being celebrated in the press for his self-awareness and emotional intelligence, for hearing alarms go off when you start thinking you're the smartest guy in the room too often.

Investing in gratitude starts with you taking stock of your own life and thanking God or the universe for your circumstances or just being appreciative for all that you do have.

It can be a simple practice you work into your daily routine – acknowledge five things you are grateful for at the end of each day. Write them down in a journal or do it digitally – the fact that you're directing your focus and attention to the positive aspects of your life, regardless of how small, will create a habit that you default to.

Warren Buffett (why am I up in this man's GRILL so much in this book? I guess he's said some sticky things over the years) has famously said that he won the "ovarian lottery" by being born in the United States where his particular talents have been rewarded. "We wouldn't be worth a damn in Afghanistan."

There is no faster and deeper transformation to a person's character than that initiated by an investment in gratitude.

I have met many wealthy people over the years and those that have been the most memorable are those that demonstrated gratitude. "Wow," I would think to myself, "They have amassed significant financial wealth AND they still have time to thank everyone around them for their help?!? I want to be like THEM."

Back on the hunt for affordable real estate in Los Angeles (there's a joke in there), we sent in our paperwork to a mortgage broker and, as part of their welcome package, they mailed us a gratitude journal. What a great idea! After this past year's medical drain on my psyche, I have started the gratitude practice and know it will provide a jolt of adrenaline as we enter the new year.

Regardless of how you feel about Oprah Winfrey, the media personality who we all turned into a self-made billionaire by watching her eponymous talk show, she has always espoused gratitude as a key growth factor for her (and anyone else's) success.

When you show up to the world supported by a pillar of gratitude, you literally change lives for the better, starting with your own.

3) Find Joy Daily

You are learning to lead with integrity – perhaps more integrity than you had in the past. And you are investing in gratitude for what you have in your life. Heck, even if you're homeless and dumpster-diving for your meals, you start with being grateful for each and every breath.

Now we're ready for the third pillar, that of finding JOY daily.

Joy is not just happiness. Joy is a swelling of the heart, much like what happens to the Grinch at the end of the story when he finally understands the meaning of Christmas and his heart grows three sizes bigger that fateful day.

Joy carries with it an air of PEACE in the moment that reminds you that all is right in the world. Even if the feeling of joy is fleeting, for that second or seconds, you have peeked behind the curtain of the physical world to sense the perfection of it all.

I hope I'm not building this up too much – we've all experienced joy, haven't we?

Perhaps you've found it in an infant's smile or squeal, in receiving a particularly thoughtful gift from a loved one, in witnessing incredible musical artistry at a concert.

Joy is a direct connection to the heart – joy is a break from the endless barrage of thought to a state of living, even briefly, in the moment.

If you don't know where to find joy, start with a smile.

We recently created a game with our daughter where we wake up in the morning and the first thing we do is smile at each other. Even if we're late to start the day and get her ready for school, starting with a smile puts us all in the best frame of mind for what lies ahead.

Don't tell her, but we started it because she was waking up on the wrong side of the bed too often, barking out demands as if we were hired help instead of her parents.

It has worked like a charm, both for her and for US, to start each day with a smile.

Finding joy is also a state of mind – a switch that you learn to turn on when you wish.

I am looking out the front window of our house right now and watching the rain fall. That brings me quite a bit of joy.

I also have the soundtrack to season two of HBO Max's *Succession* playing and that also brings me joy.

Just one thing, at minimum, to find joy in each day.

Perhaps you created an awesome human being or are raising one and just looking at them for the briefest of moments brings you joy.

The playfulness of a pet.

The delivery of a well-landed joke.

The feel of your car on the road as it responds to your commands and magically moves you through space.

A soft pillow at the end of a long day (or ANY day, for that matter).

A smile from your partner.

Again, joy is an internal feeling, but it may be safe to say that there are parts of the world where joy is not as readily available due to more stringent social norms. Not to mention the fact that there are still billions of people in the world who, by nature of their geography and where they were born and raised (Buffett's ovarian lottery - damn him!), find daily life to be a struggle.

Still, joy is available to everyone. The sun still shines. The moon still rises and falls. A faint wind blows across your face.

Find joy daily.

Observe or reflect on one thing each day that makes your heart larger.

By connecting your daily life to this profound emotion, you are tapping into deeper spiritual meaning and purpose.

Finding joy daily reminds you that you are part of a greater whole – with unique contributions to offer this spinning blue gem of a planet while you're here.

4) Express Generosity

Here we are at the final pillar of living a LIFE of Well-Rounded Wealth – express generosity.

As we discussed in the second chapter, wealth is abundance in any form it takes, financial wealth being but one of many inter-connected EFFECTS of operating from an origin point of abundance.

We can have a wealth of friends, wealth of health, wealth of love and belonging, even a wealth of shiny objects and toys that remind us that we have amassed enough commas in our net worth that we can afford the finer things in life, if we so choose.

I imagine you've caught on by now to the ultimate design of our four pillars, that well-rounded wealth starts deep within each of us INDIVIDUALLY as we focus our energy and attention on the most positive, most expansive emotions and actions available to man and womankind.

In the BE – DO – HAVE wealth journey equation, we are locking in that who we ARE in the world is someone who sees and acts from abundance.

What's more, our first three pillars are internal benchmarks – integrity is an inner compass, gratitude is a way of looking out at the world and joy is an indescribable, transcendent connection to a common spiritual core.

Any of these three pillars may motivate a person to ACT a certain way in the world, but our fourth pillar ensures that how we show up to others is often, if not always, with a generous nature.

To express generosity is to approach the world asking how you can help.

How can you help leave the planet even a little bit better than you found it?

What professional work can you do to ease the suffering of others, or even the suffering of the planet itself?

What personal approach will let those close to you know that you are there for them and want to help them succeed in any way that you can?

I don't mean that you need to be all things to all people, sacrificing your own goals to ensure that your neighbor's (whose name you can hardly remember) kitty litter box is always clean.

Generosity in action also need not have a major magnitude associated with it – sometimes a quick email or call checking in on a friend or on a mentee's progress is perceived and received as generosity of the highest order.

There is generosity of both your time and your money, but they both come from a generosity of spirit. Your wanting others to succeed and your offer to help them in the ways that you can may take different forms.

To express generosity connects us all back to one another.

To express generosity harmonizes our highest selves.

To express generosity can even restore our faith in humanity.

As a parent, and this is a goal I'm ever working on, I endeavor to tell my daughter once or twice a day what her undeniable gifts are to our family.

Compliments are a form of generosity.

My partner and I rarely argue or find ourselves on the opposite ends of an issue, but when we sometimes do, I will often be able to see his point of view and tell him so. Boy does that neutralize any mounting conflict!

Simply acknowledging another's perspective is a form of generosity – you'd be surprised how many people don't feel heard or understood in their world.

Expressing generosity signals our deeper shared, human experience together.

Where gratitude is observation, generosity is ACTION.

Acting with generosity elevates everyone's quality of life.

$$$

Well-Rounded Wealth Secret: *This Here, This Everywhere*

Here's a little peek into human behavior that may surprise you: how you operate in one area of your life is the way you operate in all areas of your life.

We human beings don't have all-powerful switches that we think we do where we can turn on our voice or our passion or our efficiency or our ability to be organized for x number of hours a day and then turn it off when the weekend arrives.

How you operate in one area of your life is the way you operate in all areas of your life.

I used to think that I could be completely dispassionate, uninspired and voiceless at a 9-to-5 but that, at home, I could flip a magic switch and turn it all on when needed. After all, friends still laughed at my jokes over dinner, nothing seemed "off" as I worked each week just to get to the weekend.

Sure, I was drinking more than usual, procrastinating, in general, and felt there was no reason to even hope for a different future or that there were any possibilities left for me in the world. You know, small things like that…

Now, however, I can plainly see how the blues or the "depression of circumstances" that I was in had a total bearing on how I acted in and viewed the other areas of my life.

I wasn't even playing in the game of life. I wasn't being creative. I wasn't alive. I was just going through the motions while only dreaming about getting home nine hours later. What happened in-between was dead air.

Turns out, my whole life was ALL dead air before I took control again.

By consciously building your LIFE with the four pillars of Integrity, Gratitude, Joy and Generosity, you will positively affect EVERY aspect of your world.

LIFE here, LIFE everywhere.

$$\$\$\$$

Well-Rounded Wealth Warning: *Fear and Failure*

Might as well bring up these two badarses since these two concepts have done immeasurable and irreparable damage to the human psyche, have snuffed out infinite dreams from the hands and hearts of amazingly talented people who never shared their gifts with the world and have driven millions to deathbed regrets.

As for **FEAR**…

Of course, you feel fear. We all feel fear. Fear is real.

The angry God of the Hebrew Bible/Old Testament punished humanity with it for eating from the wrong tree or we inherited it from our hunter/gatherer tribal past because a tiger growled in the bushes one night (or every night - ACK!) or it's a chemical reaction happening in the oldest, limbic part of the human brain as the gift that keeps on giving from some slimy ancestor thing that crawled out of the water to live on land with nothing but a dream of becoming the human race…or wherever you want to argue fear comes from…it is real and it still serves a much-needed role in our modern lives.

Fear exists to protect us from danger.

You will always feel fear. It's part of being human.

Fear is part of being alive.

When fear comes between you and your future, however, when it's based in insecurity like worrying what others will think of you or what will happen if a project you believe in all comes crashing down, it is only PERCEIVED danger – it's not real. And rather than protecting you, it is impeding you.

If you go out into the world and contribute something that you honestly feel people want or need because it will make their lives better, what is there to fear?

What we need to do is not CONQUER fear or FIGHT against it but embrace and THANK it – thank fear – for the great service it provides us. And then move forward, regardless.

Use fear to feed your intuition on a business deal that doesn't feel right or in sizing up people that you may need to work with one day (were they late to the meeting – WERE THEY?), but think of fear as an over-anxious consultant and not as a crystal ball to your future – fear doesn't always know best.

Fear is the only emotion that kills people who otherwise look alive because it paralyzes them with inaction.

Fear turns people into walking zombies who have given up on their dreams.

It is also the sneakiest lil' bugger because it lurks within the mental chatter we've learned to believe over the years without any critical questioning.

Fortunately, you understand that fear isn't going anywhere, that is has its value, and you act, anyway…you act IN SPITE of fear.

The only thing we have to fear…is fear itself.

- Franklin D. Roosevelt

(Well, "fear itself" and polio which was FDR's lifelong struggle and is still only 99% eradicated. Yet greatly more eradicated in the world thanks to The Gates Foundation – wealthy people doing good with their money!)

When you fear nothing, or at least learn to act IN SPITE of it, you have nothing to lose, and you can make calculated risks. Wealthy people take educated risks – they know of the potential upside and mitigate as many risks of the downside that they can. They won't enter into a deal just because somebody is a great pitchman, they need to see the numbers and run it past their team and then decide whether to wade into the water or not.

At this point, fear becomes your servant and provides a guiding light for intuition.

Fear is only a consultant in your life, while YOU remain firmly in the driver's seat.

As for **FAILURE**…

Unlike fear which seems to course through our veins at a cellular level, failure is a judgment, a word like "loser" that says much more about the person using the word than its intended target.

And if you think of yourSELF as a "failure" on any level or are afraid of being perceived as a "failure" by others because of something you did or didn't do, draining the word of its venom starts with YOU.

There simply is no failure if what you've learned benefits you or someone else in your next endeavor.

Even if this book only sells two copies and shows up on Amazon's Worstsellers List under Books → Business & Money → What Not to Do → BIG FAILURE → NO, REALLY, FOLKS, THIS IS RADIOACTIVE, that is just an algorithm's opinion – it has nothing to do with what I learned writing this and what people have already shared reading earlier eBook drafts.

Let's even say Amazon were to find *Think Wealthy* to be so reprehensibly bad that Jeff Bezos decides to buy up all the eye-blinding ad space in Times Square in New York City and decry what a deafening bomb of a book it is – and everywhere I go in the world people stop what they're doing to point and laugh at me – okay, at that point I MAY question my writing ability and motivation – I MAY pause for an extra second in the bathroom mirror at night and ask myself some bigger life questions – but I STILL would not label this book a failure and I would definitely never use that word as a way to define myself.

I'm not joking when I say that "failure" does not exist in my vocabulary any longer. It is a label that gets slapped onto a collection of circumstances that most people know nothing about.

If you take the path of helping others (as I have done with this book), and you know in your heart that it WILL help them, then any criticism either provides valuable feedback for the next edition or only serves to highlight a person's own unhappiness in the world which is not your job to fix.

Truth be told, both "success" and "failure" are words other people use who are looking from the outside in – they don't really pertain to those of us who are living our lives with integrity, playing on the court of life, who know our inherent value and who have the goal of helping others wherever we can.

Embrace FEAR and drop the word FAILURE (and SUCCESS, for that matter) from your vocabulary.

A Final Word on Well-Rounded Wealth

I have tried my best to communicate in this book the key financial concepts that underpin wealth creation and wealth management. I have repeated myself ad nauseum to drive home certain core concepts that I feel most people do not understand on a gut level (where it matters most). I have asked you to dream BIG with your financial goals and to use the concepts of The Money Dam™ to build the infrastructure to support those goals. I have also written a lot about human behavior and the psychology of wealth.

At the end of the day, each of us is pure potentiality, pure possibility, having a human experience. Yet we play too small by waking up each day and narrowly experiencing the world based on the habits we've created over our lifetimes to maximize pleasure and minimize pain – perceived pain.

But you are that limitless possibility. In every moment of every day.

When you pair that incredible possibility that is your birthright with an outstretched hand to help your fellow man and fellow woman, operating from the four pillars of Well-Rounded Wealth, happiness and financial wealth can be yours.

It is my sincerest hope that you know that and seize every opportunity to leave the world a better place than you found it.

It has been my honor to share this time with you – I truly thank you for taking this journey with me. From my family to yours, I wish you a long life of health, wealth and happiness.

Conclusion: Your Money, Your Self

That's it, my friend - we have reached the end of *Think Wealthy*!

Do you feel you have a better handle on the purpose of money in your own life...how you can take control of it...and do amazing things with it because you, yourself, are amazing?

There's a little trick to this book that I'd like to share with you. It's a gift for the statistical minority of readers who have actually arrived at this last section – without just skipping ahead, Cheater McCheaterson!

The secret is this: Where I have written the word "money," replace that word with "Self."

For example, with the final chapter, every subtitle that says *Money*, let's replace with *Self*:

Collect Your Money	**Collect Your Self**
Respect Your Money	**Respect Your Self**
Protect Your Money	**Protect Your Self**
Grow Your Money	**Grow Your Self**
Share Your Money	**Share Your Self**

Do you see why money is not about the digital dollars and cents of your bank account but about how you PERCEIVE yourself?

And how money is just a mirror for who we are and who we show up as in the world each day?

The amount of money you have, your net worth, says nothing about your TRUE worth, or anyone's, which is infinite – the amount of money you have only indicates where you are on the journey of connecting the limitless potential that is YOU to a common (and some might say arbitrary) measure of value out in the world.

Your money, your self.

Now that you are fully in charge and in control of your life, it's up to you to decide if you want to be part of the problem or part of the solution.

That is what I call TRENDING.

Which way are you TRENDING in life – are you trending positive or negative?

CONCLUSION

Is your net worth trending positive or negative?

As the works-in-progress that each of us are, trending is the only barometer we have for evaluating ourselves and others.

If it's not obvious, life is more rewarding when we're trending positive, to be part of the solution, because it shows up as creativity, problem-solving and helping one another succeed.

Each of us has the choice of how we trend.

In life, do you respond with courage or do you seek comfort? With curiosity or fear? With resolve or resignation?

Will people look back on your life and say that you were on the right side of history?

Life is not about how much excess money you collect.

Life is only about the value you provide around you and how you can leave this sloshing blue marble a wee bit better than you found it.

Some days the only thing you have to do is smile. And listen.

I wrote this book because I needed to choose life when I'd become lost. It is my hope that you will choose your life, too, if you haven't yet.

You are enough, with money or without it.

You have every opportunity to positively impact those around you.

Money matters because you matter.

The world is already a better place just because you're here – now let's make it even better and worthwhile for even just one other person and, what the heck, let's increase our net worth in the process.

This is now officially the book I wish I had read when I was younger.

I hope you feel the same passion and excitement for your future that I do.

Be the bow (take control and steer your financial ship), be the bank (always be investing in appreciating assets) and be grateful every step of the way.

One final time…because why the heck not?

Earn more than you spend and always be investing your time and your money in appreciating assets – dam it! ☺

Now go be a confident and amazing human being in the world – we will toast to your incredible financial success together one day soon.

Appendix A: The Money Dam™

I came up with the idea for The Money Dam™ while looking for a powerful way to think about money in my own life. One day while nerding out online about man-made water reservoirs and dams (I have *no idea why*, but I've always been entranced by these feats of engineering), it hit me that water sitting behind a dam is no different than a person's own pool of assets, or net worth.

I knew I was onto something when the concept wouldn't leave me alone – like a puppy with a full bladder – regardless of what I was doing, The Money Dam kept creeping back into my consciousness as a great metaphor for how to think about the crucial financial decisions I was making each month. The concept kept developing itself in the background of my mind from there!

How to Use The Money Dam

Think of the accumulation of your money as water being saved up behind a dam, thereby creating a lake. Just like water in a real reservoir, any money you have to your name (your net worth in the form of cash or any assets you own) is sitting, in reserve, behind your money dam.

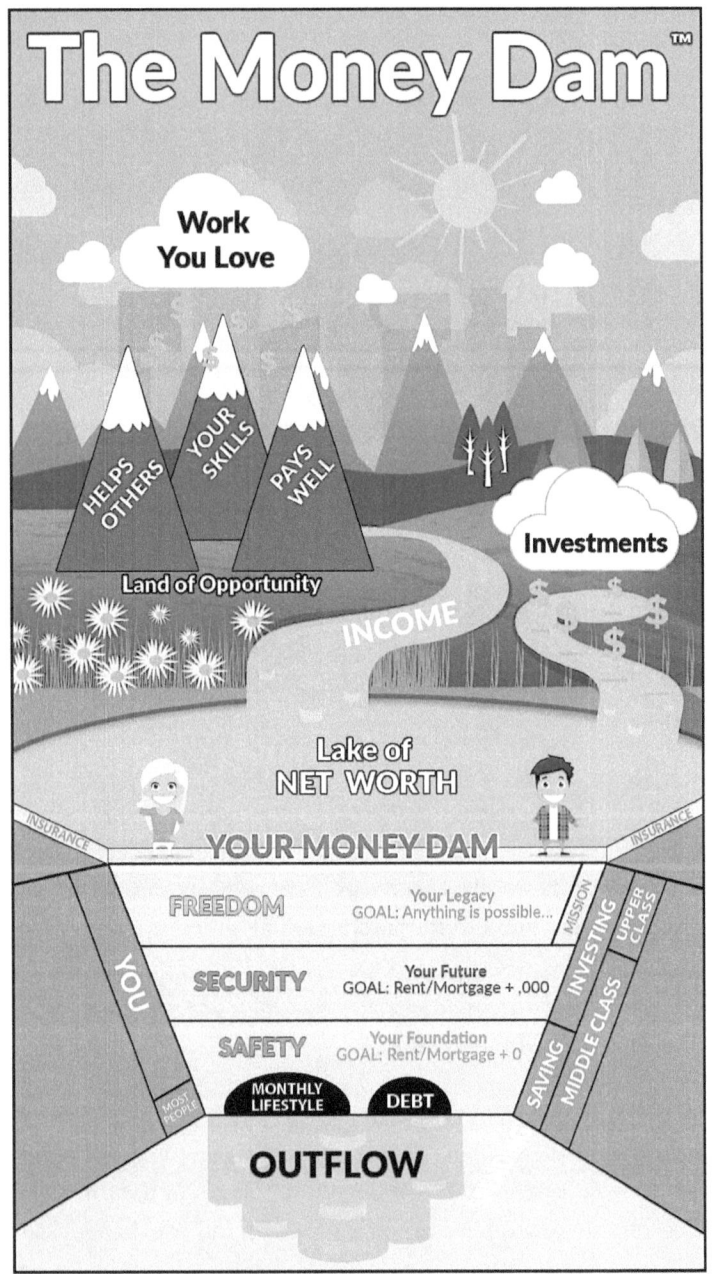

Just as dams let water through to generate electricity or to fulfill contracts to provide water downstream, you do this, too, when you pay for anything in your daily life. The biggest dams don't completely block the flow of water, but they do limit its flow downstream from what they receive upstream. The same goes for you when you earn more than you spend.

To build our dam as high as we can, regardless of whether we have anything to store behind it yet, we need nothing more than the power of our own minds and learning to Think Wealthy.

There are three (3) levels to the face of the dam, one each for short-term SAFETY, long-term SECURITY and total financial FREEDOM.

To determine the dollar amount required for each level, you only need one number – what you pay each month in rent or for a mortgage!

SAFETY: To feel SAFE, add one zero (0) to your monthly rent/mortgage number. This is your 3-6 month emergency fund.

SECURITY: To feel SECURE, add three zeroes (,000) to your monthly rent/mortgage number. This is the goal for your net worth when you reach retirement – be that at the more traditional age of 60+ or earlier if you have your sights set on joining the FIRE movement.

FREEDOM: To feel financially FREE, add four zeroes (0,000) to your monthly rent/mortgage number. At this level, you can easily live off the interest of your assets alone, if you wish. Either way, you are solidly on track to set you and your family up for generational wealth.

As I say until I'm blue in the face, like a Smurf, "If you don't give a dam about your money, no one else will!"

The Full Money Dam Infographic

Throughout the *Think Wealthy* book, I have used a simplified version of The Money Dam™. For the full, free version, go to:

ThinkWealthyBook.com

APPENDICES

Appendix B: The Million Dollars Game

If you just finished reading Chapter 1, let's play a game – The Million Dollars Game!

I'm giving you ONE MILLION DOLLARS…right now!

(Legal disclaimer: I am not giving you a million real dollars…these are IMAGINARY dollars…which means they're totally tax free! Which makes them the best KIND of dollars, right?)

Quick – what do you do with your surprise bonus of a million dollars?

$$$

Pause here while you think about it.

$$$

If you're like most people, you'll immediately think of how you're going to *spend* it.

Which is awesome. Just think of EVERYTHING you can do with it. It will feel SO GOOD when you:

- Pay off that credit card debt

- Get a new car or at least upgrade the bucket of bolts you've got now

- Move into a bigger house in a better neighborhood

- Help your parents out with anything they need

- Gift a little money to your siblings because you made a pact you'd always look out for each other

- Celebrate with your friends with a few really nice meals or buy rounds of drinks for everyone at your favorite bar (after the global pandemic ends)

- Help out any close friends who need a quick loan so they don't miss their car or mortgage payment because you've known them for years and they're like family

- Finally take that dream vacation (after the global pandemic ends) and do it up right!

With a million dollars hitting your bank account, it's natural to want to spend it on family and friends and upgrade your lifestyle – after all, you deserve it, right?!?

You've slogged the hard road of life long enough, you're long overdue for a few of the finer things by now.

$$$

At this point in the book, the end of Chapter 1, if I gave you a million dollars what you'd probably do with it is SPEND IT on yourself and others and you'd love every second of it. It'd feel great and everyone would sing your praises everywhere you went.

You'd SPEND IT because all you've known is how to make ends meet and this surplus has a lot of work to do to get you caught up on the life you've always wanted to live.

But before you'd know it, you'd be completely out of money and unable to support the new lifestyle you'd created for yourself. This would put you in the same boat as most lottery winners and around 80% of pro NFL and NBA players who declare bankruptcy five years after retirement.

When the money spigot runs out, you'll probably have a different relationship with your family members and may lose a few friends in the process, too.

And all of this is perfect. At this early point in the book, I NEED you to spend it all because that's what MOST of us would do with an influx of cash like that.

We're really just thinking of the million dollars as CASH for spending, we're not yet thinking of it as MONEY.

Pat yourself on the back – you done good and we're right where we need to be.

APPENDICES

Appendix C: The Game of Wealth

If you just finished Chapter 5, welcome to the **Game of Wealth** where we're going to find out where your hidden passions and interests lie along with your larger WHY for wealth.

And we're going to do that by spending a lot of money. Virtual money, but a lot of it!

For anyone who's ever said they wish they had more money at some point in their life, here's your chance!

The rules are simple:

1. Spend one hundred million dollars as quickly as possible. That's $100,000,000 of (virtual) money sitting in your checking account just waiting for you to tell it where to go and what to do.

2. You must spend the full one hundred million on things for you or other people, creating businesses, buying other investments, traveling, giving to charity, whatever…be as creative as you are unique in all the world.

3. Follow the levels of The Money Dam™ - how much would you save to feel safe (short term) and invest to feel secure (long term) for you and your family's future and where would you put that money? After those financial needs are met, you get to create your own life...what do you do with it and where do you spend it?

That's it! Spend a hundred million dollars and ENJOY doing it.

You *have* to spend it all, but don't forget that you need to support your life for as long as you live, too. Longevity and sustainability of your current or new lifestyle is something to think about.

You can play the Game of Wealth on a sheet of paper or a Word doc or Google doc or even in the body of an email draft like I did.

The point of the Game of Wealth is to dam up whatever you need for the future, spend as much as you want on any immediate wants or needs for yourself and others and then see where your current interests lie after you're completely free of life's financial obligations.

The more specific you are, the more real it will be for you. Attach specific numbers to purchases as you make your list...don't just say you'll buy three private islands in the Pacific to make Richard Branson jealous. Find out how much they are – you can find a price for most anything online nowadays. Of course, buying an island is not enough – does it need a staff that lives there year-round?

It's interesting to see what comes up when you can afford most anything you want.

As for me...

I was shocked at how hard it was to spend money after I was safe and secure...which is funny because we've daydreamed all our lives about having massive financial means but then when you get to play with that type of money, it may not be the experience you thought it would be.

In the end, the Game of Wealth opened many hidden interests I wasn't expecting to uncover and helped me break through my hidden financial psychology, or how I was brought up to think about money.

Learnings from the Game of Wealth

The Game of Wealth is a lesson in what you would do in the world at the level of Financial Freedom.

The learnings, to me, from playing the Game of Wealth are that, after safety and security are in the rearview mirror, it feels good to give away money, either to lessen someone else's financial burden or to surprise them, even when you do it anonymously.

It feels great to be charitable with your money and with your time. Tithing to your church or to a charity of your choice reminds you that you are part of a larger community and that you care (enough) to share.

In essence, once you have everything you need to keep your own financial future secured, what becomes important is often to help others, either through creating businesses that employ people and that create products and services that help others or by supporting businesses financially (think *Shark Tank*) or giving money through a foundation for philanthropy.

In the end, if you haven't spent it all – and even if you have, which has enriched others' lives just through the transfer of money – you get it to give it away, anyway.

Because you have to.

Because you can't take it with you.

Ideally, what you will realize is *why* you want to be wealthy beyond protecting you and your family (safety and security). You now see what causes are important to you. You see what kind of businesses you would create if money were no object. You see where your passions lie.

You're starting to see who YOU are after peering into your soul a little deeper.

Now that you are thinking about your bigger why, now that you see that you are a kind-hearted and generous human being when money flows freely, you can start integrating some of those newly discovered passions and interests RIGHT NOW when the money spigot isn't fully open just yet.

That is how you expand your own life TODAY so that, as the money flows in later in life, you already know what matters to you most and you can simply share more. And help more.

A Checklist for The Game of Wealth

Playing this game can bring up a lot of questions. For example, do you use The Money Dam numbers from your current rent or mortgage payment, or with one hundred million dollars, do you upgrade to a new location or property and what is that NEW number that you run through The Money Dam?

If you shave off a chunk of the money to live off each year, do you even NEED to set aside money in retirement accounts or have you already figured out Income Stream for Life by never touching the principal of that chunk you're living off of?

APPENDICES

Here are a few thought-starters to help you navigate your decision-making as you spend away and imagine your new life:

- Did you upgrade your living situation to a new house or condo somewhere else in the world? Did you budget for any additional expenses of upkeep, staff salaries, property taxes in that new city, etc.? You can ballpark these numbers – I just want you to be thinking more holistically about your purchases and expenses.

- Did you shave off some of the $100,000,000 to create an income stream for the rest of your life? If billionaires keep a certain amount in cash for annual living expenses and purchases, did you follow a similar approach? What percentage of a return will that chunk kick off each year for you to live off of?

- Did you invest in any startups that you believe in? If so, what industries are they trying to disrupt? Did you put any rock-bottom basement pre-IPO stock prices into a Roth IRA like Peter Thiel did in the event those companies take off one day (like PayPal)?

- For charitable giving, did you set up a foundation or an endowment that will continue to grow through appreciating assets, but that kicks off a certain return that you can disburse each year? What is the foundation's giving "mission" or core strategy for who it helps?

- Did you buy any luxury real estate or investment properties outright or did you opt to use a bank's money for the leverage it can provide? Besides, maybe you can rent them out to the rich and famous when you're not staying in them so they can help generate revenue for you, too.

- What were the causes that you cared about most and are you doing anything yet to support them with your current net worth and lifestyle? $100 now or $10,000 in the future is often just as meaningful to nonprofits.

- What were the companies and industries you invested in because it just *fascinates* you? Do you currently work in those fields or do you have a plan to move into them?

- Did you buy any investments with the idea of starting generational wealth for your family? Or do you know how you want your estate to be distributed after your last breath?

- Or did you just spend all 100 million dollars on cool things and awesome experiences for you, your friends and your family? ☺

There's no right or wrong way to play The Wealth Game – it is my hope, however, that you learned something new about yourself (or perhaps learned MUCHO new about yourself) that will inform not only what you might do one day when you have more money, but that can inform changes you can make starting right now to bring added layers of satisfaction into your life.

Maybe you'll want to add new hobbies into your current life or start the process of shifting into a new career.

Perhaps you want to start donating what you can to charities you hadn't even thought of before. Or spend some of your valuable time volunteering to support them.

What about giving back to the world in terms of future generations? Is there something you have learned in your unique life that you would like to pass down via teaching to others?

The Game of Wealth is a fantastic ride through your own imagination – which, as we've seen, is the greatest wealth-building tool you possess to begin with!

I hope you had fun playing the game – you can always come back to it in the future as your life's circumstances change to see if anything has shifted in your interests and passions.

Enjoy!

About the Author

As a debt-free (and now cancer-free) dad, **Todd Havens** loves talking and writing about money because, for years and years (and years), he was the poorest guy in any room. Who else but the broke guy would dream of one day having a zero net worth and feel like he was a financial genius?

No one taught him everything they knew about money, so he had to do it himself – he has studied the financial habits of millionaires and billionaires – and has now, as a first-gen millionaire himself, made it his mission to help others learn to Think Wealthy and completely transform their lives, too.

Todd is a brand and marketing executive in Hollywood who, in his spare time, serves as a board member on a nonprofit that both celebrates and preserves the very best in digital movie marketing.

ThinkWealthyBook.com

www.ingramcontent.com/pod-product-compliance
Lightning Source LLC
Chambersburg PA
CBHW020430130626
46549CB00001B/74